The Work of Love

The Work of Love

CREATION AS KENOSIS

Edited by

John Polkinghorne

WILLIAM B. EERDMANS PUBLISHING COMPANY
GRAND RAPIDS, MICHIGAN / CAMBRIDGE, U.K.

Published jointly 2001
in the United States of America by
Wm. B. Eerdmans Publishing Co.
255 Jefferson Ave. S.E., Grand Rapids, Michigan 49503 /
P.O. Box 163, Cambridge CB3 9PU U.K.
www.eerdmans.com
and in Great Britain by
Society for Promoting Christian Knowledge
Holy Trinity Church
Marylebone Road
London NW1 4DU

Printed in the United States of America

05 04 03 02 01   5 4 3 2 1

Library of Congress Cataloging-in-Publication Data

The work of love: creation as kenosis / edited by John Polkinghorne.
p.   cm.
Includes bibliographical references.
ISBN 0-8028-4885-0 (alk. paper)
1. Creation.   2. Philosophical theology.
I. Polkinghorne, J. C., 1930-

BT695.W665   2001
231.7'65 — dc21
2001019357

British Library Cataloguing-in-Publication Data

A catalogue record for this book is available from the British Library

SPCK ISBN 0-281-05372-3

To the memory of
the late Canon W. H. Vanstone

Contents

vii

CONTENTS

Acknowledgments

All members of the group that wrote this book are very grateful to the John Templeton Foundation for the active encouragement we were given in our enterprise and for the generous financial support that made our work together possible. We would also like particularly to thank Dr. Mary Ann Meyers for her excellent efficiency in dealing with all the administrative arrangements and for the close interest she has taken in our work.

Introduction

In October 1998, a group of theologians and scientists met in Queens' College, Cambridge, under the auspices of the John Templeton Foundation, to discuss the insights afforded by a kenotic view of creation, understood as being brought about by the action of the God of love. The meeting had as its initiating inspiration the writings of Jürgen Moltmann and W. H. Vanstone, and both of these scholars were able to take part in the discussions. It was agreed to develop the theme further by preparing the series of essays that are the substance of this book. Drafts of these writings were further discussed at a meeting held in New York City in November 1999. Sadly, between these two meetings Canon Bill Vanstone had died. It is the unanimous wish of the contributors gratefully to dedicate this volume to his memory. Each chapter is prefaced by a quotation from his seminal book, *Love's Endeavour, Love's Expense.*

The backgrounds of the members of the group are very diverse, varying from systematic theology to neuropsychology. It is hoped that the resulting breadth of perspective will be found to be helpful for the exploration of the doctrine of creation. In our view, the kenotic approach to that doctrine represents the most insightful development in recent thinking about these issues.

Ian Barbour gives five reasons why he finds the classical concept of God's unqualified omnipotence to be problematic today. They are: the scientifically discerned integrity of natural process; the widespread presence of evil and suffering in the world; the role of human freedom; Christian insights derived from the cross of Christ; and feminist critiques of patriarchal models of control. Barbour sees process theology as presenting important responses to these criticisms. He acknowledges that process thought understands limitation of divine power as being inherent in the divine nature and not a kenotic act of self-restraint. God acts through persuasion and this is held to offer the ground for sufficient transformative power. Barbour's essay concludes with some thoughts about process approaches to cosmic and eschatological issues.

Arthur Peacocke places before us the dynamic epic of evolution, with its continuous emergence of new forms of life. God is immanent within this process, which is, therefore, capable of unfolding through the naturalistic powers with which the Creator has endowed it. Peacocke identifies what he calls 'propensities' for the coming to be of such phenomena as complexity and also, significantly, pain and suffering. An evolutionary world must involve both predation and death. Just as we may believe the Creator to take delight in the rich diversity of living forms, so we must also believe God to share in creation's suffering and travail. The God revealed in human form in Jesus Christ is consistent with these deep insights.

Holmes Rolston presents us with a carefully nuanced meditation on the processes of nature. Talk of 'selfish genes' must be tempered and corrected by talk of self-actualizing organisms. Lineages are generated by the sharing of genetic information, and adaptation is an ecological word, not a genetic one. Sexual reproduction involves the merging of the self with the alien, in the bringing into being of the next generation. In Rolston's opinion, "Redemptive suffering is a model that makes sense of nature and history." Yet true kenosis is not found in nature, because voluntariness is not present there either. Only humans can choose the truly altruistic preservation of the interests of the other at the expense of one's self.

Malcolm Jeeves takes a neuroscientific approach to discussing the presence of self-giving behavior in the animal and human worlds. He argues that human beings are not to be understood in dualist terms but as psychosomatic unities. "I do not *have* a soul, I am a living being or soul." Some form of non-reductive physicalism is his favored approach. Jeeves discusses the evidence that brain damage can lead to stark changes in moral behavior. He is inclined to see signs of 'soulishness' in non-human primates. We are given a careful discussion of the relationship between genetic endowment and behavior, including altruistic activity. Jeeves emphasizes that considerations of bottom-up instincts need to be complemented by the top-down consequences of conscious choice.

John Polkinghorne seeks a middle way between classical theology and process theology, in which God interacts with creation but does not overrule its divinely granted freedom to be itself. Such a concept of continuous creation is helpful in facing the perplexities posed by theodicy. The death of mere mechanism in modern scientific thinking offers the metaphysical possibility of an appropriate concept of divine action within the cloudy unpredictabilities of physical process. Divine kenosis can then be understood as having four dimensions — relating to the self-limitation of divine power, of divine eternity, of divine knowledge, and of divine participation in the causal nexus of creation. This last possibility leads Polkinghorne to question the theological assumption that it is improper to consider divine providence as acting as a cause among causes.

George Ellis sees kenosis as being a unifying theme, expressing God's character and capable of generating an overarching understanding embracing both the ethical duties of human life and also a meaningful interpretation of cosmic process. The master exemplar is the life of Christ, kenotic in its character from the temptations in the wilderness to his sacrificial death on the cross. Ellis considers the evidence for this primacy of kenotic love and he gives a careful discussion of its implications for praxis, including political action in the face of an oppressive regime.

Michael Welker sees Western society as being caught in the tension between expectation and disappointment that results from its concentration on love as a reciprocal relationship of a one-to-one kind. Release from this trap can come from resort to the biblical sources. In their understanding, the scope of love is greatly enlarged, finding its focus in attention to the commandments of God. When God's name is made known — that is to say, when the divine power and identity are revealed — growth into a covenantal relationship is made possible. The kenotic love of God made known in Christ is of the widest possible scope, embracing the whole of creation.

Jürgen Moltmann gives us an account of kenotic ideas in Christian and Jewish thinking. Lutheran theologians from the seventeenth and nineteenth centuries applied Philippians 2:1-11 to their thought about the incarnation. In the twentieth century, Hans Urs von Balthasar took the step of locating kenosis within the inner life of the Trinity. Jewish thinking has centered on the Shekinah, God's indwelling glory present with his exiled people. Kenotic thought in relation to creation can find expression through the Kabbalistic concept of *zimzum,* a divine contraction making way for the created other. Moltmann tells us that "It is not God's power that is almighty. What is almighty is his love." He urges us to replace a metaphysics of reality with a metaphysics of possibility, emphasizing the role of the future.

Keith Ward presents us with a vision of truly cosmic scope. He believes that God suffers because God has affective knowledge of creation. In creation, God realizes possibilities that are eternally present in the divine being and comes to experience new forms of value that otherwise would not have been actualized. For Ward, kenosis is also pleroma (fullness), involving self-realization as well as self-giving. It is concerned with divine creativity as well as with the incarnation. "There are necessities in the divine nature which mean that God cannot exist in a state of unmixed bliss, all-determining power and unrestricted knowledge, if there is to be a world of free and creative personal agents." This is the way in which power is exercised by love, so that "the lesson of kenosis is a moral one." The incarnation is the expression of these timeless truths about the divine nature, revealed within history. Kenosis is the first stage of a threefold creative redemptive process, to be followed by enosis (the unity of divine and finite personhood) and theosis (the ultimate sharing of the redeemed cosmos in the life of God).

For Paul Fiddes "The claim that love is at the heart of the universe is both problematic and immensely illuminating." He is emboldened to say that God needs creation, defending this by an analogy with human love, with its mixture of agape and eros. God's perfection is dynamic, not static, and divine desire finds satisfaction in creatures. But do not these considerations threaten freedom, both human and divine, for might not the necessity of divine love constrain creaturely contingency? Fiddes believes that the answer lies in God's free choosing to need a particular creation. The context is the Trinitarian movement interweaving love. The God of love will act through persuasion. This involves both risk and the possibility of creaturely co-creativity. Fulfillment is attained through suffering, and not despite it. Tragedy and victory intermingle, in that "While creatures will know blessing in the contemplation of their Creator, God may know that they are not all that they could have been."

Sarah Coakley helpfully analyzes the various ways in which her colleagues have employed the concept of kenosis, distinguishing three broad categories of use: Christological, Trinitarian, and God's general relationship with creation. She links these differences with differing approaches to theological method. Coakley emphasizes how much of the discussion has turned on an incompatibilist concept of human freedom, and she urges that the resources of classical theology should not be abandoned too readily. Finally, three gender-linked issues are discussed: the masculine character of incompatibilism, the role of self-sacrifice, and the significance of 'otherness.'

JOHN POLKINGHORNE

God's Power: A Process View

IAN G. BARBOUR

> *. . . to interpret creation as the work of love is to interpret it as the new, as the coming-to-be of the hitherto unknown, and so as that for which there can be no precedent and no programme.*
>
> *Love's Endeavour, Love's Expense*, p. 66

In both Medieval and Reformation thought, God was said to be omnipotent, omniscient, unchanging, and unaffected by the world. According to the classical view, God is the absolute ruler of the universe. Every event is predestined in accordance with God's eternal will. This understanding of divine omnipotence is widely questioned today for five reasons that are set forth in the first half of this essay: (1) the integrity of nature in science and in theology; (2) the problem of evil and suffering; (3) the reality of human freedom; (4) the Christian understanding of the cross; and (5) feminist critiques of patriarchal models of God. Such considerations have led many contemporary theologians to speak of God's voluntary self-limitation (or kenosis) in creating a world. Most of these authors also hold that God participates in the suffering of the world. They reject the classical belief that God is unchanging and unaffected by the world.

The second half of this essay explores the contribution of process theology in developing each of these five themes in a distinctive way. Process theology is the attempt of theologians to use the process philosophy of Alfred North Whitehead in the expression and reformulation of the beliefs of a religious tradition — particularly the Christian tradition, though Jewish and Buddhist thinkers have pursued similar goals. Process theologians hold that the limitation of God's power should not be thought of as a voluntary self-limitation, as if retaining omnipotence was an option that God decided to give up. I will suggest that the process view of the social character of all beings (including God) leads to an understanding of God's power as the empowerment of other beings rather than as power over them. This provides an alternative to omnipotence or impotence by redefining the nature of divine power without denying its universal scope. The idea that God participates in the world's suffering is strongly supported by the process conviction that God is affected by events in the world. I will try to show that the God portrayed in process theology also has adequate resources for the redemptive transformation of suffering.

I. Kenosis as God's Self-Limitation

Five themes are prominent in recent criticisms of the classical understanding of divine omnipotence.

1. The Integrity of Nature in Science and Theology

With the rise of modern science nature was increasingly seen as a self-sufficient mechanism in which God could act only by intervention from outside in violation of the laws of nature. Of course, if God created the laws of nature, God is presumably free to abrogate them or to make use of higher laws. Moreover, many laws of science are now known to be probabilistic or statistical, describing the way a system usually behaves when no additional influences (natural or supernatural) from outside the system are introduced. Nevertheless, dependable regularities are characteristic of most domains of nature, and science itself would not be possible without them. The long and wasteful history of evolution suggests that God does not intervene frequently or coercively. If God is active in the process it must be in a more subtle way that always builds on the structures and activities already present. If there is any role for God, it must be by working with the powers of existing creatures rather than by overruling them.

In their previous writings several of the authors in the present volume

2

have said that their accounts of divine action do not involve violations of the laws of nature or divine intervention in gaps in the scientific account (the "God of the gaps" who retreats as each gap is closed by advances in science). Instead they have tried to show how new scientific concepts either permit divine action or suggest analogies for it.[1] George Ellis holds that God determines the indeterminacies left open by the laws of quantum physics. John Polkinghorne proposes that God acts by the communication of "pure information" at the exquisitely sensitive bifurcation points described in chaos theory, without violating the conservation of energy. Arthur Peacocke argues that God acts by "top-down causality" similar to the top-down influence of higher levels within an organism on its lower-level components (by setting boundary conditions and constraints rather than by violating lower-level laws). He also speaks of God's action in the world as an extension of the way in which larger wholes can affect changes in their parts within organisms. In all these cases God is seen as working subtly in cooperation with the structures of nature rather than by intervening unilaterally.

There are also theological reasons for affirming the integrity of nature. The intelligibility, rationality, and dependability of nature can be interpreted as plausible evidence for an intelligent creator, though not as a conclusive argument. It would be a deficient design if God had to correct it frequently. Michael Welker has commented on the passage in Genesis: "Let the waters bring forth swarms of living things. . . . Be fruitful and multiply . . ." (Gen. 1:20-22). He says that such passages do not portray the "absolute dependence" of creatures on God, as often claimed, but point instead to the cooperation of the creatures in divine creativity.[2]

Authors in the Thomistic tradition have tried to reconcile divine omnipotence and the integrity of nature. They say that God as primary cause works omnipotently through the secondary causes of nature. All events in

---

1. See essays by George Ellis, John Polkinghorne, and Arthur Peacocke in *Chaos and Complexity: Scientific Perspectives on Divine Action*, ed. Robert John Russell, Nancey Murphy, and Arthur R. Peacocke (Rome: Vatican Observatory and Berkeley: Center for Theology and the Natural Sciences, 1995). Ellis and Peacocke also have essays in *Evolution and Molecular Biology: Scientific Perspectives on Divine Action*, ed. Robert John Russell, William R. Stoeger, S.J., and Francisco Ayala (Rome: Vatican Observatory and Berkeley: Center for Theology and Natural Sciences, 1998).

2. Michael Welker, "What Is Creation? Rereading Genesis 1 and 2," *Theology Today* 47, no. 1 (April 1991): 56-70.

the world are said to be the product of a divine plan in which everything has been predestined in accordance with God's will. God's primary causality is on a completely different level from the chain of secondary causes, which is complete and without gaps at its own level. God's control was never sheer power, of course, for it was always the power of love. Dante ends *The Divine Comedy* with a vision of God as "the Love that moves Sun and other stars."[3] The Thomistic view of natural causes as instrumental to God's absolute governance of nature was also defended by Calvin, and more recently by Karl Barth and Austin Farrer, among others.[4] Critics reply that evil in the world and human freedom are incompatible with the assertion that all events are ultimately determined by God. I will suggest that process thought offers a detailed critique of both natural determinism and divine determination. It articulates roles for God and for natural causes in every event while rejecting traditional ideas of divine omnipotence.

2. The Problem of Evil and Suffering

Pain and suffering are widespread in nonhuman nature. In evolutionary history, increased capacity for pain was apparently a concomitant of increased sentience and was selected for its adaptive value in providing warning of danger and bodily harm. The behavior of animals gives evidence that they suffer intensely, and even invertebrates under stress release endorphins and other pain-suppressant chemicals similar to those in the human brain.[5] Predators live off their prey, and many organisms consume organisms lower in the food chain as a source of complex organic molecules. Evolutionary history has involved struggle and competition in which the vast majority of species have become extinct. Holmes Rolston gives an example of a tragic dimension in nature. The white pelican lays its eggs two days apart. The later, smaller chick is allowed to survive only if the larger chick has succumbed at an early age. The usual fate of the

3. Dante Alighieri, *The Paradiso*, trans. John Ciardi (New York: New American Library, 1970), canto 33.

4. Karl Barth, *Church Dogmatics* (Edinburgh: T. & T. Clark, 1956-75), vol. 3, part 3, pp. 49, 94, 106, 133, 148, etc.; Austin Farrer, *Faith and Speculation* (London: Adam and Charles Black, 1967), ch. 4 and 10.

5. Donald R. Griffin, *Animal Thinking* (Cambridge, Mass.: Harvard University Press, 1984).

smaller chick is to be attacked and fed to the larger one or pushed out of the nest.[6]

To be sure, what is harmful to the individual may benefit the group or the larger system. The predator's prey contributes to the ecosystem, and the back-up chick contributes to future generations of pelicans. Death is a necessary feature of evolution in which changes occur between generations and finite resources can support only limited populations. Even in nonlinear thermodynamic systems, disorder is a condition for the emergence of new forms of order. In other writings and in the present volume, Rolston says that nature is "cruciform" when suffering serves a wider purpose and new life arises from the old. In "suffering through to something higher" nature offers a pattern that is fulfilled in the suffering Redeemer and the suffering of God with and for creation.[7]

With the emergence of higher levels of sentience and consciousness in evolutionary history, the capacity for greater suffering and the capacity for greater enjoyment were inescapably linked together. In human life, suffering contributes to moral growth, as Paul asserts (Rom. 5:3). Courage would be impossible without danger and temptation. The suffering of others calls forth our sympathy and compassion, and undeserved suffering can have a redemptive effect on other people. Moreover, the free choice of the good would not be possible without the alternative choice of evil. John Hick, following Irenaeus, sees the world as an opportunity for moral development and "soul-making." The injustice of undeserved suffering, he says, can be rectified in the afterlife. Hick sees the presence of evil and suffering as evidence of God's self-limitation. He also holds that God withholds divine power to provide the "epistemic distance" that allows us to respond freely to divine love rather than being overwhelmed and coerced into belief.[8]

I question whether moral development alone can justify the extent and pervasiveness of suffering in human life, or the depths of human evil, brought home to me anew by a recent visit to Auschwitz. Some people do indeed gain courage and strength in encountering suffering, but others are broken and embittered by it. Voluntary self-limitation exonerates God

6. Holmes Rolston, III, *Science and Religion: A Critical Survey* (Philadelphia: Temple University Press, 1987), pp. 137-38.

7. Holmes Rolston, III, *Science and Religion,* ch. 3.

8. John Hick, *Evil and the Love of God* (San Francisco: Harper and Row, 1966).

from direct responsibility for specific instances of evil and suffering, but presumably God is ultimately responsible for them. How would we view a human father who withheld measures that could have prevented the protracted suffering of a person with AIDS or a prisoner at Auschwitz? A human father does not of course establish the ground rules for ongoing life, but the analogy may give us pause in claiming divine omnipotence behind self-limitation. At this point process thought differs from most versions of kenotic theology by claiming that the limitations of divine power are the product of metaphysical necessity rather than voluntary self-limitation.

3. The Reality of Human Freedom

From the scientific side, human freedom appears to be threatened by biological determinism. Comparisons of twins (having identical genes) with non-twin siblings (sharing half their genes) and adopted children raised together (with few shared genes) show that in the case of many behavioral traits roughly half of the similarities are genetically inherited. This does not prove that human freedom is illusory, but it does suggest that our decisions are severely constrained by our genes. We can make choices only within a limited range of possibilities.[9] In other studies, damage to particular areas of the brain and changes in the balance of chemicals in the brain have been shown to affect particular mental abilities dramatically. The dependence of mental and spiritual life on biological processes calls into question the traditional dualism of body and soul. Freedom can be defended only if we can show that a human being is at the same time a biological organism, an embodied self, and a responsible agent.[10]

The experience of choice seems to be an indelible feature of firsthand personal experience. Even the philosopher or scientist who defends determinism assumes in daily life that other people are responsible for their actions. In this essay, however, we are primarily concerned with the threat to human freedom from divine determination rather than from biological

9. Ted Peters, *Playing God: Genetic Determinism or Human Freedom?* (New York and London: Routledge, 1997).

10. See Ian G. Barbour, "Neuroscience, Artificial Intelligence, and Human Nature: Theological and Philosophical Reflections," *Zygon* 34 (1999): 361-98.

determinism. Moral choice is frequently called for in the bib.
ture. "Choose this day whom you will serve" (Josh. 24:15). Pa
with the paradox of human freedom and divine grace. "I work
than any of them, though it was not I but the grace of God which is with
me" (1 Cor. 15:10). "Work out your own salvation, for God is at work in
you" (Phil. 2:12). Paul also recognizes that true freedom requires not only
the absence of external constraints but the resolution of internal conflicts:
"For I do not do the good I want, but the evil I do not want is what I do"
(Rom. 7:19). Both Paul and Luther held that human sin results in a
"bondage of the will" from which we can be liberated only by our acceptance of God's love.

Writers in the Thomistic tradition have tried to reconcile human
freedom with divine foreknowledge and predestination. Human freedom
occurs in the realm of successive temporal events; God desires our free response, not coerced obedience. But God transcends time; divine knowledge is eternal and unchanging. God knows the future, not as it is unpre-
dictably produced by human choices and worldly causes, but as it is
determinately specified by divine decree. Within the world, an act is un-
certain before it takes place, but for God there is no "before." All time is
present to God simultaneously.[11]

I would reply that this solution implies that time is unreal to God.
Divine interaction with human life would be more like the staged performance of a prepared script than an intimate involvement in an ongoing
relationship. Here I join those who say that God is omniscient in knowing all that can be known, but this does not include choices that are unknowable until they are made. The "free-will defense" in theodicy asserts
that the price of human freedom is the possibility of the choice of evil.
Polkinghorne has used the term "free-process defense" to refer to divine
self-limitation in the nonhuman domain.[12] Process theologians have in-
sisted that if time is real in God's experience, human freedom implies limitations in God's knowledge of the future.

11. E. L. Mascall, *He Who Is: A Study in Traditional Theism* (London: Longmans Green and Co., 1945); Richard Creel, *Divine Impassibility: An Essay in Philosophical Theology* (Cambridge: Cambridge University Press, 1986).

12. John Polkinghorne, *The Faith of a Physicist* (Princeton: Princeton University Press, 1994), pp. 83-85.

4. The Christian Understanding of the Cross

The Bible presents diverse images of God. In some parts of the Hebrew scriptures, God is the Lord mighty in battle in defense of the chosen people. Isaiah is overwhelmed by the majesty and mystery of God in his vision in the temple (Isaiah 6). But God is also compared to a grieving husband, strong in judgment but tender in forgiveness toward an unfaithful wife (Hosea 1–4). Later chapters of Isaiah portray Israel as God's "suffering servant" whose suffering can redemptively affect other nations (Isaiah 53), a role which early Christians believed was fulfilled in the person of Christ.

Paul writes that Christ "did not count equality with God a thing to be grasped, but emptied himself, taking the form of a servant . . . and became obedient unto death, even death on a cross" (Phil. 2:7-8). Christians have understood the cross on the one hand as the result of Christ's choice of the path of self-sacrificial love in decisions throughout his life — from the temptations in the wilderness at the start of his public career to his free decision and faithful response in the Garden of Gethsemane near its end. But they have also claimed that in the incarnation and in Christ's death God participated in human suffering and showed the power of redeeming love. The cross thus represents the nature and will of God as well as the fully human decisions of Christ. Such a God would act kenotically in creation as well as incarnation.

Among modern writers, W. H. Vanstone has shown that a characteristic of authentic love is its vulnerability, and he concludes that this would be true for God as well as for humanity:

> Thou art God; no monarch Thou
> Thron'd in easy state to reign;
> Thou art God, Whose arms of love
> Aching, spent, the world sustain.[13]

In *The Creative Suffering of God,* Paul Fiddes presents a critique of traditional ideas of God's self-sufficiency and immutability. Fiddes gives a sympathetic discussion of process philosophy, though in the end he ar-

---

13. W. H. Vanstone, *Love's Endeavour, Love's Expense* (London: Darton, Longman and Todd, 1977), p. 120.

8

gues that God's temporality and vulnerability are better expressed by the trinitarian interaction within the life of God.[14] He develops some of these themes further in his essay in the present volume.

In the Bible, the Holy Spirit is God's activity in nature, in the experience of the prophets and the worshiping community, and in the life of Christ. Reference to the Spirit allows us to bring together the doctrines of creation and redemption which have so often been separated in Christian life and thought. Geoffrey Lampe maintains that Christ was inspired by the Spirit, as appears in the account of his baptism.[15] In many biblical passages the Spirit is said to work from within to renew, inspire, empower, and guide — all of which are noncoercive actions, of which the dove at Christ's baptism is an appropriate symbol. Some images of the Spirit (as wind or fire, for example) suggest a stronger influence, but the active participation of the individual is still required. There are thus distinctive biblical grounds for defending a kenotic theology.

5. Feminist Critiques of Patriarchal Models of God

Feminist theologians are concerned that the virtues that are taken to be "masculine" in our culture (such as power, control, independence, and rationality) are held to be superior to the "feminine" virtues (such as nurturance, cooperation, interdependence, and emotional sensitivity). The cultural priority of the first set of virtues can be seen as both a cause and an effect of male dominance in western social structures. Patriarchal models of God in Christian thought are the product of a history in which both church leadership and theological reflection have been controlled almost exclusively by men.[16]

Feminist authors have given attention to the caring and nurturing aspects of human nature — and of God — that have been less highly respected historically than the characteristics of power and justice. Feminine images of God not only support the self-respect of women but allow stronger representation of neglected aspects of the divine nature. Feminist writings often emphasize the Spirit as the only nongendered member of

14. Paul S. Fiddes, *The Creative Suffering of God* (Oxford: Clarendon Press, 1988).
15. Geoffrey Lampe, *God as Spirit* (Oxford: Clarendon Press, 1977).
16. Rosemary Radford Ruether, *Sexism and God-Talk* (Boston: Beacon Press, 1983).

the Trinity, or they turn to the feminine expression of God as Sophia (Wisdom).[17] Such images may seem to diminish God's power, but they can better be understood as expressing a different form of power — not power as control over another person, but power as empowerment of another person. Creative empowerment is not a "zero-sum" game (in which one person loses something when the other person gains it) but rather a "positive-sum" game (in which both parties can gain).

However, feminist authors have pointed to the dangers when Christ's self-sacrificial death is used to justify self-sacrifice on the part of women. Women have too often been given the role of "suffering servant," and have themselves accepted this role, enduring abuse with patience. Elizabeth Johnson says that voluntary suffering for the sake of a greater good may indeed be admirable — as when civil disobedience on behalf of social justice results in imprisonment. But many women are involuntary victims of sexual and domestic violence and lack the courage to resist. Self-respect and self-affirmation are not incompatible with love of others and can contribute to mutually fulfilling relationships. The literature of psychotherapy suggests that the capacity to care for others correlates more frequently with self-acceptance than with self-abnegation or low self-esteem.[18]

Joanne Brown and Rebecca Parker argue that Christ's death must never be used to justify suffering. According to the substitutionary atonement theory, developed by Anselm, the Son was obedient to the Father and "died for our sins," taking the punishment we deserve. Brown and Parker criticize the idea of a propitiatory sacrifice that vicariously satisfies the retributive demands of divine justice. Such a theory also endorses obedience and sanctifies suffering, which are not messages women need to hear. Brown and Parker see some advantages in the "moral influence theory" (following Abelard), which says that Christ's undeserved suffering brings us to repentance and acceptance of forgiveness; this interpretation emphasizes divine love more than justice. But even this theory does not encourage victims to resist those that oppress them. These authors insist that Christ did not deliberately seek suffering. He suffered when his message of radical love challenged the prevailing structures of religious and

---

17. Sallie McFague, *Models of God for an Ecological, Nuclear Age* (Philadelphia: Fortress Press, 1987).

18. Elizabeth A. Johnson, *She Who Is: The Mystery of God in Feminist Theological Discourse* (New York: Crossroad Press, 1992).

10

political power. Both divine and human love are active in resisting and overcoming suffering, not in welcoming it.[19] We must take these caveats from feminist authors into account in any formulation of kenotic theology that emphasizes self-sacrifice.

Some Protestant theologians have advocated the ideal of *agape,* unconditional love that expects no return, and contrasted it with *eros,* a more limited love that expresses desire and fulfills needs.[20] Stephen Pope points out that the Thomistic tradition defends a greater variety of forms of love, including some that are mutual and reciprocal as expressed in friendship, family ties, and fellowship within a community. He says that while some situations may call for radical self-sacrifice, love more typically involves both giving and receiving.[21] Similarly, God's love for Israel involves both giving and receiving, and not kenosis alone; it is compared to the love of a man for a woman or to the mutuality of a covenant binding a community.

II. Kenotic Theology and Process Theology

All five themes of kenotic theology outlined above are prominent in the writings of process theologians. Whitehead himself is explicit in rejecting the monarchial model of God as "imperial ruler." Instead, he speaks of God as "the fellow-sufferer who understands."[22] He defends "the Galilean vision of humility," in which God offers "tender care that nothing be lost." While the "primordial nature" of God is the source of all possibilities, the "consequent nature" of God is influenced by the world.[23] Extending Whitehead's analysis, Charles Hartshorne gives a critique of traditional

19. Joanne Carlson Brown and Rebecca Parker, "For God So Loved the World?" in *Christianity, Patriarchy, and Abuse: A Feminist Critique,* ed. Joanne Carlson Brown and Carole R. Bohn (New York: Pilgrim Press, 1989).

20. Anders Nygren, *Agape and Eros* (London: SPCK, 1938).

21. Stephen Pope, *The Evolution of Altruism and the Ordering of Love* (Washington, D.C.: Georgetown University Press, 1994). See also Stephen Post, "The Inadequacy of Selflessness: God's Suffering and the Theory of Love," *Journal of the American Academy of Religion* 50 (1988): 213-28.

22. Alfred North Whitehead, *Process and Reality* (New York: Macmillan, 1929), p. 352.

23. For an introductory account of process theology, see John B. Cobb, Jr., and David Ray Griffin, *Process Theology: An Introduction* (Philadelphia: Westminster Press, 1976).

concepts of divine impassibility and immutability. He defends "dipolar theism" in which God is temporal and changing in interaction with the world but eternal in character and purpose.[24] According to both authors, God shares our suffering by participation in the world, and this in turn affects us, as another person's sympathy can affect us in human life.

In describing the unfolding of every event Whitehead includes the influence of past events, the ordering of potentialities by God, and an element of novelty. This is a God of persuasion rather than coercion. Such a conceptuality is particularly helpful in representing the evocative character of divine love in human life. It would not be relevant to the inanimate world if the world were conceived as a deterministic mechanism. But it is relevant to nature seen as a hierarchy of levels with downward causation and the communication of information from higher to lower levels, or to the view of nature set forth in process philosophy.

In place of either mind/matter dualism or materialism, process thought presents a pluralistic two-aspect monism in which all events have a subjective and objective aspect but a pluralism of diverse levels of organization. This view should be called *panexperientialism* rather than *panpsychism* since experience is postulated at all levels in integrated events (but not in unintegrated aggregates like rocks or loosely integrated structures like plants). Mentality and consciousness are said to occur only in the last phase of complex processes in higher organisms.[25] God's influence on separate cells or molecules is minimal though not totally absent — which would be consistent with the long and slow course of evolutionary history before higher levels were present. Let us ask how the process understanding of divine power differs from most versions of kenotic theology.

1. Voluntary Self-Limitation or Metaphysical Necessity?

Process thought is distinctive in holding that limitations of divine knowledge and power arise from metaphysical necessity rather than from voluntary self-limitation. In analyzing omniscience, process authors claim that if temporal passage is real for God, and if chance, novelty, and human

24. Charles Hartshorne, *The Divine Relativity* (New Haven: Yale University Press, 1948).

25. David Griffin, *Unsnarling the World Knot: Consciousness, Freedom, and the Mind/Body Problem* (Berkeley and Los Angeles: University of California Press, 1998).

freedom are features of the world, then the details of future events are simply unknowable, even by God, until they occur. It would make no sense to say that God might have had knowledge of the future but set aside such a capacity. Similarly, process thinkers present a view of reality in which divine omnipotence is in principle impossible.

Charles Hartshorne elaborates a metaphysics in which all beings including God are inherently social and interactive. Every being has passive and receptive capabilities as well as active and causally effective ones. No being can have a monopoly of power or effect unilateral control. It is not as if the presence of the world limits God's otherwise unlimited power, since any valid concept of God must include sociality and relationality. Hartshorne says that in some aspects God is temporal and affected by the world but in other aspects God exemplifies classical divine attributes. God alone is everlasting, omnipresent, and omniscient (in knowing all that can be known). God is perfect in love and wisdom and unchanging in purposes and goals. God offers an initial aim to every entity and orders the world through cosmic laws that limit but do not exclude creaturely freedom. God's power is universal in scope. It "influences all that happens but determines nothing in its concrete particularity."[26]

To say that the limitation of God's power is a metaphysical necessity rather than a voluntary self-limitation is not to say that it is imposed by something outside God. This is not a Gnostic or Manichean dualism in which recalcitrant matter restricts God's effort to embody pure eternal forms in the world. If God's nature is to be loving and creative, it would be inconsistent to say that God might have chosen not to be loving and creative. We cannot say that God was once omnipotent and chose to set aside such powers temporarily. If behind God's kenotic actions there was an omnipotent God who refrained from rescuing the victims of pain and suffering, the problem of theodicy would still be acute, as noted earlier. Hartshorne objects to divine omnipotence on moral as well as metaphysical grounds. Within a social view of reality, persuasion has a higher moral status than coercion, even if it entails greater risk of evil and suffering. He says that God does all that it would be good for a supreme being to do, though not all that it would be good for other beings to do for themselves.[27]

---

26. Charles Hartshorne, *Omnipotence and Other Theological Mistakes* (Albany: State University of New York Press, 1984), p. 25.

27. Charles Hartshorne, *Reality as Social Process* (Glencoe, Ill.: Free Press, 1953).

2. The Adequacy of God's Power

The limitation of divine power in process thought may make the problem of theodicy more tractable, but does it leave God powerless to overcome evil? Hartshorne goes further than Whitehead in portraying God's ability to transform evil redemptively and to empower people with courage to resist evil. Daniel Day Williams writes:

> I think Dr. Hartshorne is right in stressing also the coercive aspects of religious experience. To worship God in dependence on his holiness does transform the self, far beyond its conscious intent and understanding. When we oppose God we discover the boundaries of our action, which are starkly there, and the consequences which are visited upon us whether we will or no. There are large coercive aspects in the divine governance of the world.[28]

Williams in turn goes beyond Hartshorne in defending divine initiative in history and in the person of Christ. He holds that for God, as for human beings, "to love is to be vulnerable," but he maintains that in some respects God is invulnerable. "God's love is absolute in its integrity forever. In this sense it is invulnerable."[29] Events in the world may threaten the fulfillment of God's purposes, but God's being is not threatened. God remains faithful to the creation.

Williams cannot accept the divine monarch who controls all things and guarantees victory over evil, but he also cannot accept the divine aesthete who can only take up the tragic elements of life into a larger and more harmonious picture, as some passages in Whitehead suggest. Between these extremes Williams portrays the divine companion whose influence is transformative and redemptive.[30] He describes a client who

28. Daniel Day Williams, "How Does God Act? An Essay in Whitehead's Metaphysics," in *Process and Divinity*, ed. W. L. Reese and E. Freeman (LaSalle, Ill.: Open Court Press, 1964), p. 177.

29. Daniel Day Williams, *The Spirit and the Forms of Love* (New York: Harper and Row, 1968), p. 185. See also Daniel Day Williams, "The Vulnerable and the Invulnerable God," *Christianity and Crisis* 22 (March 1962): 27-30. On Williams's views, see Warren McWilliams, *The Passion of God: Divine Suffering in Contemporary Protestant Thought* (Macon, Ga.: Mercer University Press, 1985), ch. 6.

30. Daniel Day Williams, "Deity, Monarchy, and Metaphysics: Whitehead's Cri-

finds that a psychotherapist can hear his story without being threatened by it. Such sharing of suffering is a form of acceptance and communication. Healing can arise from the sharing and reinterpretation of suffering. So, too, God's participation in Christ's suffering and in ours is "God's act of self-identification for us, his way of communication to us, and his healing power among us."[31] Moreover, God's action in Christ can empower us to cooperate in the alleviation of the suffering of others. For Williams, divine love, like human love at its best, seeks neither power over others nor powerlessness, but reciprocity and mutual empowerment.

Anna Case-Winter proposes a synthesis of process and feminist thought. She argues that the strength of process thought lies in its conceptual framework and in its critique of the intellectual adequacy of classical views; she draws particularly from Hartshorne's analysis of divine power. She says that the strength of feminist theology, on the other hand, is its attention to the experience of people in particular life situations and social contexts. Feminists have been more aware of the social and political consequences of theological ideas and the way concepts of God have been used to legitimate patterns of domination and oppression. But process and feminist authors share a commitment to starting from experience and to using holistic, social, relational, and organic models of reality. Both groups understand God's power not as overpowering but as empowering. Case-Winter suggests that God is like a mother who empowers a child *in utero* and in subsequent life by working with other powers, not by displacing them. Such views of divine power would encourage forms of human power that are consistent with freedom, responsibility, and an ethics of solidarity with the oppressed.[32] Other writers have also noted the similarities between feminist and process thought.[33]

---

tique of the Theological Tradition," in *The Relevance of Whitehead*, ed. I. Leclerc (New York: Macmillan, 1961).

31. Daniel Day Williams, "Suffering and Being in Empirical Theology," in *The Future of Empirical Theology*, ed. Bernard Meland (Chicago: University of Chicago Press, 1969), p. 191.

32. Anna Case-Winter, *God's Power: Traditional Understanding and Contemporary Challenges* (Louisville: Westminster/John Knox, 1990).

33. Sheila Devaney, ed., *Feminism and Process Thought* (New York and Toronto: Edwin Mellen Press, 1981).

3. The Beginning and the End

Whitehead, who wrote before scientific evidence of the Big Bang was available, held that God and the world have always coexisted, and that God creates by working with what already exists. Whitehead postulated an infinite sequence of "cosmic epochs" differing significantly from each other.[34] Subsequent process thinkers have generally followed him in defending an infinite temporal past, and some have suggested that "cosmic epochs" might be identified with successive cycles of *an oscillating universe,* expanding and contracting, with a Big Crunch before each Big Bang. Process authors have said that God is always creative and social, bringing order and novelty out of chaos. They have criticized the doctrine of creation *ex nihilo* for overemphasizing divine transcendence, and they have defended continuing creation which gives greater prominence to divine immanence.[35] But recent evidence suggests that our universe may be expanding too rapidly for it to slow down in the future and then eventually contract.

An alternative to an oscillating universe is the theory of *quantum vacuum fluctuations,* which is supported by many cosmologists today. Quantum theory permits very brief violations of energy conservation. In the laboratory, a vacuum is really a sea of activity in which pairs of virtual particles come into being and almost immediately annihilate each other. Perhaps our universe started from an enormous fluctuation that rapidly expanded, following the scenario of current inflationary theory. Our universe would be one of many coexisting universes which expanded too rapidly to be in communication with each other.[36] In this theory, as in the *ex nihilo* tradition, our universe did not arise from the remains of a previous universe. However, in this theory the universe did not originate totally *ex nihilo* but from a Superspace of quantum fields and quantum laws.

34. Alfred North Whitehead, *Process and Reality,* corrected edition, ed. David Ray Griffin and Donald Sherborne (New York: Free Press, 1978), p. 91.

35. Charles Hartshorne, *Man's Vision of God* (Chicago: Willet Clark, 1941), pp. 230-34; John Cobb and David Griffin, *Process Theology: An Introduction,* pp. 64-67; Lewis Ford, "An Alternative to Creatio Ex Nihilo," *Religious Studies* 19 (1983): 205-13.

36. Andre Linde, "The Self-Reproducing Inflationary Universe," *Scientific American* 271 (November 1994): 48-55; Alan Guth, *The Inflationary Universe* (Reading, Mass.: Addison-Wesley, 1997); John Gribbin, *In the Beginning* (Boston: Little, Brown, 1993).

Atheistic cosmologists are attracted to the *quantum fluctuation theory* partly because it allows them to avoid the unique beginning associated with traditional theism. Rem Edwards suggests, however, that the theory is compatible with a revised process theism that includes both distinctive events in the initiation of universes and a continuing divine activity in each universe. God's everlasting creativity and sociality would be expressed both in Superspace and in innumerable finite universes. Edwards holds that the space and time of our universe are finite but were created within an infinite Superspace — not by chance but by God's selection among potential universes. In such a scheme God is always related to some universe but not always to our particular cosmic history.[37] But this is a highly speculative theory because other universes are in principle unobservable from our universe.

The simplest cosmological option is a *unique Big Bang,* a view that does not postulate unobservable cycles or unobservable universes. This option assumes a beginning of time and it is closest to the *ex nihilo* tradition. Whitehead himself said that God's primordial nature transcends our cosmic epoch. In process thought, the limitation of God's power over the events within cosmic history arises not only from God's nature but also from the influence of past events on subsequent events. Moreover, in the course of cosmic history beings at higher levels of organization have greater self-determination, culminating in human freedom, and they have a greater capacity to resist God's initial aims for them. Neither of these limitations were present in the early moments of the universe before even quarks were present. The pure potentialities in the primordial nature of God could have been more readily and rapidly realized in those early moments than in subsequent history, and would represent an essentially unilateral exercise of divine power, as the *ex nihilo* tradition affirms. However, Whitehead maintained that the primordial and consequent natures of God are abstractions from the divine unity, and this option would require more drastic modifications in his thought than the other cosmological theories mentioned earlier.

Scientific theories concerning the long-term future of the universe appear rather bleak. According to one scenario, the expansion of the universe will slow down and reverse itself, collapsing to a "heat death" that will end

37. Rem Edwards, "How Process Theology Can Affirm Creation Ex Nihilo," *Process Studies* 29 (2000).

all forms of life. Astronomers have been searching for the "missing mass" (perhaps in neutrinos or interstellar dark matter) that might produce such a "closed universe." An alternative scenario expects the expansion to continue forever (an "open universe") leading to a "cold death" when temperatures are too low to support life. Recent evidence that the universe has been expanding more rapidly than previously assumed favors the second scenario. But before either of these cosmic catastrophes, our sun will have burnt itself out and life on our planet will be impossible. Long before then human folly may have ended human life by nuclear war or ecological disaster.

The Bible includes a wide variety of expectations of the future. The early prophets saw God's judgment in the disasters threatening the nation, but they believed that if Israel returned to the covenant faith it would enter a new era of peace, justice, and prosperity under a divinely appointed leader. Later, in the midst of oppression, the apocalyptic literature looked to the establishment of God's Kingdom by the supernatural defeat of the oppressing powers. Within the New Testament, the Kingdom was sometimes portrayed as growing slowly like a grain of mustard seed (Matt. 13), and in other passages as coming rapidly by a dramatic intervention (as in the book of Revelation). Christ's return was sometimes imminently expected (as in Mark 13), while other authors held that it had already occurred spiritually in Christ's presence with his followers (the "realized eschatology" of John's gospel).[38]

Liberals today, including process theologians, have usually favored a prophetic rather than an apocalyptic eschatology. But in reaction to the historical optimism of earlier decades they acknowledge that the Kingdom will not come by human effort alone. David Griffin points out that classical Christianity faced the problem of reconciling an omnipotent God and the continued existence of evil, and it sought an eschatological solution. He claims that process thought does not face this problem. It leads us to believe that God empowers us to resist evil now rather than to expect God's unilateral action in the future. It provides grounds for hope of God's victory over evil, but it offers no risk-free guarantee.[39]

38. Claus Westermann, *Beginning and End in the Bible* (Philadelphia: Fortress Press, 1972).

39. David Ray Griffin, *God, Power, and Evil: A Process Theodicy* (Philadelphia: Westminster Press, 1976); also his "Creation Out of Chaos and the Problem of Evil," in *Encountering Evil: Live Options in Theodicy,* ed. Stephen Davis (Atlanta: John Knox Press, 1988).

4. *Immortality and the Resurrection*

Most scholars maintain that the idea of an immortal soul temporarily in-habiting a mortal body found in the early centuries of Christian history was more indebted to Greek than to Hebrew thought. The Hebrew scrip-tures portrayed the human self as a unified bodily activity of thinking, willing, and acting. Paul defends the resurrection of the whole person by God's action, not the inherent immortality of a separate soul. I have ex-plored elsewhere some historical and contemporary interpretations of hu-man nature.[40] In the present context I can only note that process thinkers have articulated two forms of immortality. Objective immortality, de-fended by Whitehead, refers to our effect on God and our participation in God's eternal life. Our lives are meaningful because they are preserved everlastingly in God's experience, in which evil is transmuted and the good is saved and woven into the harmony of the larger whole. God's goal is not the completed achievement of a static final realm but rather a con-tinuing advance toward richer and more harmonious relationships.[41]

Other process writers defend subjective immortality in which the hu-man self continues as a center of experience in a radically different environ-ment, amid continuing change rather than changeless eternity, with the po-tential for continued communion with God. John Cobb speculates that we might picture a future life as neither absorption in God nor the survival of separate individuals but as a new kind of community transcending individ-uality.[42] Marjorie Suchocki suggests that subjective and objective immortal-ity can be combined, because God experiences each moment of our lives not merely externally as a completed event but also from within its subjec-tivity. In that case our subjective immediacy would be preserved in God as it never is in our interaction with other persons in the world.[43]

Finally, Christ's resurrection is a challenge to kenotic theology. If Christ's death on the cross revealed God's nature as suffering love, was this only a temporary strategy until God's true nature as omnipotent ruler was revealed in the resurrection? Religious art and popular piety have in-

40. Ian G. Barbour, "Neuroscience, Artificial Intelligence, and Human Nature."
41. See Cobb and Griffin, *Process Theology,* ch. 7.
42. John B. Cobb, Jr., "What Is the Future? A Process Perspective," in *Hope and the Future,* ed. Ewart Cousins (Philadelphia: Fortress Press, 1972).
43. Marjorie Hewett Suchocki, *The End of Evil: Process Eschatology in Historical Con-text* (Albany: State University of New York Press, 1988), ch. 5.

19

cluded images of both the agony of the crucifixion and the risen Christ ruling in glory. Luther advocated both a "theology of the cross" and a "theology of glory." But theologians today who speak of God's voluntary self-limitation have the task of showing that the message of the resurrection does not cancel out the message of the cross.

Process theologians face a different challenge. Can process thought account for Easter? To be sure, scholars have questioned the historical accuracy of the resurrection stories. There are discrepancies among them, and Paul's letters, written earlier than the gospels, never mention the empty tomb. But clearly the lives of the disciples were transformed in a dramatic way that changed the course of history. We could start by saying that the disciples became aware that in the midst of suffering God is present and new life is possible. They realized that God's love was not defeated by Christ's death. But we must also acknowledge their conviction that God had acted in a new way and that Christ had been taken up into the life of God and was a continuing influence on their lives. Marjorie Suchocki speaks of both confirmation and transformation: "The resurrection is the confirmation of that which Jesus revealed in his life and death, and it is the catalyst that transforms the disciples, releasing the power that led to the foundation of the church."[44] In process thought, God provides initial aims relevant to particular occasions, so very specific divine initiatives are possible, though always in cooperation with finite beings in the world. The events at Easter can be understood as such a new divine initiative and not just a new realization by the disciples of the meaning of Christ's life.

In sum, I have suggested that in its critique of divine omnipotence process thought offers a distinctive rendition of five themes prominent in kenotic theology: the integrity of nature; the problem of evil and suffering; the reality of human freedom; the Christian understanding of the cross; and feminist critiques of patriarchal models of God. I have tried to answer some possible criticisms of process theology concerning: metaphysical necessity rather than voluntary self-limitation; the adequacy of God's power for redemptive action; the beginning and end of the cosmos; and the interpretation of immortality and the resurrection. Process thought offers a path between omnipotence and impotence by reconceptualizing divine power as empowerment rather than overpowering control.

44. Marjorie Hewett Suchocki, *God, Christ, Church: A Practical Guide to Process Theology* (New York: Crossroad Press, 1982).

The Cost of New Life

ARTHUR PEACOCKE

The activity of God in creation must be precarious. It must proceed by no assured programme. Its progress, like every progress of love, must be an angular progress.

Love's Endeavour, Love's Expense, p. 62

The perception that in the act of creation God may be conceived of as self-offering and self-limiting, as in some way exposing Godself to suffering, and thereby becoming vulnerable to the history of the created order cannot be justified without reference to the evolutionary character of the actual process of creation. One can only speak of creation *as* a process because of the evidence for what is often now called the 'epic of evolution': the whole sequence, as unveiled by a gamut of the sciences, from the origin of the universe in the 'hot big bang' to the arrival of *homo sapiens* on planet Earth. It is notorious that the discovery of the biological phase of this process by Darwin in the nineteenth century led him and many of his contemporaries into a crisis of doubt about the nature and existence of any Creator God as they perceived in it the role of chance. Even more so today, any belief in divine creation has to come to terms with and, better, be integrated with and informed by these scientific perceptions of the way in which life, including that of humanity, has come into existence. In pursuing those objectives, I hope to show how the insight into God's relation to the world as a 'kenotic' one — one of self-offering and self-limitation

— may be illuminated and amplified. With reference to our understanding of God's relation to and interaction with the world the significant features of the process of biological evolution as uncovered by science are as follows.

God and Biological Evolution

(a) *Biological evolution is continuous and evidences emergence of new forms of life.* The evidence for the continuous emergence of new forms of life from original self-reproducing conglomerations of previously inorganic components is now overwhelming. Since the more general inferences by Darwin, and Wallace, of this process as the best explanation of widely disparate observations of the relation of the variation of both past and present living organisms to a multiplicity of environmental factors and its subsequent reinforcement by genetics, there has now been added, with the rise in the twentieth century of molecular biology, the conclusive evidence *inter alia* of: the universality in all living organisms of the otherwise arbitrary genetic code (that between DNA nucleotide triplets and the amino acids of proteins); the matching of the genealogy of amino acid sequences in particular proteins common to a wide range of disparate species with evolutionary trees derived on paleontological and morphological grounds; and the matching of changes in nucleotide sequences of DNA with those same evolutionary trees. Indeed the genealogies based on this molecular detective work has amplified and bridged many gaps in the fossil record of creatures with survivable bony structures and has illuminated the evolutionary relationships of organisms, such as bacteria. The very gradualness of the molecular changes so discovered emphasizes yet again the slowness but real continuity of the processes of biological evolution over the three or so billion years since the Earth was cool enough to allow the existence of macromolecular complexes, some of which became self-copying and therefore 'alive'.

The processes that have occurred can be characterized also as displaying *emergence,* for new forms of matter, and a hierarchy of organization of these forms themselves, appear in the course of time. These new forms have new properties, behaviors, and networks of relations that necessitate not only specific methods of investigation but also the development of new epistemologically irreducible concepts in order to describe and refer

22

to them. To these new organizations of matter it is justifiable to ascribe new levels of what can only be called 'reality': new kinds of reality may be said to 'emerge' in time. On the surface of the Earth, new forms of *living* matter (that is, living organisms) have come into existence by this continuous process — that is what we mean by evolution.

There is inexorably impressed upon us a dynamic picture of a world of living structures involved in continuous and incessant change and in process without ceasing. Any static conception of the way in which the 'God' gives existence to all-that-is and sustains and holds everything in being is therefore precluded. For in the world new structures and processes appear in the course of time, so that God's action as Creator is both past and present: it is continuous. The scientific perspective of a cosmos, and in particular that of the biological world, as developing continuously in time with the emergence of the new re-introduces into our understanding of God's creative relation to the world a *dynamic* element which, even if obscured by the allocation of 'creation' to an event in the past, was always implicit in the Hebrew conception of a 'living God'. We are here a far cry away from any static model of an Atlas-like god holding the World on his shoulders. Any notion of God as Creator must now assert that God is continuously creating, continuously giving existence to what is new; that God is *semper Creator;* that the world is a *creatio continua*. The traditional notion of God *sustaining* the world in its general order and structure now has to be replaced by one with a dynamic and creative dimension — a model of God giving continuous existence to a process that has an inbuilt creativity, built into it by God and manifest in a 'time' itself given existence by God. As Frederick Temple said in his Bampton Lectures of 1885, "God did not make the things, we may say, but he made them make themselves."

Biological evolution impels us to take more seriously and more concretely than hitherto the notion of the immanence of God-as-Creator — that God is the Immanent Creator creating in and through the processes of the natural order. I would urge that all this has to be taken in a very strong sense. If one asks where do we see God-as-Creator during, say, the processes of biological evolution, one has to reply: "The processes themselves, as unveiled by the biological sciences, *are* God-acting-as-Creator, God *qua* Creator." This is not pantheism for it is the *action* of God that is identified with the creative processes of nature, not God's own self. God gives existence in divinely created time to a process that itself brings forth the new: thereby God is creat*ing*.

23

(b) *Biological evolution proceeds 'naturally'* — that is, by processes accessible to and made intelligible by biology and other natural sciences. This implies that there is no need to look for God in any way as a kind of *additional* nonscientifically accessible factor supplementing these creative processes of the world whose existence is indeed given them *by* God. If this is so, the processes revealed by evolutionary biology are, for theists, in themselves God-acting-as-Creator. To justify this we have to ask whether the sciences provide a *sufficient* explanation of biological changes and the overall sweep of evolution.

All biologists would agree that natural selection is a major factor operative in biological evolution and most would say it is by far the most significant one. For some, such as Richard Dawkins,[1] it is the only one. It must be accepted that it can be demonstrated how subtle, and indeed often counterintuitive, the effects of natural selection can be in bringing into existence complex structures and in affecting behavior patterns. It certainly operates at the level of the gene and in group selection, which was once rejected but has recently been re-introduced.[2] Among biologists many other factors continue to be advocated,[3] all of them naturalistic — that is, within the purview of, and investigatable by, scientific methods. One of the most interesting recent considerations brought to bear on how evolution can occur is the theoretical work of Stuart Kaufmann[4] showing how the constraints and selectivity effected by self-organizational principles can shape the possibilities of elaboration of structures and even direct its course. This theme has been expounded further by Ian Stewart,[5] who shows how mathematical theories of complexity may help explain the origin and evolution of life and how mathematical laws control the growing organism's response to its genetic instructions — the key to understand-

1. Richard Dawkins, *The Selfish Gene* (Oxford: Oxford University Press, 1976); *The Blind Watchmaker* (London: Longmans, 1986).

2. D. S. Wilson and E. Sober, "Reintroducing Group Selection to the Human Behavioral Sciences," *Behavioral and Brain Sciences* 17 (1994): 585-654.

3. For example: the 'evolution of evolvability' (S. A. Kaufmann); genetic assimilation (C. H. Waddington); the effect of an organism's state and individual behavior (R. C. Lewontin and A. Hardy); 'top-down causation' (D. Campbell); the role of 'neutral' mutations (M. Kimura); 'molecular drive' in multigene families (G. A. Dover); and the context of adaptive change in hierarchies of biological entities (N. Eldredge).

4. Stuart A. Kaufman, *At Home in the Universe* (London: Penguin Books, 1995).

5. Ian Stewart, *Life's Other Secret: The New Mathematics of the Living World* (London: Penguin Books, 1998).

ing its growth and form.[6] All of which may lead to less reductionistic and more holistic ways of interpreting, purely scientifically, living organisms and their evolution.

It must be stressed that all these proposals are entirely naturalistic in their content, requiring the intervention of no *deus ex machina,* no special forces or divinely directed events. They are part of the ongoing inquiries, and inevitably debate, within experimental and theoretical biology, and they assume a basically Darwinian process to be operating, even when they disagree about its speed and smoothness. That being so, it has to be recognized that the history of life on Earth involves chance in a way unthinkable before Darwin. There is a creative interplay of 'chance' and law apparent in the evolution of living matter by natural selection. For biological evolution depends on a process in which changes occur in the genetic-information-carrying material (DNA) that are purely physicochemical and random with respect to the biological form and needs of the organisms possessing the DNA — random with respect to its need to produce progeny for the species to survive. What we call 'chance' is involved both at the level of the mutational event in the DNA itself; and in the intersecting of two causally unrelated chains of events — namely, the changes in the DNA and the consequences of such changes for survival in its particular biological niche. The interaction with the biological niche in which the organism exists then filters out, in an entirely understandable fashion, those changes in the DNA that enable the organisms possessing them to produce more progeny. That is what 'natural selection' is.

As I shall suggest, the involvement of what we call 'chance' at the level of mutation in the DNA does not, of itself, preclude these events from displaying regular trends and manifesting inbuilt propensities[7] at the higher levels of organisms, populations, and ecosystems. To call the mutation of the DNA a 'chance' event serves simply to stress its randomness with respect to biological consequence. As I have earlier put it (in a response later supported and amplified by others[8]):

6. In this context, Stewart writes inspired by an earlier biological pioneering classic: D'Arcy Wentworth Thompson's *On Growth and Form* (Cambridge: Cambridge University Press, 1942).
7. See below for a discussion of this term.
8. David Bartholomew, *God of Chance* (London: SCM Press, 1984).

25

Instead of being daunted by the role of chance in genetic mutations as being the manifestation of irrationality in the universe, it would be more consistent with the observations to assert that the full gamut of the potentialities of living matter could be explored only through the agency of the rapid and frequent randomization which is possible at the molecular level of the DNA.[9]

This role of 'chance', or rather randomness (or 'free experiment') at the micro-level is what one would expect if the universe were so constituted that the range of possible forms of organizations of matter (both living and nonliving) that it contains might be thoroughly explored. This 'exploration' occurs within the limitations of the irreversibility of historical processes and with the closing off therefore of some potentialities as others are actualized. Each stage of evolution constitutes the launching pad for the next so that the process involves an element of contingency. It is the interplay of chance and law that is creative within time, for it is the combination of the two that allows new forms to emerge and evolve — so that natural selection appears to be opportunistic. As in many games, the consequences of random events, the fall of the dice, depend very much on the rules of the game.[10] It has become increasingly apparent that it is chance operating within a law-like framework that is the basis of the inherent creativity of the natural order, its ability to generate new forms, patterns, and organizations of matter and energy. If all were governed by rigid law, a repetitive and uncreative order would prevail; if chance alone ruled, no forms, patterns, or organizations would persist long enough for them to have any identity or real existence, and the universe could never be a cosmos and susceptible to rational inquiry — it would be either a rigid repetitive machine or a primeval Hesiodic chaos. It is the combination of the two that makes possible an ordered universe capable of developing within itself new modes of existence. The 'rules' of the evolution 'game' are what they are because of the properties of the physical environment and of the already evolved other living organisms with which the organism in question interacts.

9. A. R. Peacocke, *Creation and the World of Science* [henceforth *CWS*] (Oxford: Clarendon Press, 1979), p. 94.

10. R. Winkler and M. Eigen, *Laws of the Game* (New York: Knopf, 1981; London: Allen Lane, 1982).

These properties, this 'givenness', for a theist, can only be regarded as an aspect of the God-endowed features of the world. The way in which what we call 'chance' operates within this framework to produce new structures, entities, and processes can then properly be seen as an eliciting by the Creator of the potentialities that the physical cosmos possessed *ab initio*. Such potentialities a theist must regard as written into creation by the Creator's intention and purpose and must conceive as gradually being actualized by the operation of 'chance' stimulating their coming into existence.

For a theist, God must now be seen creating in the world by giving existence to processes involving chance. God is the ultimate ground and source of both the 'rules of the game' (law or necessity) and of 'chance'. The Creator, it seems, unfolds the divinely endowed potentialities of the universe, in and through a process in which these creative possibilities, inherent by God's own intention within the fundamental entities of that universe and their interrelations, become actualized within a created temporal development shaped and determined by those selfsame God-given potentialities. But the means involve randomness, so that there is an open-endedness in the direction the processes at any instance might take — an open-endedness that looks in retrospect like mere contingency to the human observer. Moreover, the theist has to accept that there is a sense in which God is, as it were, 'taking a risk' in creating through such a process built at the level of DNA mutations on randomness, and at the environmental level on the contingency of macroscopic events affecting the viability of the organism possessing the mutations.

(c) *Biological evolution manifests significant trends.* Is there any objective, non-anthropocentrically biased, evidence for directions or at least trends in biological evolution? Biologists have been especially cautious not to answer this question affirmatively, for evolution is best depicted biologically not as a kind of Christmas tree, with *homo sapiens* accorded a pseudo-angelic position crowning the topmost frond, but rather as a bush. As Stephen J. Gould puts it, "Life is a copiously branching bush, continually pruned by the grim reaper of extinction, not a ladder of predictable progress." Later, Gould poses the challenge to any idea of direction in evolution towards humanity, thus:

> If humanity arose just yesterday as a small twig on one branch of a
> flourishing tree, then life may not, in any genuine sense, exist for us

or because of us. Perhaps we are only an afterthought, a kind of cosmic accident, just one bauble on the Christmas tree of evolution.[11]

Nevertheless, G. G. Simpson can affirm that "Within the framework of the evolutionary history of life there have been not one but many different kinds of progress."[12] While admitting that such lines can be traced in the evolutionary 'bush', other biologists would, understandably, be more chary of calling them 'progress'.

One must not be misled by the randomness of the mutations — some kind of lesion and/or alteration of the DNA in an organism so that the gene encoded around this point is changed — into thinking that no directions whatever could ever be manifest in the evolutionary process. For the consequences for an organism of a mutation in its DNA depend on the environment of the whole organism, which includes not only its physical surroundings (food resources, habitat, etc.) but also the presence *inter alia* of predators and symbionts. In the light of the dominant role of natural selection in evolution, the pertinent question is therefore, "Are there any particular properties and functions attributable to living organisms that could occur as the result of mutations in DNA and that could be said to be in themselves helpful for evolution to occur because they are advantageous in natural selection (for survival of progeny) of organisms possessing them?"

We have here a situation in which what F. Dretske has called 'structuring causes' are operative, namely, the influence of independent (maybe random) triggering events on the subsequent form and state of the systems in which the triggering events occur.[13] It also corresponds to what Karl Popper called a 'propensity' in nature for certain properties to ap-

11. S. J. Gould, *Wonderful Life: The Burgess Shale and the Nature of History* (London and New York: Penguin Books, 1989), pp. 35, 44.

12. G. G. Simpson, *The Meaning of Evolution* (New Haven: Bantam Books, Yale University Press, 1971), p. 236. He instances the kinds of 'progress' (prescinding from any normative connotation) as: the tendency for living organisms to expand to fill all available spaces in the livable environments; the successive invasion and development by organisms of new environmental and adaptive spheres; increasing specialization with its corollary of improvement and adaptability; increase in the general energy or maintained level of vital processes; protected reproduction/care of the young; individualization, increasing complexity, and so forth.

13. F. Dretske, "Mental Events as Structuring Causes of Behavior," in *Mental Causation,* ed. J. Heil and A. Mele (Oxford: Clarendon Press, 1993), pp. 121-36.

pear. He argued that a greater frequency of occurrence of a particular kind of event may be used as a test of whether or not there is inherent in a sequence of events (equivalent to throws of a die) a tendency or propensity to realize the event in question. This is not any non-randomness in the initial event (say, the fall of the die — they are not 'loaded') but in the *consequences* of that initial event in the particular context in which it is set. Propensities are simply the effects of the context on the outcomes of random events. Popper pointed out that the *realization of possibilities,* which may be random, *depends on the total situation within which the possibilities are being actualized* so that "there exist weighted possibilities which are *more than mere possibilities,* but tendencies or propensities to become real"[14] and that these "propensities in physics are properties of *the whole situation* and sometimes even of the particular way in which a situation changes. And the same holds of the propensities in chemistry, in biochemistry, and in biology."[15]

I suggest that there *are* propensities, in this Popperian sense, in evolution towards the possession of certain characteristics, propensities that are built into an evolutionary process because natural selection of the best procreators in general favors the acquisition of certain features. For there are some features that *naturally* enhance survival for procreation in certain widely occurring environments, that is, they are favorable to natural selection of the organism possessing them. Among the plethora of such features of living organisms there are a number that characterize *homo sapiens* and are pertinent to our wider concerns. They are as follows.

(i) *Complexity.* The human brain is the most complex natural system known to us. Is there a propensity to complexity in *biological* evolution? There certainly seems to be, and 'increasing complexity' was included in Simpson's list (see note 12) as characteristic of it. What significance is to be attributed to this? Is it simply that biological "evolution is a process of divergence and wandering rather than an inexorable progression towards increasing complexity"[16] so that evolution merely allows[17] the emergence

14. Karl Popper, *A World of Propensities* (Bristol: Thoemmes, 1990), p. 12.

15. Karl Popper, *A World of Propensities,* p. 18.

16. W. McCoy, "Complexity in Organic Evolution," *Journal of Theoretical Biology* 68 (1977): 457.

17. But note the judgment of S. Conway Morris (*The Crucible of Creation: The Burgess Shale and the Rise of Animals* [Oxford: Oxford University Press, 1998]): ". . . within certain limits the outcome of evolutionary processes might be rather predictable. . . . Nearly all bi-

of new complexity, but does not necessitate it? Faced with some new challenge in its environment, it is reasonable to suppose that mutations would be selected that allowed the acquisition of some new structure and/or function that enabled the creature to produce more progeny in the new circumstances. The fact is that there *has* been, taking biological evolution as a whole, an emergence of increasingly complex organisms (even if in some very stable, evolutionary lines, in very static niches, there has been a loss of complexity and so of organization). So, on Popper's criterion enunciated above, we would be correct in saying that there is a propensity towards increased complexity in the evolution of living organisms.

The need for *organization* for survival was beautifully demonstrated by H. A. Simon,[18] who showed that the simplest modular organization of, say, the structure of a watch, so that each module had a limited stability, led to an enormous increase in survivability during manufacture in the face of random destructive events. Hence the increases we observe during evolution in complexity and organization (subsumed under 'complexity' from now on) in the biological world are entirely intelligible as contributing to success in natural selection and are not at all mysterious in the sense of requiring some non-naturalistic explanation.

(ii) *Information-processing and -storage ability.* The more capable an organism is of receiving signals, recording and analyzing them, and using the information to make predictions useful for survival about changes in its environment, the better chance it will have of surviving under the pressures of natural selection in a wide variety of habitats. In other words, there is a propensity towards the formation of systems having the functions we now recognize in nervous systems and brains. Such ability for information-processing and -storage is indeed the necessary, if not sufficient, condition for the emergence of consciousness.

---

ologists agree that convergence is a ubiquitous feature of life. . . . The underlying reason for convergence seems to be that all organisms are under constant scrutiny of natural selection. . . . convergence shows that in a real world not all things are possible. . . . again and again we have evidence of biological form stumbling on the same solution to a problem. . . . It is not very important if the many details of an alternative history are different, because in broad outlook the study of evolutionary convergence demonstrates that the world, perhaps even any world [*cf.* R. Dawkins, below and note 20], would have to look broadly similar" (pp. 201, 204, 205).

18. H. A. Simon, "The Architecture of Complexity," *Proceedings of the American Philosophical Society* 106 (1962): 467-82.

(iii) *Pain and suffering.* This sensitivity to, this sentience of, its surroundings inevitably involves an increase in its ability to experience pain, which constitutes the necessary biological warning signals of danger and disease. It is impossible to envisage an increase of information-processing ability without an increase in the sensitivity of an organism's signal system to its environment. Hence an increase in 'information-processing' capacity, with the advantages it confers in natural selection, cannot but have as its corollary an increase, not only in the level of consciousness, but also in the experience of pain.

Each increase in sensitivity, and eventually of consciousness, as evolution proceeds inevitably heightens and accentuates awareness both of the beneficent, life-enhancing, and of the inimical, life-diminishing, elements in the world in which the organism finds itself. The stakes for joy and pain are, as it were, continually being raised, and the living organism learns to discriminate between them. So pain and suffering, on the one hand, and consciousness of pleasure and well-being, on the other, are emergents in the world; and there can be said to be a propensity for them to occur. From a purely naturalistic viewpoint, the emergence of pain and its compounding of suffering as consciousness increases seem to be inevitable aspects of any conceivable developmental process characterized by a continual increase in ability to process and store information from the environment. In the context of natural selection, pain has an energizing effect and suffering is a goad to action: they both have survival value for creatures continually faced with new problematic situations challenging their survival. Holmes Rolston has developed this characteristic of biological evolution — he calls it 'cruciform naturalism'. Sentience, he argues, evolves with a capacity to separate the 'helps' from the 'hurts' of the world: with sentience there appears caring. "Pain is an energizing force" so that "where pain fits into evolutionary theory, it must have, on statistical average, high survival value, with this selected for, and with a selecting against counterproductive pain. . . . Suffering is a key to the whole, not intrinsically, not as an end in itself, but as a transformative principle, transvalued into its opposite."[19]

In relation to any theological reflections, it must be emphasized that pain and suffering are present in biological evolution as a necessary condi-

19. Holmes Rolston, III, *Science and Religion: A Critical Survey* (New York: Random House, 1987), pp. 287ff.; and see his chapter in this volume.

tion for survival of the individual long before the appearance of human beings. So the presence of pain and suffering cannot be the result of any particular human failings, though undoubtedly human beings experience them with a heightened sensitivity and, more than any other creatures, inflict them on each other and on other living creatures.

(iv) *Self-consciousness and language.* If an information-processing and -storage system can also monitor its own state at any moment, then it has at least the basis for communicating what that state is to other similar systems. Hence, provided the physical apparatus for communication has also evolved, the capacity for language becomes possible and especially in the most highly developed such systems. In other words, there is an inbuilt propensity for the acquisition of language, as we see in many other forms in the nonhuman living world, and so for developing the necessary basis for *self*-consciousness. This would be an advantage in natural selection, for it is the basis of complex social cooperation in the creatures that possess it (so far, supremely *homo sapiens*) with all the advantages this gives against predators and in gaining food.

It is interesting to note that Richard Dawkins[20] also includes among the thresholds that will be crossed *naturally* in "a general chronology of a life explosion on any planet, anywhere in the universe . . . thresholds that any planetary replication bomb can be expected to pass," those for: high-speed information-processing, achieved by possession of a nervous system; consciousness (concurrent with brains); and language.

Given the immanentist understanding of God's presence 'in, with, and under' the processes of biological evolution adopted up to this point, can God be said to be implementing any purpose in biological evolution? I have given reasons for postulating that, arising from the naturally selective nature of the interaction between organism and environment, there are propensities[21] in evolution towards the possession of certain characteristics. We must recall that use of this term does not mean that in any sense 'the dice are loaded' — that the mutational basis for natural selection is in any way non-random — but that the *consequences* for the species of random mutations depend on the environment of the organism (in the widest sense) and that this can favor some rather than others. Among

20. Richard Dawkins, *River Out of Eden* (London: Weidenfeld and Nicholson, 1995), pp. 151ff. (The 'thresholds' mentioned in the main text are his numbers 5, 6, and 7.)
21. Defined above on pp. 28-29.

such consequences inherently built into an evolutionary process based on natural selection, we have identified: increase in complexity; information-processing and -storage; consciousness; sensitivity to pain; and even self-consciousness (a necessary prerequisite for social development and the cultural transmission of knowledge down the generations). *Some* successive forms, along *some* branch or 'twig' (à la Gould), have a distinct probability of manifesting more and more of these characteristics. The actual physical form of the organisms in which these happen is contingent on the history of the confluence of disparate chains of events, including the survival of the mass extinctions that have occurred. However, the recognition of these built-in propensities in evolution suggests that, providing there had been enough time, a complex organism with consciousness, self-consciousness, social and cultural organization (that is, the basis for the existence of 'persons') would likely have evolved and appeared on the Earth (or on some other planet amenable to the emergence of living organisms) — though not necessarily, indeed probably not in view of the historical contingencies in human history, in the actual physical form of *homo sapiens*. There can, it seems to me (*pace* Stephen Gould),[22] be overall direction and implementation of divine purpose through chance (mutations) operating in a rule-obeying context (the environment) without a deterministic plan fixing in advance all the details of the structure(s) of what eventually emerges with personal qualities. Hence the emergence of self-conscious persons capable of relating personally to God can still be regarded as an intention of God continuously creating through the processes that God has given an existence — of this contingent kind and not some other.

I see no need to postulate any *special* action of God — along the lines, say, of some divine manipulation of mutations at the quantum level, or of some special 'lure' of God in the process — to ensure that persons emerge in the universe, and in particular on Earth. Not to coin a phrase, "I have no need of that hypothesis"! In other words, the whole process leading to the emergence of persons can be satisfactorily accounted for as a purely naturalistic one and as therefore implemented by God's *general* providential ordering of and immanent presence in the world. There is no obligation on the part of theists to invoke any *special* providential action by God, least of all any intervention in natural processes (whether quantum

22. Gould, *Wonderful Life*, p. 51 and *passim*.

or 'chaotic'), to account for the emergence of self-conscious persons, since this appears to be an inbuilt consequence of the very nature of those processes as discovered by the sciences — those God-given processes in and through which God is acting as Creator. It is interesting that these processes appear increasingly to embody holistic, directional principles that have a mathematical basis, and so one can account naturalistically for much that has previously led to the inference of some kind of 'lure' or pull directing evolution to higher complexities.

(d) *Biological evolution is costly, involving pain, suffering, predation, and death.* We have suggested that experience of pain is inevitable in any creature that is going to be aware of and can gain information from its environment and so avoid dangers. The pain associated with breakdown of health due to general organic causes also appears to be simply a concomitant of being a complex organized system incorporating internal as well as external sensors. When pain is experienced by a conscious organism, the attribution of 'suffering' becomes more appropriate and, with self-consciousness, empathy with the suffering of others emerges. The ubiquity of pain and suffering in the living world appears to be an inevitable consequence of creatures acquiring those information-processing and -storage systems (observed as nerves and brains in the later stages of evolution) that are so advantageous in natural selection.

Complex living structures can only have a finite chance of coming into existence if they are not assembled *de novo,* as it were, from their basic subunits, but emerge through a kind of modular process through the accumulation of changes in simpler forms, as demonstrated by H. A. Simon in that classic paper (see note 18). Having come onto the scene, they can then survive, because of the finitude of their life spans, only by building preformed complex chemical structures into their fabric through imbibing the materials of other living organisms. It is difficult for the chemist and biochemist to conceive how complex material structures, especially those of the intricacy of living organisms, could be assembled in times of the requisite order of magnitude otherwise than from less complex ones, that is, by predation. So there is a kind of *structural* logic about the inevitability of living organisms preying on each other — almost as 'analytical' as the impossibility is for the mathematician of conceiving of a universe to which the laws of arithmetic are inapplicable. For we cannot conceive, in a lawful, non-magical universe, of any way whereby the immense variety of developing, biological, structural complexity might appear in a finite time, except by utilizing structures already existing, either by way of modification (as in biological evolution) or of incorporation (as in feeding). Plants feed on inorganic materials and animals have to feed on plants and some animals on other animals. The structural logic is inescapable: new forms of matter arise only through incorporating, imbibing, the old.

Moreover, new patterns can only come into existence in a finite universe ('finite' in the sense of the conservation of matter-energy) if old patterns dissolve to make place for them. This is a condition of the creativity of the process, of its ability to produce the new which at the biological level we observe as new forms of life only through death of the old. For the death of individual organisms is essential for release of food resources for new arrivals, and species simply die out by being ousted from biological 'niches' by new ones better adapted to survive and reproduce in them. Hence biological death of the individual is the prerequisite of the creativity of the biological order, that creativity which eventually led to the emergence of human beings. To summarize, we can say that "new life through death of the old" (what J. H. Fabre called the "sublime law of sacrifice")[23] is inevitable in a finite world composed of common 'building blocks' (atoms, molecules, macromolecules) having regular properties.

Divine Delight, Yet Self-Offering and Suffering in Evolution?

Any understanding today of God's relation to the world cannot ignore these features of the way in which it now appears God has been and is creating the living world, including that of humanity. Some of the impact of this knowledge about the processes of creation has already been adverted to as we have been describing them. But now we must stand back and look at the whole panorama in relation to our understanding of God.

Certain new positive features in this perspective need first to be stressed. The process of biological evolution by natural selection has been caricatured as "nature, red in tooth and claw," first by the poet Tennyson (actually in *In Memoriam,* before the publication of Darwin's *Origin of*

23. Quoted by C. E. Raven, *Natural Religion and Christian Theology,* 1951 Gifford Lectures, Series 1, *Science and Religion* (Cambridge: Cambridge University Press, 1953), vol. 1, p. 15.

Species), then taken up by anti-theist biologists — though it has to be recognized that Darwin was led into agnosticism both by this aspect of evolution and the role of chance. Nevertheless, caricature it is, for — as G. G. Simpson has pointed out[24] — natural selection is not even in a figurative sense the outcome of struggle, as such. Natural selection involves many factors that include better integration with the ecological environment, more efficient utilization of available food, better care of the young, more cooperative social organization — and better capacity of surviving such 'struggles' as do occur (remembering that it is in the interest of any predator that its prey survive as a species!).

We also have to stress that the natural world is immensely variegated in its hierarchies of levels of entities, structures, and processes, in its 'being'; and abundantly diversifies with a cornucopian fecundity in its 'becoming' in time. The multiply branching bush of terrestrial biological evolution appears to be primarily opportunist in the direction it follows and, in so doing, produces the enormous variety of biological life on this planet. We can only conclude that, if there is a Creator, then that Creator intended this rich diversity, the *whole* tapestry of the created order in its warp and woof — and not simply as stages on the way to *homo sapiens*. We can only make sense of that, utilizing our resources of personal language, if we say that God may be said to have something akin to 'joy' and 'delight' in creation — and not only in humanity (indeed perhaps more than in humanity, considering the history of the twentieth century!). We have a hint of this in the first chapter of Genesis: "And God saw everything he had made, and behold, it was very good."[25] This naturally leads to the idea of God's 'play' in creation[26] in relation to Hindu thought *(lila)* as well as to that of Judaism[27] and Christianity.

But there is, as we have seen, a darker side — the ubiquity of pain, predation, suffering, and death in the creative evolutionary process. The theist cannot avoid asking, "If the Creator intended the arrival in the cosmos of complex, reproducing structures that could think and be free — that is, self-conscious, free persons — was there not some other, less costly and painful way of bringing this about? Was that the only possible way?"

24. Simpson, *The Meaning of Evolution,* p. 201.
25. Genesis 1:31.
26. Q.v., A. R. Peacocke, *CWS,* pp. 108-11.
27. Cf. Proverbs 8:27-31.

This is one of those unanswerable metaphysical questions in theodicy to which our only response has to be based on our understanding of the biological parameters (already described) discerned by science to be operating in evolution. These indicate that there are inherent constraints on how even an omnipotent Creator could bring about the existence of a law-like creation that is to be a cosmos not a chaos, and thus an arena for the free action of self-conscious, reproducing complex entities and for the coming to be of the fecund variety of living organisms whose existence the Creator delights in. All of which is predicated on the attribution of the very existence of all-that-is to a self-existing Ultimate Reality, named 'God' in English, whose inherent nature is of such a kind as to give existence to other entities to enable them eventually to share in the ineffable, divine life of that Reality. Such a Creator God has to be conceived of now not only, as in pre-Darwinian days, as giving existence to everything and of sustaining all in existence, but, I have suggested, as deeply involved in, with, and under the very evolutionary processes of creation. These processes are indeed to be seen as the very action of God *as* Creator.

But if that is so, then the ubiquity of pain, predation, suffering, and death as the means of creation through biological evolution entails, for any concept of God to be morally acceptable and coherent, that we cannot but tentatively propose that *God* suffers in, with, and under the creative processes of the world with their costly unfolding in time. In other words, the processes of creation are immensely costly *to God* in a way dimly shadowed by the ordinary experience of the costliness of creativity in multiple aspects of human existence — whether it be in giving birth, in aesthetic creation, or in creating and maintaining human social structures. We are *not* the mere 'playthings of the gods', or of God, but sharing as co-creating creatures in the suffering of God engaged in the self-offered, costly process of bringing forth the new.

I have been speaking, analogically, of suffering *in* God, this suffering being an identification with, and participation in, the suffering of the world. Elsewhere[28] I have given reasons for the talking in panentheistic terms of God being 'more than' the world yet of the world as being

28. A. R. Peacocke, *CWS*, pp. 141, 201-2, 207; *Theology for a Scientific Age* (London: SCM Press and Fortress Press, 2nd enlarged edition, 1993), pp. 158-59, 370-72. For a recent, cogently argued case for resuscitating this, not new, Christian perception, see Philip Clayton, "The Case for Christian Panentheism," *Dialog* 37 (1998): 201-8; and *God and Contemporary Science* (Edinburgh: Edinburgh University Press, 1997), ch. 4.

'within God'; and also for using female metaphors for the creating by God and of the world 'in God'. The dimension of suffering we are here incorporating into our understanding of this relation now gives an enhanced significance to this feminine pan*en*theistic model. Moreover, it gives a new and poignant pertinence to St. Paul's poetic vision of creation as being in the pangs of childbirth:

> For the creation waits with eager longing for the revealing of the children of God; for the creation was subjected to futility, not of its own will but by the will of the one who subjected it, in hope that the creation itself will be set free from its bondage to decay and will obtain the freedom of the glory of the children of God. We know that the whole creation has been groaning in labour pains until now.[29]

Christian theology has long attributed self-limitation to God in the very notion of God creating something other than Godself with a given degree of autonomy. For example, this has been depicted by the idea of God "making a space" *(zimzum)* for the created order.[30] Now, as we reflect on the processes of creation in biological evolution, we can begin to understand that this self-limitation involved a costly, suffering involvement on behalf of their ultimate fruition in the divine purposes and their ultimate consummation.

We can perhaps dare to say that there is a creative self-emptying and self-offering (a *kenosis*) of *God,* a sharing in the suffering of God's creatures, in the very creative, evolutionary processes of the world. Such a perception now enriches the Christian affirmation of God's nature as best understood as inherently that of Love. God, we find ourselves having to conjecture, 'suffers' the natural evils of the world along with ourselves because — we can but tentatively suggest at this stage — God purposes *inter alia* to bring about a greater good thereby, namely, the kingdom of living organic creatures, delighting their Creator, and even free-willing, loving persons who have the possibility of communion with God and with each other. Indeed, the creation may in one sense be said to exist *through* suffering: for suffering is recognized to have creative power when imbued with love. God's suffering must be construed as not merely passive but ac-

---

29. Romans 8:19-22 (NRSV).
30. See J. Moltmann elsewhere in this volume.

tive with creative intention, the activity manifest in the creative processes of the world. God brings about new creation through suffering and, as we shall infer below in the light of the significance of Jesus the Christ, thereby also overcomes the evil introduced into the creation by free human beings. For humanity is free to go against the grain of the creative processes, to reject God's creative intentions, to mar God's creation, and to bring into existence disharmonies uniquely of its own — and has perennially done so. Hence humanity has the ability to cause God to suffer in an especially distinctive way.

Human pain and suffering are increased by our very self-consciousness, by our empathy with each other, and by that emergent ability we have of questioning our actual relation to the Creator while enduring such experiences. When we do so question we are free to rebel against God and, more generally in our lives, to ignore the divine presence, thereby augmenting the suffering of God in the divine, creative process. For God, this was clearly a risky and costly enterprise.

God's Purposes in the 'Risk' of Creating Humanity?

As we reflect on the nature of humanity we are bound to ask that our conclusions cohere with the intelligibility which, it can be claimed, is provided by the affirmation of the world as created, that is, of the existence of God as Creator. This intelligibility is in danger of collapsing in view of the enigmatic and paradoxical nature of the human person so evolved. What did and does God think God is up to in evolving this "glory, jest and riddle of the world"[31] with its enormous potentiality both for creative good and for degradation and evil, destructive of itself and of the rest of the created world? What are God's purposes? What meaning is God expressing in creating humanity?

The sequence from the inanimate to the conscious, and then to the self-conscious, is concomitant with an increasing independence of and freedom over against the environment. This independence and freedom in humanity attains the critical point where it can attempt an independence of, and freedom from, the intentions of the Creator. This independence and freedom are an inevitable consequence of that very self-

31. A. Pope, *An Essay on Man,* Epistle ii.1.28.

consciousness that has emerged naturalistically through the evolutionary processes in God's regular way of making effectual God's creative intentions. We cannot help concluding that God intended that out of matter persons should evolve who had this freedom, and thereby allowed the possibility that they might depart from God's intentions. To be consistent, we must go on to assume that God had some overarching intention that made this risk worth taking, that there was and is some fundamental way of God being God that allows God's relationship with freely responding persons to be valued by God. So our 'model' of God as the personal agent of the creative process must be amplified to include a recognition of the Creator as suffering in, with, and under the creation as new and hazardous possibilities come into existence — most of all those implicit in the creation of self-determining human persons.[32]

If God willed the existence of self-conscious, intelligent, freely willing creatures as an end, he must, to be self-consistent, presumably have willed these means to achieving that end. This divine purpose must be taken as an overriding one, for it involves as a corollary an element of risk to the purposes whereby God renders God's own self vulnerable in a way that is only now becoming perceivable by us. This idea that *God took a risk in creation* is not new — as evidenced by the traditional theology implicit in the creation 'narratives' in the Old Testament — but is now, I am suggesting, reinforced and given a wider context by these considerations based on the nature of biological processes.

To instantiate truth, beauty, and goodness in the created order, the possibility of generating a *free* being necessarily capable of valuing them had to be incorporated as a potential outcome of the cosmic processes, with all its risks. The cost to God, we may venture to say, was in a continuing self-limitation which is the negative aspect of God's creative action, and also in a self-inflicted vulnerability to the created processes in order to achieve an overriding purpose: the emergence of free persons. Creation is

32. This is not meant to be at all dismissive of the significance of the nonhuman creation. For at every level in the operation of the creative process, something is reflected in its own measure of the divine purpose. As Charles Raven put it, "from atom and molecule to mammal and man each by its appropriate order and function expresses the design inherent in it and contributes, so far as it can be failure or success, to the fulfilment of the common purpose." But in human beings this ability to express God's 'design' becomes personal and capable of responding freely, or not doing so, to God: it is this we must suppose God intended (*Natural Religion and Christian Theology,* vol. 2, p. 157).

then indicated as involving for God a kind of risk, incurred lovingly and willingly and with suffering, for the greater good of a freely responsive humanity coming into existence within the created world. Love and self-sacrifice are, from this perspective, seen as inherent in the divine nature and expressed in the whole process of creation. Perhaps this is what the author of the Revelation was hinting at when he described Christ, whom he saw as now present within God, as "the Lamb slain *from the foundation of the world.*"[33]

Divine Self-Offering in Jesus the Christ and in Creation

So far the suggestion of a divine self-offering involvement in creation can be no more than a reasonable conjecture, an attempt to make sense of certain features of natural processes that are also seen as created by God. But this suggestion is reinforced, indeed overtly revealed — that is, communicated by God — if God is truly self-expressed in Jesus the Christ. For his path through life was preeminently one of vulnerability to the forces that swirled around him, to which he eventually succumbed in acute suffering, and, from his human perspective, in a tragic, abandoned death.

Because sacrificial, self-limiting, self-giving action on behalf of the good of others is, in human life, the hallmark of love, those who believe in Jesus the Christ as the self-expression of God have come to see his life as their ultimate warrant for asserting that God is essentially 'Love',[34] insofar as any one word can accurately encompass God's nature. Jesus' own teaching concerning God as 'Abba', Father, and of the conditions for entering the 'Kingdom of God' pointed to this too, but it was the person of Jesus and what happened to him that finally, and early, established this perception of God in the Christian community.

We see therefore that belief in Jesus the Christ as the self-expression of God in the confines of a human person is entirely consonant with those conceptions of God, previously derived tentatively from reflection on natural being and becoming, which affirm that God, in exercising divine creativity, is self-limiting, vulnerable, self-emptying, and self-giving

33. Revelation 13:8 (AV).
34. 1 John 4:16.

— that is, supremely Love in creative action. It is this action and expression of Love, we believe, that eventually overcomes the evil in humanity. On this understanding Jesus the Christ is the definitive communication from God to humanity of the deep meaning effected in creation — and that is precisely what the prologue to the fourth gospel says in terms of God the Word/*Logos* active in creation and now manifest in the person of Jesus the Christ.

Furthermore, we inferred even more tentatively from the character of the natural processes of creation that God has to be seen as suffering in, with, and under these selfsame processes with their costly, open-ended unfolding in time. But if God was present in and one with Jesus the Christ, then we have to conclude that *God* also suffered in and with him in his passion and death. The God whom Jesus obeyed and expressed in his life and death is indeed, therefore, a 'crucified God',[35] and the cry of dereliction can be seen as an expression of the anguish also of God in creation. If Jesus is indeed the self-expression of God in a human person, then the tragedy of his actual human life can be seen as a drawing back of the curtain to unveil a God suffering in and with the sufferings of created humanity and so, by a natural extension, with those of all creation, since humanity is an embedded, evolved part of it. The suffering of God, which we could infer only tentatively in the processes of creation, is in Jesus the Christ concentrated into a point of intensity and transparency that reveals it as expressive of the perennial relation of God to the creation.

35. As definitively expounded in J. Moltmann's *The Crucified God* (London: SCM Press, 1974).

Kenosis and Nature

HOLMES ROLSTON, III

Every commonplace detail of nature, every stone and tree, includes an immense richness and variety of lesser detail: in every fragment of it a thousand million lesser fragments cohere and interact.

Love's Endeavour, Love's Expense, p. 84

Unless a grain of wheat falls into the earth and dies, it remains alone; but if it dies, it bears much fruit.

John 12:24

1. Selfish Genes, Selfish Organisms, and Survival of the Fittest

If one compares the general worldview of biology with that of theology, it first seems that there is only stark contrast. To move from Darwinian nature to Christian theology, one will have to change the sign of natural history, from selfish genes to suffering love. Theologians also hold that, in regeneration, humans with their sinful natures must be reformed to lives that are more altruistic, also requiring a change of sign. But the problem lies deeper; all of biological nature can seem to run counter to what Jesus teaches: that one ought to lay down one's life for others. In nature, there is no altruism, much less kenosis.

43

Life, coded by the genes, is always encapsulated in particular organisms. In biology we find, at once and pervasively, the organism as a bounded somatic "self" — something quite unknown in physics, chemistry, astronomy, meteorology, or geology. The general Darwinian interpretive framework moves from the coding genes to the coping organisms and sees organisms so constituted genetically that self-interested (typically labeled "selfish") behavior is inevitable. Organisms behave so as to benefit themselves at cost to others. A bird grabs a seed, and others foraging nearby do not get it. A bird eats a worm, and benefits; the worm loses. Genotypes program selfish phenotypes. With genotypes, Richard Dawkins's most fundamental biological truth is "the gene's law of universal ruthless selfishness."[1] With phenotypes, George Williams claims, "Natural selection . . . can honestly be described as a process for maximizing short-sighted selfishness."[2] So runs the current dogma.

But claims that genes and organisms are "selfish" may depend not so much on empirical evidence as on the choice of a general interpretive framework within which to view the phenomena. Such biologists could be committing Whitehead's "fallacy of misplaced concreteness," where, selecting out some particular feature of a situation, one forgets the degree of abstraction involved from the real world, and mistakenly portrays the whole by over-enlarging a factor of only limited relevance. The "self" question, much discussed in biology, is, philosophically speaking, an "identity" question, which proves also to be an "integration" question. The question is of "belonging": What is the gene's and the self's suitable role and place?

2. Self-Defense and Self-Actualizing

In less pejorative language, one can more simply say that an organism is "self-actualizing." An organism pursues its integrated, encapsulated identity; it defends its life, conserves its own vitality as an intrinsic value. This involves "self-defense," without which life is not possible. An or-

1. Richard Dawkins, *The Selfish Gene*, new edition (New York: Oxford University Press, 1989), p. 3.
2. George C. Williams, "Huxley's Evolution and Ethics in Sociobiological Perspective," *Zygon* 23 (1988): 383-407, citation on p. 385.

ganism must make claims on its environment, for food, mates, territory. Heterotrophs must use, instrumentally, other organisms, for example as prey. Heterotrophs and autotrophs alike must resist being made use of by other organisms, where this is detrimental to their interests, for example again, as prey. An organism is "self-constituting," "self-realizing," "self-developing," "self-conserving," "self-generating"; an organism acts "for its own sake" — all these things can be said in a descriptive language that, though still Darwinian, stops short of framing organisms with the ultra-Darwinian "selfish" overtones. Self-maintenance and self-propagation are not evils; both are necessary and good. Without them no other values can be achieved or preserved.

An organism can only conserve what identity, or vitality, or value, it has, and not some other that it does not have. Any particular organism has a "good-of-its-kind," that is, a species identity. But it does not have all of the good-of-its-kind, since other alleles, which it does not have and which are not expressed in its structure and behavior, are not present. They are elsewhere in the population. So the organism expresses as much of the good-of-its-kind as it possesses, both that conserved from its inherited past and that ventured in novel recombinations and mutants. This genetically based knowledge will be tested in the trials of life. Others, conspecifics, do likewise. Some reproduce better than others. In the contests of life, natural selection operates to optimize the good-of-that-kind in the niche in which that species resides, sacrificing the less fit, increasing the more fit. The outcome is species-actualizing, a species whose members are later more fit on their adaptive landscapes than they were before.

3. Self-Identity, Species Identity, Inclusive and Shared Fitness

An organism has a somatic self-identity, but the organism is itself an expression of a genetic identity. Such genetic identity is, in the particular combinatorial genome that the organism possesses, unique to itself (excepting twins and clones). But this genetic identity is also, more and less, scattered about. By contemporary biological theory, the organismic individual competently defends its "self" (still so-called), wherever and to the extent that this "like-self" is manifested, which will be most among nearby family, also in tribe, population, fanning out in the whole gene pool. The organismic self can hold what values it holds intrinsically only as such values are inclusively distributed in kin outside self somatically, though like self genetically, what biologists call "inclusive fitness."[3] When an organism is faced with defending similarities against differences, in competition with others of its species, with different alleles, each organism has been selected to defend its kin and therefore its similarities in offspring and relatives. That way, if its alleles have a survival advantage, the fittest (best-adapted) will survive.

Already, genetic identity is getting mixed up. We hardly know whether to say that some helping behavior, directed at a relative, who partially contains a copy of one's "self" (and who also partially contains "non-self" genes) is a "self-sacrificing" or a "self-interested" act. It depends on where one posts the boundaries of "self." Richard Alexander sums this up: "We are evidently evolved not only to aid the genetic materials in our own bodies, by creating and assisting descendants, but also to assist, by nepotism, copies of our genes that reside in collateral (nondescendant) relatives."[4] Assistance to a relative will be favored if the benefit to the relative, proportioned to the degree of relationship, exceeds the cost to the donor.

What gets defended and selected is not just the genes of any particular individual but some set of genes-in-relatives, wherever they are in the kinship group. From this perspective, the behaviors selected are not so atomistic and individualistic as first seems the case; they are diffused in the kin, in the nearby kind. Many of a particular self's genes are copresent in relatives, copies within kin in a different skin; indeed all of a particular self's genes are somewhere carried also by others, in rather similar and somewhat variant combinations, save for those rare mutants it might possess. The organism, in addition to its own self-actualizing, assists in the self-actualizing of its kin.

Any such "inclusive" self clouds the seeming clarity of having located a "self" that can be identified, much less one that can be "selfish." It is not just the organismic (somatic) self that counts; it is the reproductive (genetic) self. All that an organism can really transmit to future generations

3. William D. Hamilton, "The Genetical Evolution of Social Behavior. I and II," *Journal of Theoretical Biology* 7 (1964): 1-52. Uses of "inclusive" in biological theory, when compared and contrasted with uses in theological circles, are quite revealing.

4. Richard D. Alexander, *The Biology of Moral Systems* (New York: Aldine de Gruyter, 1987), p. 3.

are genetic elements of itself, slivers of a self. The life that the organismic individual has is something passing through the individual as much as something it intrinsically possesses. All such selves have their identity in kinship with others, not on their own. Identity does not attach solely to the centered or modular organism; it can persist as a discrete pattern over time. The individual is subordinate to the species, or at least that portion of the species line for which it has alleles — not the other way around. Any one genetic set is as evidently the property of the larger species gene pool as of the individual through which this part of it passes.

The organism can only conserve what form of life, what value it embodies, and none other. But the biological system, in which the individual self-actualizing and self-reproducing organism plays its role, is more selective. Individuals are evaluated for their increased fitness, for what geneticists call their "adaptive value."[5] Individuals that have more of such capacities survive; but when they survive they pass along genes that have survival value in the species line, enabling it to continue by re-forming on its evolving adaptive landscape. What is conserved is what any individual "knows" that is better than its less well-"informed" competitors, the losers. Such vital information gets distributed, portioned out, increasing in frequency in the next generation, more and more actualized. Now we begin to see more than mere self-defense. We see organisms whose function is given over to the success of their lineages. To put the point provocatively, organisms are "devoted to" their lineages.

Genes are a flow phenomenon. The genes are caught up in an impulse to thrust through what they know vitally to the next generation, and the next, and the next. Genes live in a lineage, dynamically evolving over time. Ultra-Darwinians, swept along by strong undertow from their theory, will insist on a gestalt in which the gene is said to be protecting itself "selfishly" in the next generation. David Barash puts it this way: "The ultimate benefit is clear enough: genes help themselves by being nice to themselves, even if they are enclosed in different bodies."[6] The trouble with that kind of claim, besides the bald anthropomorphism, is that the

5. Robert H. Tamarin, *Principles of Genetics,* 5th edition (Dubuque, Iowa: William C. Brown, 1996), p. 558; Francisco J. Ayala, *Population and Evolutionary Genetics* (Menlo Park, Calif.: Benjamin-Cummings, 1982), p. 88.

6. David Barash, *The Whisperings Within* (New York: Harper and Row, 1979), p. 153.

"self" essential to the claim has no firm identity, being now scattered about, divided around in dozens of bodies.

When one clarifies that identity in terms of a cybernetic flow of information — familial, populational, species — the phenomenon under discussion is more appropriately viewed in another gestalt. A single gene is tested for what it can "contribute" to the whole organism. The organism, in turn, an expression of its genome, is tested for its adapted fit in an ecosystem. But that is not so much for the somatic survival of that organism as for the organism's power to sustain the ongoing population and species line, what it can "contribute" to the species line. Fitness is the ability to "contribute" more to the welfare of later-coming others of one's kind, more relative to one's "competitors." The organism contributes all that it has to contribute, its own proper form of life, what it has achieved that is of value. The organism gets lost as an individual, we might say, and gains a role in the lineage that transcends it. The system facilitates congruence between generations.

When the individual self has become implicated into an "inclusive" fitness, we can introduce, rather provocatively, the word "shared" to help interpret this genetic "allocating" and "proliferating." "Share" has the Old English and Germanic root *sker,* to cut into parts, surviving in "shears," "plowshare," and "shares" of stock. As used here, to "share" is to distribute in parts the self's genetic information, thereby conserving it. Genes generate ongoing species lines, instantiated in individual lives. To accomplish this, genes reproduce or communicate what survival value they possess. They share [= distribute in portions] their information, literally, although preconsciously and premorally.

The central feature of genes is that they can be copied and expressed, again and again. They replicate. Their power to send information through to the next generation is what counts. The genetic information gets allocated and reallocated, portioned out, and located in various places. Whatever the process, rather obviously genetic information has been widely distributed, communicated, networked, recycled, and shared throughout natural history. In cumulative result, there is the genesis of diversity and complexity in natural history. There is the transgenerational distributing and contributing of genetic values. Put one way, the organism is "sacrificed" to its species line; put still another way, the organism is "empowered" for such contribution.

Here we must take some care. When used in ethics and theology,

48

"share" has a positive moral tone, and our point in using it biologically, additionally to describing what is going on, is to neutralize, to un-bias, the negative moral tones left by "selfish." "Share" is difficult to interpret selfishly. When genetic information is passed on to a next generation, when that information overleaps death, it would seem as appropriate to say that it has been "shared" (distributed) as that it has been "selfishly" kept. *Genes are no more capable of "sharing" than of being "selfish" — it must at once be said — where "sharing" and "selfish" have their deliberated, moral meanings.* Since genes are not moral agents, they cannot be selfish; and, equally, they cannot be altruistic. But they can transmit information. If one is going to stretch a word sometimes employed in the moral world and make it serve in this amoral, though axiological, realm, then "share" is as descriptive as "selfish" and without the pejorative overtones. Sometimes one has to lean into the wind to stand up straight. "Dividers" and "multipliers" too find it hard to be selfish. The survival of the fittest turns out to be the survival of the sharers.

We do need to choose our words carefully — "distribute," "disperse," "allocate," "proliferate," "divide," "multiply," "transmit," "recycle," or "share" in "portions." We want a nonhumanistic, nonanthropocentric account, one unbiased by our morals either for worse or better. The distributive account is a much more descriptive paradigm, because there is no good reason to think that genes are selfish; there are no moral agents in wild nature even at the organismic level, much less the genetic one. But there is good reason to think that there are objective, nonanthropocentric values, adaptive values, in nature, on which survival and flourishing depend, and that these are defended and distributed by wild creatures in their pursuit of life. Only humans are moral agents, but myriads of living things defend and reproduce their lives.

The genetic information is divided out in the population, various alleles here and there, various recombinatory and mutant trials, and the good of the species vitally depends on such distributed and shared genetic information. Though the individual organism does not act for the good of the species, which it is incapable of doing, it is good for the species that the individual organism acts as it does. The losers, used in the genetic search, get sacrificed, relatively, for the good of the species, but that does not mean they have no share in the generative process. Though their alleles are less frequent in the next generation, the species line in which such organisms also have their identity continues for the better. Losers in one sense can be winners in another — rather like those who lose an argument win, if, in the discipline or tradition with which they identify, better arguments prevail. Most ball teams are losers; but the champions require the testing that the losers provide, and the sport that the losers love is a better sport in result. In the genetic development being discussed here, the winners win if — and only if — they can contribute survival value to oncoming generations.

Evolutionary genesis depends on such individuals, both winners and losers, to comprise the variation over which natural selection can act. The individual organism, self-actualizing as it is, is a player in a bigger drama that is going on "over its head," so to speak, or that is "bigger than itself." The uniqueness of any particular genetic makeup is a one-off event — temporary, instantiated in an organism, tested for its fitness; and thereby it has a role in a recombinatorial process by which the species survives, making possible the myriads of other lives that ensue in that species lineage.

This places this organismic self-actualizing in a more inclusive context, but, some will insist, it does not yet allow for self-emptying. An organism can only defend its own proper life (recalling the Latin: *proprius*, one's own), and in that sense it cannot be kenotic. Oak trees and warblers cannot be altruistic, behaving so as to benefit others at cost to self, for, if they do, they go extinct. Meanwhile, the picture coming into focus does portray individual lives discharged into, flowing into, "emptied into" these larger populational and species lines. Maybe some precursor of kenosis is beginning to evolve. Fitness means dying to self for newness of life in a generation to come. Our inquiry continues.

4. Interdependence and Symbiosis

The life of every organism, plant or animal, is situated within an ecology, a life support system. Nothing lives alone. Any "self" is embedded in an environment. Only those organisms survive that find a fitness in a biotic community. The organism can only conserve what value it has, and none other. But the biological system, in which the individual self-actualizing and self-reproducing organism plays its role, is more comprehensive, more inclusive. The individual is immersed in a field of forces transcending its individuality.

A grass plant survives with other plants, more and less kin, as well as other species, embedded in the same soil, capturing nutrients released by fungal and microbial decomposers, as well as by the ungulates who eat the grass. Plants depend on the carbon dioxide released by animals, who depend on the oxygen released by plants. An animal must eat the grass, or eat what has eaten the grass, and so trophic pyramids build up. Energy and materials cycle and recycle through the system. Hypercycles develop, loop-linking several species; the rate of replication of each species is an increasing function of the concentration of the replicator immediately preceding it in the cycle. *Chlamydomonas* (a single-celled green alga) is eaten by *Daphnia* (a waterflea), and the stickleback, a fish, feeds on the *Daphnia;* the stickleback excretes nitrate, which fertilizes the *Chlamydomonas.*[7] Meanwhile too, each species defends its kind with defenses against being eaten.

In this system, the only capacity that the individual organism has is to be "self-interested," to defend its self and its kind; but the truth is that the system requires the organism to operate within the interdependencies, resources, and constraints of its situation. So we need to place any organismic self-actualizing in an even more inclusive context than that of species lines. Insisting on seeing everything from the perspective of either individual genes or organisms or even individuals in species lines could be a metaphysical atomism that fails to appreciate how these self-units are structured into ecological communities, parts within larger wholes. These networks constitute their identity quite as much as does anything internal to their genetic or organismic "selves," or their species lines. The truth could be more social, or ecological, than ultra-Darwinists envisage. Life must be encapsulated in selves, and such selves reproduce and spread in an environment in which they both play a part and have an integrated fit. They must have a part, a "share" of the resources in their environment, and they themselves will, sooner or later, enter that resource chain and become parts claimed, or shared, by others.

The genes within an organism are dependent on the genes in many other species with which it significantly interacts. One can think of this as value capture and contest, which it is; but it is also value dependency. Any particular organism, with its genes, must live "together with" those on

---

7. John Maynard Smith and Eörs Szathmry, *The Origins of Life: From the Birth of Life to the Origin of Language* (New York: Oxford University Press, 1999), pp. 49-50; Manfred Eigen and Peter Schuster, *The Hypercycle: A Principle of Natural Self-Organization* (Berlin: Springer-Verlag, 1979).

whom it is dependent, more and less. In turn, others will be dependent on it. That genes "co-act," or, rather more provocatively, "co-operate" (operate together), evidently true from the skin in, does not cease to be part of the truth from the skin out, although the character of the co-operation shifts from the organismic to the ecosystemic. Each species is a node in a network, and genes elsewhere in that network are quite vital to it, "alien" or "other" genes in the somatic sense, but genes with which it is quite "at home" in the ecological sense.

Animals occupy niches in a trophic pyramid; they eat and will be eaten. Animals have no genes for photosynthesis; such genes, in plants, are quite vital to them. Ungulates cannot digest cellulose without the bacteria in their rumen. Carnivores eat herbivores. The raptors eat the warblers that eat the insects that eat the leaves. That makes raptors dependent on the successes of all the genes with survival value in warblers, insects, and the plants they eat. Higher animals may lose enzymes, rather than gain them, because they depend on the lost enzymes remaining in species on which they feed. Natural selection shapes animal behavior according to such dependencies, which may involve several trophic levels.

Life preys on life; all advanced life requires food pyramids, eating and being eaten. If the higher forms had to synthesize all the life materials from abiotic materials (also degrading their own wastes), they could never have advanced very far. The upper levels are freed for more advanced synthesis because they depend on syntheses (and decompositions) carried out by lesser organisms below. Heterotrophs must be built on autotrophs, and no autotrophs are sentient or cerebral. From a systemic point of view, we see the conversion of a resource from one life stream to another — the anastomosing of life threads that characterizes an ecosystem. Plants become insects, which become chicks, which become foxes, which die to fertilize plants.

Sometimes genes jump around. Two life lines, once independent, can fuse into a single identity. Now that scientists can couple molecular genetic analysis with traditional fossil paleontology, the tree of life is turning out to have surprisingly complex roots, because there are not just splits and branches, but gene exchanges by organisms that reconnect and interconnect the splits and branches.[8] Genetic information has been widely

8. Nicholas Wade, "Tree of Life Turns Out to Have Surprisingly Complex Roots," *New York Times*, April 14, 1998, pp. B11, B14.

distributed, redistributed, multiplied, divided, or "shared," not only within but across species lines.

Two of the most important processes energizing life on Earth use endosymbionts. One, involving mitochondria, powers animals; the other, with chloroplasts, powers plants; and, of course, plant power is the basis of animal power. Mitochondria, which anciently had a free-living identity, have been incorporated into the organisms they now empower. Similarly with chloroplasts. Multicellular organisms may have formed by one-celled organisms joining up, as well as by their differentiation.

Fitness is not something a gene, or even an organism, has as such. Adaptation, the central word in Darwinian theory, is an *ecological* word, not a *genetic* one. One does not know the fitness when one knows the output of a gene, not even when one knows how this output integrates hierarchically in the whole organism. We know fitness only when we know how this output operates in the environmental niche the organism inhabits. Although the mutants bubble up "from below," the shape that the microscopic molecules take is controlled "from above," as the molecular information stored is what has been discovered about how to make a way through the macroscopic, terrestrial-range world. Identity is identity in an environment.

Sometimes it is hard to say which level is prior and which is subordinate; perhaps it is better to say that there are vital processes at multiple levels. Biological identity is multi-leveled. *Ecosystem* is as ultimate a truth as is *gene*. Biological phenomena take place at multiple interconnected levels, from the microscopic genetic through the organismic to the ecosystemic and bioregional levels. Bigger networks are superposed on smaller networks, and these on lesser networks still; there is descent from continental and global scales to those in nanometer ranges. Genes have what identity they have only as they play a part in this larger biotic community in which they code a role.

That the myriad creatures are in contest and competition cannot be denied; nor can it be denied that they are bonded together in interdependencies. Genes are cross-wired not only within individuals, within families, within populations, within species; they are cross-wired within ecosystems. Any particular self, with its integrated genes from the skin-in, distributed genes round about, and its web-worked connections from the skin-out, is a kind of holon, a genuine whole but one in which also its environment, its niche, is fully reflected. True, the co-actors are not so much co-operators as are they enmeshed in a series of checks and balances, controls and feedback loops; but equally true, just this system is the vital context of all life. Seen in this more comprehensive scheme of things, plants function for the survival of myriads of others. We could even say, provocatively for our "kenosis" inquiry, that they are "emptied into," given over to, "devoted" to, or "sacrificed" for these others in their community.

5. Sexuality and Reproduction

Interpreting sexuality is philosophically revealing. In sexual reproduction, which nature requires for survival in most fauna and flora, the offspring will be half-different even in the first generation — half-different at least from the perspective of the diploid-haploid-diploid recombination of genes that takes place at meiosis. Sexually reproducing organisms cannot make identicals; offspring must be *others (alteri)* and in this sense sexual reproduction is by necessity "altruistic" in an others-unlike-self sense. It is hard to be selfish, if one is a genome and must be split in half at every reproduction. "Sex," says Michael Ghiselin, is "synonymous with 'mixis' — literally 'mingling'."[9]

Further, the system encourages outbreeding. If an animal must mate, then mating with siblings would more nearly preserve the particular set of genes that an organism has. Given the necessity to breed sexually, it might be thought advantageous to breed with near kin. That way the organism can transmit its own genes somatically coupled with its genes also in relatives. This sometimes happens, but the system discourages close inbreeding. Breed an organism must with its own kind, breed it often does within its tribe, perhaps even its larger family, but breed it should not with immediate relatives. There are selective pressures toward outbreeding, where an animal mates with kind, not kin.

Inbreeding costs, known also as inbreeding depression, include reduced viability and fecundity of offspring and susceptibility to disease and genetic deformities, so that close inbreeding is selected against rather strongly and is virtually absent in natural populations of animals. These detrimental effects have also resulted in suppressed self-pollination in

9. Michael T. Ghiselin, *The Economy of Nature and the Evolution of Sex* (Berkeley: University of California Press, 1974), pp. 52-53.

plants. The system discourages kin selection in sexual pairing; it forces outbreeding, against the "selfish" tendencies of the genes.[10] It requires spreading genes around, mixing them up.

To reproduce themselves selfishly one's genes have to join with an alien set. That interlocks any "selfish" set of genes with those of another line; it must outbreed at a fifty-fifty split to protect its genes within. From the gene's-eye view this is a curious system, in which the chances of transmission are fifty-fifty by required coupling with nonkindred lines. If one still wants to think of it that way, the system limits, or mixes, the permitted "selfishness" with other-directedness. Competitors are forced to be cooperators, the selfish to share. An organism must mate to breed. Sexuality means, for our inquiry, that an organism must contribute to, flow into, discharge its genes into a broader populational pool.

The whole thrust of sexual reproduction is toward bonding the individual into a community exceeding itself. Sexuality dilutes or divides out any "selfishness." The system is, so to speak, "self"-limiting. What one in fact confronts is survival by way of incorporation into, and cooperation with, others. Genes do not stay within individuals, they are spread around families; and, beyond that, they cannot stay within families either. In mating, outbreeding, they must be mingled with those of others in the population, and those of populations can (as mobility and opportunity permit) be shared throughout the species.

Reproduction is typically assumed to be a need of individuals, but since any particular individual can flourish somatically without reproducing at all, indeed may be put through duress and risk or spend much energy reproducing, one can interpret reproduction as the species keeping up its own kind by reenacting itself again and again. In the species line, individuals are devoted to this task, their absolutely essential function. The female mammal's liver is of benefit to her somatically; the female's mammary glands benefit the next generation at cost to her. The female's reproductive system is not maintained for her identity but to preserve her species identity. This preserves her genes, if you like, but these genes of hers flow in reproduction into the populational and species pools. The gene flow at one level is the species flow at another scale.

In this sense a tigress does not bear cubs to be healthy herself, any

10. With enough unrelatedness, in populations evolved more or less differently in more or less distant environments, there can also be outbreeding depression.

more than a woman needs children to be healthy. Rather, her cubs are *Panthera tigris* recreating itself. She plays a part, or has a role, or a "share" in the ongoing line. Her behavior may be "self-propagating" or even "self-interested" from the point of view of genetic or species identity, although the vocabulary of "self" or "interest" applied to a species line seems awkward. In any case, what she does is not "self-interested" from the point of view of somatic identity.

Richard Alexander says, "In a sense somatic effort is personally or phenotypically selfish, while reproductive effort is self-sacrificing or phenotypically altruistic but genetically selfish."[11] Well, perhaps, but it is also difficult to figure out what "genetically selfish" means, because the "self" is "inclusive" of others, kin, mated to, and instantiated in and representative of a species line. Meanwhile, genetic survival often requires somatic sacrifice.

Both reproductive morphology and behavior are defending the line of life bigger than the somatic individual. The lineage in which an individual exists dynamically is something dynamically passing through it, as much as something it has. The locus of the value that is really defended over generations seems as much in the form of life, the species, as in the individuals, since the individuals are genetically impelled to sacrifice themselves in the interests of reproducing their kind. Value is something dynamic to the specific form of life. The value resides in the dynamic form; the individual inherits this, exemplifies it, defends it, and passes it on.

So now at various levels — inclusive fitness, sexuality, ecosystem interdependencies — the picture coming more and more into focus has a great deal of one kind of thing being sacrificed for the good of another. The lives of individuals are discharged into, flow into, "emptied into" these larger currents of life. Maybe there is kenosis in nature after all.

6. Life, Death, and Regeneration

With living things, questions of level mingle with questions of identity, which mingle with questions of persisting and perishing. Whole organisms are ephemeral. The genes have more of an eye on the species (so to

11. Alexander, *The Biology of Moral Systems*, p. 41.

speak) than on the individual. The solitary organism, living in the present, is born to lose; all that can be transmitted from past to future is its kind. Though selection operates on individuals, since it is always an individual that copes, selection is for the kind of coping that succeeds in copying, that is re-producing, producing again the kind, distributing the information coded in the gene more widely. Survival is through making *others* (altruism, even if similar others), who share the same valuable information. Survival is of the better transmitter of whatever is of genetic value in self into others, descendants. Survival of the fittest turns out to be survival of the senders.

Individual organisms must die. Species do not have to die; most, of course, do die. Ninety-eight percent of all species that have ever existed have gone extinct, so there are high probabilities; but there is no law of nature or inevitability about species extinction. But here a puzzling aspect of the matter strikes us. By virtue of the innovative genes, in their reproducing, the death of the organism feeds into the nondeath of the species. Only by replacements can the species track the changing environment; only by replacements can the descendants evolve into something novel. Genera and species sometimes do die, that is, go extinct without issue; but they are often transformed into something else, new genera and species; and, on average, there have been more arrivals than extinctions — resulting in the increase of both diversity and complexity over evolutionary history.

Life demands the unrelenting conservation of biological identity above all else, an identity that is threatened every moment, every hour, every generation. Life came forth from the formless void, and each life must constantly struggle lest it relapse into that chaos. Life must be perpetually redeemed in the midst of its perishing.[12] In the Psalmist's metaphors, life is lived in green pastures and in the valley of the shadow of death, nourished by eating at a table prepared in the midst of its enemies. The organism ever stands in close proximity to failure, a failure (death) that will sooner or later overtake every individual life. These individual failures are kept from being final only by regeneration from life to life. Every species

12. This idea, even the phrase, goes back through Whitehead to Locke and eventually Heraclitus, where it is not necessarily restricted to living organisms. See Alfred North Whitehead, *Process and Reality*, corrected edition (New York: Free Press, [1927-28], 1978), pp. 29, 60, 146-47, and others.

has to reproduce itself from generation to generation; it absolutely must regenerate or else go extinct.

The conservation of life is through the reproduction of life.

7. Cruciform Nature

In the Hebrew beginning, the "wind" ("Spirit") of God "animates" ("inspires") the waters and the earth; God commands the earth to "bring forth" or "bear" the swarms of creatures, each reproducing after its kind, multiplying and filling the earth (Genesis 1). In the Greek, "nature" has, as root idea, "giving birth." If we must use metaphors, after Darwin, the Earth is as much like a womb in these gestating powers as it is, after Newton, a clockwork machine, or, after Einstein, energy and matter bubbling up out of a spacetime matrix. This "giving birth" requires "labor," and the birthing metaphor, making possible this continued reproduction, seems inseparable from elements of struggle. Biological nature is always giving birth, regenerating, always in travail. Something is always dying, and something is always living on. "The whole creation has been groaning in travail together until now" (Romans 8:22). Perhaps we can begin to recognize in creative nature dimensions both of redemptive and of vicarious suffering, one whereby ongoing success is achieved by sacrifice.

That is what was right about Darwin's "struggle to survive," and, though biologists now prefer to speak of an organism's finding an "adapted fit," they remain fully aware of this dimension of striving. An instinctive biological drive to survive is present at every biostructural level. Each individual organism must, throughout its life, maintain and regenerate its somatic structures. But death comes, and life is maintained only in the effort demanded to pass life from one generation to the next. When we deal with nature in physics and astronomy, we meet a causal puzzle, one of creation *ex nihilo*. Biology adds creation *ex nisus*, creation *per laborem*. To cause, there is added care. To movement, there is added concern. To energy, there is added effort. Something is at stake, requiring defense. There is success, and failure. There is death, but, with labor and regeneration, life ongoing. There is a kind of death that bears much fruit, like a seed fallen into the earth; and here (in the verse used as epigraph) John can use a botanical analogy to the passion of Jesus.

The flora and lower faunal forms participate in this struggle, though only in later, higher forms, does the capacity for suffering evolve. Now there must also be endurance — in the more sentient creatures, passionate endurance. We meet an existential puzzle, one of creation *per passionem*. The goings on become going concerns. Life on earth is not a paradise of hedonistic ease, but a theater where life is earned by toil and sweat. We do not really have available to us any coherent alternative models by which, in a hurtless, painless world, there might have come to pass anything like these dramas in botanical and zoological nature and that have happened, events that in their central thrusts we greatly treasure. There are sorts of creation that cannot occur without death, without one life seeded into another, and these include the highest created goods. Death can be meaningfully integrated into the biological processes as a necessary counterpart to the advancing of life.

There is a creative upflow of life transmitted across a long continuing turnover of kinds, across a natural history that includes a struggle resulting in more diverse and more complex forms of life. This whole evolutionary upslope is a calling in which renewed life comes by blasting the old. Life is gathered up in the midst of its throes, a blessed tragedy, lived in grace through a besetting storm. In nature there is first simply formation, and afterward information. Only still later does nature become cruciform. But the story on Earth does develop so.

Things perish with a passing over in which the sacrificed individual also flows in the river of life. Each of the struggling creatures is delivered over to preserve a line. In the flesh and blood creatures, each is a blood sacrifice perishing that others may live. We have a kind of "slaughter of the innocents," a nonmoral, naturalistic harbinger of the slaughter of the innocents at the birth of the Christ, all perhaps vignettes hinting of the innocent lamb slain from the foundation of the world. In their lives, beautiful, tragic, and perpetually incomplete, they speak for God; they prophesy as they participate in the divine pathos. All have "borne our griefs and carried our sorrows." They share the labor of the divinity.

The abundant life that Jesus exemplifies and offers to his disciples is that of a sacrificial suffering through to something higher. The Spirit of God is the genius that makes alive, that redeems life from its evils. The cruciform creation is, in the end, deiform, godly, just because of this element of struggle, not in spite of it. There is a great divine "yes" hidden behind and within every "no" of crushing nature. God, who is the lure toward rationality and sentience in the upcurrents of the biological

59

pyramid, is also the compassionate lure in, with, and under all purchasing of life at the cost of sacrifice. Long before humans arrived, the way of nature was already a *via dolorosa*. In that sense, the aura of the cross is cast backward across the whole global story, and it forever outlines the future.

In the biblical model, to be chosen by God is not to be protected from suffering. It is a call to suffer and to be delivered as one passes through it. The election is for *struggling* with and for God, seen in the very etymology of the name Israel, "a limping people." The divine son takes up and is broken on a cross, "a man of sorrows and acquainted with grief." Redemptive suffering is a model that makes sense of nature and history. So far from making the world absurd, suffering is a key to the whole, not intrinsically, not as an end in itself, but as a transformative principle, transvalued into its opposite. The capacity to suffer through to joy is a supreme emergent and an essence of Christianity.

The enigmatic symbol of this is the cross, a symbol Christians adopt for God, and for an extrahistorical miracle in the atonement of Christ, but one which, more than they have known, is a parable of all natural and cultural history. The cross here is not nature's only sign, but it is a pivotal one. It would also be a mistake to say that life is nothing but a cross, for life is gift and good news too. Still, all its joys have been bought with a price.

"I believe in Christ in every man who dies to contribute to a life beyond his life," confessed Loren Eiseley.[13] That theme of dying to contribute to a life beyond one's own is, however, willingly or unwillingly, everywhere in the plot. It does not emerge with humans, though the capacity to be deliberate and responsible about such dying and contributing may emerge with humans. All the creatures are forever being sacrificed to contribute to lives beyond their own.

Every organism is plunged into a struggle in which goodness is given only as it is fought for. Every life is chastened and christened, straitened and baptized in struggle. Everywhere there is vicarious suffering. The global Earth is a land of promise, and yet one that has to be died for. The story is a passion play long before it reaches the Christ. Since the beginning, the myriad creatures have been giving up their lives as a ransom for many. In that sense, Jesus is not the exception to the natural order, but a chief exemplification of it.

13. Loren Eiseley, "Our Path Leads Upward," *Reader's Digest*, March 1962, pp. 43-46, citation on p. 46.

If so, kenosis, so far from being in stark contrast with selfish genes, might be integral to the plot. This is only a precursor to the level of kenosis exemplified in the Christ. But, contrary to what first appeared when we began this analysis, theologians do not have to change the sign of natural history as given to them by biologists.

8. Choosing Kenosis: Objection and Opportunity

There is a sense in which there can no more be self-emptying in nature than there can be selfishness. Both are equally category mistakes, projecting human possibilities onto a nature incapable of either. Nature, including botanical and zoological nature, just *is*. Period. There is neither good nor bad about such an amoral nature. But there are other senses in which organismic selves both can be and regularly are limited in nature, checked by and poured out ("emptied") into processes transcending such selves, discharging themselves into the resulting genesis of biodiversity on Earth. When we humans get into the picture, that amoral but valuable genesis has to be evaluated, both the products and the process.

One objection to this search for precursors of kenosis in natural history is that there is little or nothing voluntary in these animal and plant behaviors, which is also why there is nothing moral there.[14] We can take

---

14. After a careful survey, Helmet Kummer concludes, "It seems at present that morality has no specific functional equivalents among our animal relatives" ("Analogs of Morality Among Nonhuman Primates," in Gunther Stent, ed., *Morality as a Biological Phenomenon* [Berkeley: University of California Press, 1980], p. 45). Contesting this, some recent studies find significant choices made in some animals, especially primates. Some of these may be called premoral or even moral.

Frans de Waal finds precursors of morality, but concludes: "Even if animals other than ourselves act in ways tantamount to moral behavior, their behavior does not necessarily rest on deliberations of the kind we engage in. It is hard to believe that animals weigh their own interests against the rights of others, that they develop a vision of the greater good of society, or that they feel lifelong guilt about something they should not have done. Members of some species may reach tacit consensus about what kind of behavior to tolerate or inhibit in their midst, but without language the principles behind such decisions cannot be conceptualized, let alone debated" (*Good Natured: The Origins of Right and Wrong in Humans and Other Animals* [Cambridge, Mass.: Harvard University Press, 1996], p. 209).

After her years of experience, Jane Goodall writes: "I cannot conceive of chimpanzees

61

into account how what are, from one perspective, self-fulfilling activities, are from another perspective, activities in which a self is limited with respect to others. But no action can be kenotic unless it is freely chosen. Trees do nothing voluntary, therefore nothing kenotic. The creatures can only acquiesce in this order of evolutionary generation in which they are embedded; they cannot do otherwise. So there is nothing to commend them for, and this is a radical difference with a voluntary self-limiting on behalf of others, as found in the life of Jesus or the lives of the saints.

True, but! Anyone who thinks much about freedom soon finds complex contexts in which freedom blends with determinism, with destiny. Even those actors that might seem to be most free can equally sense an inescapable calling to roles in which they must acquiesce. "Thy will, not mine, be done." "Here I stand, I cannot do otherwise." Humans inherit a world, and roles and opportunities in that world, as givens within which they must operate. Freedom is never freedom from an environment; seldom is there much freedom to choose another environment. Freedom is within an environment. Persons, like other creatures, find themselves with their particulars in time and space, a setting within which they must work. Any blending of option, openness, indeterminacy, or contingency, with inevitability, determinism, controls, or givenness is elusive and permits no simple resolution.

There is autonomy in the creatures, in botanical and zoological senses. Plants are on their own in the world, defending their own forms of life, and reproducing this generation after generation. There are external controls, but these defenses are innate in their genes (as they are also in ours). Animals do what they spontaneously desire, and they are so made as instinctively to desire reproduction and distributing their form of life as widely as is in their power. All organisms, in reproduction, also spontaneously generate variations, novelties vital to their searching for better adapted modes of life.

No organism voluntarily chooses its form of life; no organism has the power to consider self-limitation on behalf of others as one of its options.

---

developing emotions, one for the other, comparable in any way to the tenderness, the protectiveness, tolerance, and spiritual exhilaration that are the hallmarks of human love in its truest and deepest sense. Chimpanzees usually show a lack of consideration for each other's feelings which in some ways may represent the deepest part of the gulf between them and us" (*In the Shadow of Man* [Boston: Houghton Mifflin, 1971], p. 194).

That level of choice only appears with humans. Even they do not choose to be *Homo sapiens,* though as members of the species *Homo sapiens,* they have optional lifestyles unprecedented in the fauna and flora. Neither do humans choose this life-and-death-birth-and-rebirth order of being in which they too are caught up; they can only acquiesce in it. Neither do humans choose whether life must persist midst its perpetual perishing. This Earth-world is given to humans willy-nilly, as much as to all the other species.

But humans do have novel powers for rebuilding their Earth and for choosing their forms of life upon it. Humans may choose to rise to such challenges and succeed; they may also fail. In terms of our theological interests, humans in their cultures can rise deliberately to choose moral good, or they can fall back into moral evil. This amplifies the spontaneous evils of nature and deeply compounds the story. Humans have a superiority of opportunity, capacities unattainable in animal life. Even in human life such capacities are forever unattained, only brokenly attained. There is a genesis of spirit, recompounded from nature, in which humans can and ought to break out of their animal natures. Those experiences come creatively, with struggle, with an arduous passage through a twilight zone of spirit in exodus from nature. This requires the second birth superposed on the first, transcending natural possibilities. This may indeed require divine inspiration and redemption, transcending merely human possibilities. In this sense theological experience requires experiences beyond the previous attainment and power of biology, and here the possibility of kenotic self-limitation in humans reaches levels without precedent in prehuman nature.

Self-actualizing is a good thing for humans as well as animals. Organisms do well what they have the capacities to do; and this vital, productive capacity results in the Earthen genesis, with its swarms of creatures. The amoral fauna and flora are checked in their possessive impulses by the limitations of their ecosystems, and this provides a satisfactory place, a niche, for each specific form of life. Each species is limited to its appropriate sector, where it has an adapted fit. The creatures are caught up in these creative processes in which the individual is sacrificed to species lines, embedded in ecosystems, dynamic in evolutionary history.

The human species is embedded in this system, flesh and blood that must cope in an Earth-world. But the human species is unique, with powers of dominion unparalleled in any animal, and tempted by the fearful power of hand and mind to possess the whole. The human species has no natural niche, no limits by natural selection, which is relaxed progressively as the human species rises to culture as its niche, superposed on nature. Our possessive power is tempted to concupiscence. This power can only be checked by duty or by tragedy, and not by duty alone but by duty empowered by a vision of the whole. We move out of biology into ethics, and further, out of ethics into spirituality. Now we reach the possibility of kenosis in the classical Christian sense, where a self-interested individual limits self on behalf of others.

Indeed, we can now envision the possibility of kenosis in a still richer sense, where self-interested humans impose limits on human welfare on behalf of the other species. Beyond any human capacity to actualize a self, shared with myriads of other creatures, humans are distinguished by their capacity to see others, to oversee a world. Environmental ethics calls for seeing nonhumans, for seeing the biosphere, ecosystem communities, fauna, flora, the Earth. Environmental ethics advances beyond humanistic ethics, beyond the usual Christian ethics in that it considers others besides humans. We can put this provocatively by saying that Christian kenosis is called to rise to sufficient moral vision to count real "others" (nonhumans) — trees, species, ecosystems.

An exciting difference between humans and nonhumans is that, while animals and plants can defend only their own lives, with their offspring and kind, humans can defend life with vision of greater scope. They can sacrifice themselves for the good of humans yet unborn, or on the other side of the globe, the entire human community. Humans can also care for the biotic communities with which they share this planet; they can care for their biosphere. Here we recognize a difference crucial for understanding the human possibilities in the world. Humans can be genuine altruists; this begins when they recognize the claims of other humans, whether or not such claims are compatible with their own self-interest. The evolution of altruism and the possibility of kenosis is complete only when humans can recognize the claims of nonhumans. In that sense environmental ethics is the most altruistic form of ethics. It really loves others. This ultimate altruism is, or ought to be, the human genius.

The secular world looks for the management of nature, for reducing all nature to human resource, and plans a technology and an industry to accomplish that in the next century and millennium. But in that aspiration, humans only escalate their inherited desires for self-actualizing, tempted now into self-aggrandizement on scales never before possible. Humans are no longer checked by the long-standing ecological and evolutionary forces in which they have so long resided. The Christian opportunity today is to limit such human aggrandizement on behalf of the five million other species who also reside on Earth. Such kenosis is a Christian calling for the next millennium.

The Nature of Persons and the Emergence of Kenotic Behavior

MALCOLM JEEVES

Man's choice in the endless crises of his existence is the response of free-dom — the response on which love must wait for its triumph and tragedy.

Love's Endeavour, Love's Expense, p. 92

Introduction

Jürgen Moltmann tells us that one key aspect of kenosis, namely self-giving, is "God's trinitarian nature, and is therefore the mark of all his works."[1] Today, aspects of self-giving and self-sacrificing behavior are widely discussed and debated by evolutionary biologists, psychologists, and neuroscientists. For example, the evolutionary biologist Frans de Waal[2] says that "aiding others at a cost or risk to oneself is widespread in the animal world." But is there still a 'self' to do the 'self-giving'? Some neuroscientists, for example Francis Crick, question the existence of the soul, traditionally regarded as the seat of the self. In this chapter we shall focus on some of the recent evidence that self-giving is indeed present "in the structure of God's work" while at the same time signaling the ever

---

1. Jürgen Moltmann, Chapter 8 this volume.
2. Frans de Waal, *Good Natured: The Origins of Right and Wrong in Humans and Other Animals* (Cambridge, Mass.: Harvard University Press, 1996).

present temptation to offer facile and superficial explanations of such be-havior. Unlike William Sanday's[3] discussion of kenosis a century ago, we shall not be speculating about psychology's possible contribution to dis-cussions of the two consciousnesses, the Divine and the Human, in one person Jesus Christ, though our approach will be similar to Sanday's as we ask what clues we may glean from contemporary psychobiology that will illuminate our discussions of the roots and fruits of the self-giving com-ponent of kenotic behavior.

Background

When, at the turn of the century, William Sanday asked whether psychol-ogy might have something to contribute to our understanding of kenosis he focused on it as referring to the "self-emptying of the Divine Nature of Christ" (p. 71). This, in turn, meant that he saw psychology's role as help-ing to address the notion of two "consciousnesses," the Divine and the human, in the one person. However, as Sarah Coakley[4] reminds us, "kenosis has had a bewildering number of different evocations in differ-ent contexts in the Christian tradition." She distinguishes six different meanings of kenosis. Mindful of the views of kenosis offered by the theo-logian contributors to this volume, which have much in common with the views of William Sanday, it is instructive to see how, in his *Chris-tologies Ancient and Modern,* he explored the relevance of the contempo-rary psychology to his understanding of kenosis.

First we note that Sanday's focus was almost exclusively on the two-natures aspect of the problem. We shall touch on this since today some dualist views of human nature, widely accepted in Sanday's time, are un-der serious revision in the light of developments in neuroscience. We shall also be concerned to explore ways in which developments in evolutionary biology and primatology can be seen as giving hints about the emergence of aspects of self-giving and apparent self-sacrificing behavior in the ani-mal kingdom. That in turn leads to consideration of how our increasing knowledge of the neural substrates of behavior, including its moral di-mensions, raises questions about the variability and diversity of expres-

3. W. Sanday, *Christologies Ancient and Modern* (Oxford: Clarendon Press, 1910).
4. Sarah Coakley, Chapter 11 this volume.

sion of kenotic-like behavior. All of these are issues that arise at the interface of theology and science and must all be handled with a strong dose of
semantic hygiene lest we slip into the category mistakes of which we are
reminded by Rolston.[5]

Sanday's use of psychology in his *Christologies Ancient and Modern*
drew upon William James's then recently published *Varieties of Religious
Experience,* as well as on the views of F. W. H. Myers, at the time one of
the most influential figures in the activities of the Society for Psychical
Research. It is evident from Myers's posthumously published two-volume
work, devoted to discussions of the nature of consciousness, that he was
already exploring the role of the subconscious and of subliminal processes. If Sanday had waited another twenty years, he would no doubt
have drawn heavily on the works of Sigmund Freud and Carl Jung.

Today, Sanday would have found a wealth of sources to take into account had he shared Moltmann's view (in this book) that "creative love is
self-giving and self-limiting." These sources would include neuropsychol-
ogists, evolutionary psychologists, personality theorists, and materialist
neuroscientists.

It remains a matter of debate how seriously Sanday followed his own
guidelines, which he suggested should be applied when relating "new
ideas" from psychology, such as on the subconscious, to views on christology and, in particular, to the theology of kenosis.

Sanday's guidelines (given on page 141 of his text) included:

I am myself inclined to believe that the question of what we may follow his (i.e., Myers) example of calling subliminal consciousness and
subliminal activities is destined to be of much importance and (I
would even hope) of much value in the future of theology as well as
of psychology. *It ought, however, to be worked out on the ground of psychology first by the disinterested methods of psychological science, and
then on the foundations thus laid, the theologian may build.* (my italics)

Sanday, in putting to work the then emerging ideas of the conscious
and the subconscious as a way of understanding aspects of the divinity of
Christ, struggled hard to avoid a new form of dualism. Thus he wrote,
"Whatever there was of divine in him, on its way to outward expression

5. Holmes Rolston, III, Chapter 3 this volume.

68

whether in speech or act, passed through, and could not but pass through, the restricting and restraining medium of human consciousness. This consciousness was, as it were, the narrow neck through which alone the divine could come to expression" (p. 216). At the same time he had no doubt that "The consciousness of our Lord, as I have been trying to describe it and as I conceived it as presented to us in the Gospels, is a genuinely human consciousness. But I shall doubtless be asked: If that is so, what grounds have we for thinking that there was in him a root of being striking down below the strata of consciousness, by virtue of which he was more than human? My reply is, that we know it by the marks which have been appealed to all down the centuries in proof that in him deity and humanity were combined."

Kenosis and Developments in Science Since Sanday

With the plethora of views in the scientific and philosophical marketplace today on the nature of consciousness, Sanday could have a field day seeking to explore how each might have implications for understanding the divinity of Christ and the nature of kenotic behavior. Our aims, however, will be much more circumscribed and sharply focused. We shall look at some of the developments in science, particularly in evolutionary psychology and neuroscience, which for anyone writing about the theology of kenosis and related issues raise important questions. Such questions include:

1. How have developments in neuroscience in general, and in neuropsychology in particular, called for a re-examination of our understanding of personhood?
2. What is the status of current dualistic views of the person?
3. How free is the act of self-giving or self-limiting? For example, do recent developments in neuroscience and psychology call for a radical reassessment of the extent and limits of psychological determinism?
4. In the light of developments in evolutionary psychology and sociobiology, should we continue to regard self-giving and self-limiting behavior as uniquely human?
5. What questions have behavioral genetics and personality theory raised about the variability in self-giving and self-limiting behavior in

humans and nonhumans, and how have they illuminated our understanding of the biological roots of such behaviors?

In focusing on these particular questions, we limit ourselves to considering first, changing views of the nature of persons; second, current
views on the limits of human freedom; third, the evolutionary emergence
of one aspect of the ultimate nature of love, namely, the self-giving and
self-limiting aspects; and finally, the likely polygenetic basis of aspects of
kenotic behavior.

The Nature of Persons:
Psychobiological and Theological

Kenosis is, first and foremost, about the person of Christ. Other contributors to this volume, for example, Moltmann and Ward, deal with this
from a theological standpoint. However, given the presupposition that
"truth cannot contradict truth," it must seem to some to be increasingly
difficult to hold some traditional Christian views of persons in a world of
modern neurobiology and neuropsychology. Following such views would
face one with the following contradictory propositions:
    Proposition 1: Humans are physical beings who also have nonmate-
rial souls. It is through our souls that we experience and relate to God.
    Proposition 2: Humans are neurobiological beings whose mind (also
soul, religious experience, etc.) can, in theory, be exhaustively explained
by neurochemistry and ultimately by physics.
    The second proposition, that of the reductionist materialist, is well ex-
emplified by the statement of Nobel Laureate Francis Crick,[6] that "you,
your joys, and sorrows are no more than the behaviour of a vast assembly of
nerve cells and their associated molecules." Crick continued, "the idea that
man has a disembodied soul is as unnecessary as the old idea that there was a
Life Force," and this, he believes, "is in head on contradiction to the religious beliefs of billions of human beings alive today." In a very recent paper
in *Nature Neuroscience,* the editor wrote, "the rapid progress of neuroscience
has . . . deep and possibly disturbing implications"; its findings are "inter-

---

6. Francis Crick, *The Astonishing Hypothesis: The Scientific Search for the Soul* (London: Simon and Schuster, 1994).

preted by some as providing new ammunition for a materialistic account of human nature, and thus as an attack on traditional belief systems."

Few neuroscientists any longer believe that humans are composed of two distinct parts called brain and mind, or body and soul. With every neuroscience advance comes further confirmation of the inseparable bond between brain and mind. In *Descartes' Error,* neuroscientist Antonio Damasio[7] contends that "the distinction between diseases of 'brain' and 'mind' . . . is an unfortunate cultural inheritance that permeates society . . . it reflects a basic ignorance of the relation between brain and 'mind'."

But what about the soul? It's true that many people of faith continue to speak and sing words that assume that our human nature includes an entity called a soul that interacts with our bodies but leaves at our death. This body/soul dualism — the legacy of Plato, St. Augustine, and Descartes — cannot be ruled out on scientific grounds. Another Nobel Laureate, Sir John Eccles, believed that mind and soul are indeed nonmaterial entities that interact with the physical body. Many adherents of New Age religion and some devotees of parapsychology hold a similar view. However, not all Christian neuroscientists feel led either by their science or their faith to believe that they are made up of two separate entities, body and soul. Rather, we believe we are unified human beings (which is one translation of *soul* found in some modern versions of the Bible), with physical and mental aspects. The mental dimension of one's being is as important as the physical body–brain on which it depends. The emerging scientific evidence, fueled by psychology's so-called cognitive revolution, gives as much weight to the mental aspects of our nature as to the physical. Susan Greenfield's[8] recent (1999) Michael Faraday Lecture at the Royal Society of London concluded that as we come to the end of the decade of the brain, we should make the next the decade of the mind.

As the past century of Jewish and Christian biblical scholarship has reminded us, our "soulishness" should be understood as our relatedness to God, to other humans, and to all of creation. The biblical idea is, in this respect, remarkably similar to the neuroscience view that we are psychosomatic unities, not dualistic packages. I do not have a soul, I *am* a living being or soul. As New Testament scholar Joel Green[9] reminded us very re-

7. A. R. Damasio, *Descartes' Error: Emotion, Reason and the Human Brain* (New York: Grosset/Putman, 1994).

8. S. Greenfield, Michael Faraday Lecture: Royal Society of London.

cently, although in the history of Christian thought body-soul dualism has often occupied a central place, it is, nevertheless, not the *only* position. Green argues that "a rehearsal of the biblical evidence suggests the degree to which body-soul dualism has achieved a prominence far out of proportion to the scriptural basis on which it was alleged to have been built." He continues: "Christians who today embrace a monistic account of humanity may do so not only as 'good scientists', but as persons assured that this position actually places them more centrally within the biblical material than has usually been granted over the past two millennia." Green at the same time notes that "biblical faith would naturally resist any suggestion that our humanity can be reduced to our physicality." This latter view, labeled nonreductive physicalism or dual-aspect monism, is set out in detail in the recent volume *Whatever Happened to the Soul?* Green also highlights one other, often forgotten, biblical theme on human nature, namely that "the nature of the human person can never be understood one person at a time, so to speak. If we would articulate an account of the human person that takes with utmost seriousness the biblical record, we would have far less conversation about the existence or importance of 'souls' and far more about the human capacity and vocation for community with God, with the human family and in relation to the cosmos." This latter emphasis on the capacity for community would naturally subsume some manifestations of individual and group self-giving behavior.

The need fully to recognize the unity of personhood is further underlined in the recent book by the evolutionary biologist Frans de Waal. Like some others, he refers to the now often quoted example of the experience of the railroad worker Phineas Gage, who, in 1848, in a moment of distraction, triggered a blast while leaning over a hole filled with explosive powder, which resulted in a pointed tamping iron going straight through his left eye, brain, and skull. Remarkably, Gage was not killed but only stunned! After this dramatic episode Gage was transformed from a previously upright and conscientious citizen into a man with serious character flaws brought about by damage to the ventral-medial frontal region of his brain. This remarkable pattern of changed behavior has now been observed in a dozen other similarly brain-damaged patients, who, though possessing intact logical and memory functions, have dramatically com-

9. J. Green, "Scripture and the Human Person," *Science and Christian Belief* 2, no. 1 (1999): 51-64.

promised abilities to manage their personal and social affairs. As de Waal put it, "It's as if the moral compass of these people has been demagnetized, causing it to spin out of control." De Waal continues: "What this incident teaches us is that conscience is not some disembodied concept that can be understood only on the basis of culture and religion." Morality is as firmly grounded in neurobiology as anything else we do or are. This finding has been further and very strikingly reinforced by a report of recent research by Damasio and his colleagues.[10] They report the case of two children who suffered brain damage — one a female at fifteen months, the other a male at three months. The woman is now 20, the man 23. They both display disruptive and reckless behavior, lying, stealing, inability to make friends, insensitivity, and lack of remorse. The link between personality and emotion and their neural substrates has been further documented by studies of psychopaths and murderers using modern brain neuro-imaging techniques. There is much still to be learned. The relevance of these developments in neuroscience for our discussions is that they provide hints that given time we may begin to understand something about the neural substrates of kenotic behavior. That, however, will do nothing to empty kenotic behavior of its moral significance any more than a recent study of Einstein's brain calls into question the validity of his scientific theorizing. In each instance they must be judged by appropriate criteria applicable to the domain of knowledge in question.

The possibility that animals might possess "soulishness" comes also from a nonscientific source. The opening chapters of the Hebrew scriptures refer to both animals and humans as "living beings." That does not conflict with the evidence accumulated by psychologists, which makes it clear that animals differ greatly from humans in some aspects of their degree of "soulishness" — so much so that the difference is best seen in qualitative terms. This is evidenced by the absence of libraries, cathedrals, observatories, nuclear science laboratories, and high-tech medical procedures among chimpanzees! However, as we shall see later, the possibility for the emergence of self-giving and self-sacrificing behavior in nonhuman primates, as well as in lower organisms, may equally be seen as part of the intrinsic pattern of creation. The view of personhood suggested here takes

10. S. W. Anderson, A. Bechara, H. Damasio, D. Tranch, and A. R. Damasio, "Impairment of Social and Moral Behaviour Related to Early Damage in Human Prefrontal Cortex," *Nature Neuroscience* 2, no. 11 (November 1999): 1032-37.

account of what is known of the neurobiology of human nature and suggests that a nonreductive view of the relationship between human subjective mental life and neurobiology allows a key role for top-down causal influences. At the same time it presents a view of human soulishness as embodied in the capacity for the deepest and richest forms of personal relatedness, which recognize that it is God's sovereign choice to be in relationship to humankind in a manner that bestows ultimate and irreducible dignity to persons. More specifically for our concerns here it says:

1. that it is not the implantation of a 'soul' at a particular time that confers the capacity for kenotic behavior
2. that "soulishness" as here conceived recognizes, indeed expects, indications of it in nonhuman primates, especially those capable of empathy and "mind reading," and hence also the potential for exhibiting kenotic behavior in nonhuman primates. Recent evidence from neuroscience has reported the discovery in the monkey's pre-motor cortex of "mirror neurons."[11] These are neurons that respond when a particular action is performed by the responding monkey *and* when the same action is observed to be performed by another individual. Experimental evidence suggests that a similar matching system also exists in humans. In addition, it has been suggested that there is a unique type of brain cell, which seems to separate humans and apes from lower animals. These "spindle cells" may be indications of part of the necessary neural substrates for empathetic emotional responses to others, including their facial expressions.
3. that the capacity for kenotic behavior may be altered/diminished by selective brain damage and/or by the failure of the brain to develop normally — a "bottom-up" effect.
4. that given the intactness of the normal neural substrates (as yet not fully spelled out), kenotic capacities may be enlarged and enhanced by participation in a kenotic community, i.e., a "top-down" effect.

With this changed way of looking at personhood and at human nature we may now move on to issues that are raised in the context of the nature of love and of kenosis. These include psychological determinism,

11. V. Gallese and A. Goldman, *Trends in Cognitive Sciences* 2, no. 12 (December 1998).

the genetic basis of personality traits such as self-giving behavior, and of the emergence of self-giving behavior as evidenced in the researches of evolutionary psychologists.

Determinism and the Freedom to Act in a Self-Giving and Self-Limiting Way

Why revisit the subject of psychological determinism when it has been so widely discussed and, some would say, effectively dealt with in the past? This remains, in the minds of many people, a significant issue and one that has become much more focused as a result of the exciting developments in neuroscience over the last two decades. Forms of reductionism, such as Crick's, ignore earlier warnings that in seeking parsimony of explanations in science there is a danger of cutting our throats with Occam's razor or of blowing out our brains with Lloyd Morgan's canon. Views on this issue do not divide along a neat line with theists on one side and atheists on the other. Writing of the reductionist program, John Polkinghorne, referring to "the perpetual puzzle of the connection of mind and brain," commented that "the reductionist programme in the end subverts itself. Ultimately it is suicidal." He writes, "If our mental life is nothing but the humming activity of an immensely complexly connected computer-like brain, who is to say whether the programme running on the intricate machine is correct or not?" He continues: "The very assertions of the reductionist himself are nothing but blips in the neural network of his brain. The world of rational discourse dissolves into the absurd chatter of firing synapses. Quite frankly, that cannot be right, and none of us believes it to be so." Such views were expressed differently forty years earlier by another distinguished scientist. Biologist J. B. S. Haldane wrote, "If my mental processes are determined wholly by the motions of the atoms in my brain, I have no reason to suppose that my beliefs are true . . . and hence I have no reason for supposing my brain to be composed of atoms." Haldane appeared not to have shared Polkinghorne's theistic assumptions.

Developments in neuroscience over the last two decades have indeed forced upon us, as Francis Crick claims, a careful rethinking of the limits of human freedom. Psychologists and neurobiologists make certain assumptions that are basic to their endeavors. Thus, as we study a particular behavior, if it seems to be capricious we subject it to more careful study, hoping to find the hidden laws that we expect *really* apply. This kind of determinism, which applies not only within psychology but also in other domains, has been labeled methodological determinism.

If the tentative application of methodological determinism turns out to be reasonably successful, then the next step is to say, "Well, it seems likely that in all areas of the study of behavior, if only we can understand it sufficiently, we shall find that it follows exceptionless regularities. Where there are exceptions is probably due to our lacking complete information and, therefore, from a procedural point of view we shall assume that determinism does apply." This stage has sometimes been called empirical determinism. It is then but a short step to move beyond methodological determinism and empirical determinism and adopt a reductionist position that was popular fifty years ago, when it was claimed that all human acts are instantiations of the laws of physics and chemistry. This of course is a vast extrapolation from our actual limited ability to explain and predict behavior. Certainly no psychologist can prove any such universal proposition. In practice the predictability we are normally able to obtain, even in the experimental laboratory, is largely of a probabilistic type. The next move is to go beyond this to metaphysical determinism, which asserts that all human psychological events instantiate universal laws and that we hold this view as an absolute ontological presupposition that no empirical evidence could be allowed to gainsay. With the demise of logical positivism, however, this is a much less widely held view today than it was fifty years ago.

The outcome of four decades of study of the neural substrates of mental life has, as indicated above, certainly pointed to an ever tightening link between mind and brain. That is not to deny that distinctly psychological events take place or that they are 'less' real than their physical component events. The reductionist thesis is that descriptive and causal statements made in familiar psychological language can be translated without residue, at least in principle, into statements in physiological language. More sophisticated proponents of these views readily acknowledge that a 'psychological' statement such as "Smith laughed when he saw the logical fallacy" cannot be completely translated into physiological language simply because the term *fallacy* designates a logical (normative) concept rather than a physiological state. But the reason for that is that the original statement you are trying to translate is not, in itself, purely causal or descriptive. It is the evidence for this tightening of the link between mind and brain that has led to a re-examination of determinism in human behavior and re-opened questions concerning whether we do in fact enjoy any real freedom of choice.

One simple way to deal with this problem is to adopt a dualist position. In this way, at a stroke, you cut the Gordian knot. The nonmaterial mind can, it is claimed, act freely and influence or determine the activity of the physiological substrate as it wishes. Sir John Eccles, referred to earlier, held a variant of this view, arguing that room is left in the brain events underlying mental processes for randomness of the Heisenberg variety. One problem with this view is that most brain events involve so many millions of electrons that the chances of a Heisenberg uncertainty event having a *significant* effect on most of them is virtually nil. Eccles' response to this would be to point out that when you come to something like a single synapse, you are dealing with the diffusion of molecules through maybe a dozen meshes of a membrane, where Heisenberg uncertainty *could* significantly affect the probability of a molecule getting through. It is in this context that Eccles proposes a model in which he speaks of the person inhabiting another world and acting upon the brain. However, while physical randomness in the brain might secure the *unpredictability* of a choice, it would weaken rather than strengthen the chooser's *responsibility* for the outcome of that choice. More recently, attempts have been made to invoke chaos theory to help enlighten the issues here. An example may be taken from the 1986 paper in *Scientific American*[12] on chaos theory, which suggested that "Even the process of intellectual progress relies on the injection of new ideas and on new ways of connecting old ideas. Innate creativity may have an underlying chaotic process that selectively amplifies small fluctuations and molds them into macroscopic coherent mental states that are experienced as thoughts. In some cases the thoughts may be decisions, what are perceived to be the exercise of will. In this light, chaos provides a mechanism that allows of free will within a world governed by deterministic laws." Further discussion of this issue is given by John Polkinghorne in his chapter. For our purposes, the more pressing problems are nearer to hand and cannot easily await the philosophical solution to the problems posed above. Clearly our present behavior *is* dependent on our genetic endowment, our neural

12. J. P. Cruchfield, J. D. Farmer, N. H. Parkhard North, and R. W. Shaw, "Chaos," *Scientific American,* 1986, pp. 38-49.

substrate, our early upbringing — the social, cultural, and physical environment in which we have grown up. Such factors *could* certainly make it more difficult for some people than others to act in a self-giving or self-limiting way. We shall examine aspects of this in later sections.

The Nature of Love and Kenosis
in the Light of Evolutionary Psychology

It is interesting to put side by side Moltmann's statement that self-giving is "God's trinitarian essence, and is therefore the mark of all his works" with Frans de Waal's statement that "aiding others at a cost or risk to oneself is widespread in the animal world." Moltmann was writing as a systematic theologian, and de Waal, as a primatologist. It is aspects of this convergence of thinking that we shall examine in this section. Anything that we write in this context should be guided by the penetrating comments of Pascal in 1659: "It is dangerous to show a man too clearly how much he resembles the beast, without at the same time showing him his greatness. It is also dangerous to allow too clear a vision of his greatness without his baseness. It is even more dangerous to leave him in ignorance of both."

As de Waal has pointed out, a gene-centric sociobiology still tends to dominate popular thinking. Taken to its logical extreme, the point is that genes favor their own replication — a gene is successful if it produces a trait that in turn promotes the gene. It was to describe such genetic self-promotion that Richard Dawkins introduced his psychological term in the title of his book, *The Selfish Gene*. Accordingly, what may be a generous act in common language, such as bringing home food, may be selfish from the gene's perspective. With time, perhaps not surprisingly, the important words "from the gene's perspective" were forgotten and eventually left out. Thus all behavior became selfish. However, since genes have neither a self nor the emotions to make them selfish, it should be self-evident that the phrase is simply a metaphor. But, as de Waal has already pointed out, if you repeat a metaphor often enough, it tends to assume an aura of literal truth. Dawkins himself certainly cautioned against his own anthropomorphism of the gene, but to little effect. The whole thrust of de Waal's most recent book is to begin to redress, from a scientific point of view and not a philosophical and logical one, the imbalance left by the impact of Dawkins's book.

Evolutionary theory attempts to explain the evolution of aiding others in two general ways:

1. It argues that genes favoring altruism can spread in future generations if their costs to altruists' personal reproductive success is outweighed by the benefits in reproductive success of altruists' relatives carrying copies of the same genes ('kin selection'). The ratio of these indirect benefits through relatives, versus costs to oneself, needs to be greater the less closely the altruist is related to those helped — i.e., the lower the likelihood the altruist will be helping copies of their genes in the other.
2. It proposes that genes favoring altruism could spread if the altruism is sufficiently reciprocated ('reciprocal altruism').

As regards the first mechanism, examples are widespread in the animal kingdom. Some of its most extreme forms are found, as one might expect, in those odd species where individuals in a colony are unusually highly related to each other — social insects like bees and ants, in which workers' genetic relatedness to each other and to the queen is ¾ (cf. the maximum of ½ found in mammals — i.e., between mammalian parent-child and sib-sib relationships). This is taken to explain why sterile castes of workers evolved in ants and bees — i.e., the workers are totally altruistic, spending their whole lives giving for the 'good of the group' (or the good of the queen, who is the only one to reproduce directly). One of the most graphic examples is 'honey-pot' worker ants, who do nothing but hang from the ceiling of the ant colony, acting as receptacles or storage jars for honey, which some workers fill them with, and which the colony draws on when needed. At an individual level, that is self-sacrifice![13] Examples of reciprocal altruism appear to be much rarer. Humans apart, there are only a handful of examples. A classic one is vampire bats, who are in real danger of starving if they fail to act subtly enough to get their blood meal of an evening, and are then fed, back in their colony, by an unrelated nest mate, to whom they are likely to repay the favor on another night.[14]

---

13. E. O. Wilson, *Socio-biology: The New Synthesis* (Cambridge, Mass.: Belknap/Harvard University Press, 1975).

14. G. S. Wilkinson, "Reciprocal Food Sharing in the Vampire Bat," *Nature* 308 (1984): 181-84.

As is immediately evident, the examples cited flash up the warning that we must not assume that because two behaviors are similar, the mechanisms underlying them are necessarily similar or identical. We are today familiar enough with our ability to reproduce aspects of human and animal behavior in robots, but no one suggests that the underlying mechanisms producing those behaviors are necessarily the same. They may certainly share some common features, but when it comes to questions of motivation, conscious awareness, goal-directed behavior, and such, the two may be miles apart. Likewise, because we may observe self-giving, self-sacrificing behavior in different evolutionary phyla, that in itself tells us nothing about the underlying mechanisms for those behaviors. How, for example, could it be 'self'-giving if there is no awareness of 'self'?

There remain, however, some compelling examples based on anecdotal evidence. Jane Goodall[15] described examples of chimpanzee behavior that are different in that they appear to be unusual behaviors, not something done by all chimps or even by particular chimps routinely. She describes (p. 357) a female helping her mother, who was unlikely to help her in return or reproduce again. The anecdotal nature of the observation may be scientifically problematic, but it is certainly different from the ant and bat cases. It looks like an unusual episode in which the female recognized her mother as in need of help and worked out a way to help her.

The impetus given by de Waal's book seems ready to be pushed further by Eliot Sober and David Wilson's recent book, *Unto Others: The Evolution and Psychology of Unselfish Behavior.*[16] The authors are a prominent philosopher of biology, Eliot Sober, and a well-known theoretical biologist, David Wilson. Between the 1960s and 1980s, a view prevailing in the preceding years was strongly denounced and largely dismissed. This was the idea of 'group selection' — that whole groups of individuals could act as the units that natural selection either favored or disfavored. If this view were correct, then the evolution of altruism could be explained by the success of groups of cooperating altruists, outcompeting groups of relatively selfish individuals. This was an idea Darwin had himself put forward. In the latter half of this century, however, evolutionary biology has

15. Jane Goodall, *The Chimpanzees of Gombe: Patterns of Behavior* (Cambridge, Mass.: Belknap/Harvard University Press, 1986), ch. 11.

16. E. Sober and D. Wilson, *Unto Others: The Evolution and Psychology of Unselfish Behavior* (Cambridge, Mass.: Harvard University Press, 1998).

forthrightly rejected this. Theoretical models indicated that the conditions required for group selection made it most unlikely to occur in nature. In simple terms, individuals helping others for the good of the group alone would always be outcompeted by any selfish competitors, who would bequeath more genes to future generations. Consistent with this, empirically supported cases of group selection were not demonstrated.

Sober and Wilson mount a vigorous new defense of group selection and offer a thorough review and analysis. The crux of their argument is that the idea of group selection has been interpreted too narrowly. It is not necessary that whole groups must be selected over others; rather, genes favoring altruism could rise in frequency where the positive effects on between-groups competition are more significant than the costs in within-group competition, even where the altruism is directed towards non-kin or non-reciprocators. Sober and Wilson argue that the conditions necessary for this plausibly existed in hominid evolution, and that psychological predispositions for genuine altruism were the results. It is too early to judge whether Sober and Wilson's case will gain acceptance. The jury is still out, and it is evident from the reviews that have already appeared that it contains both exciting and stimulating material and also material that may be over interpreted. As John Maynard-Smith[17] stated in his review, "This book should come with a health warning. Read critically, it will stimulate thought about important questions. Swallowed whole, its effects would be disastrous." Iver Mysterud[18] echoes Maynard-Smith's comments when he writes, reviewing the book, "*Unto Others* is one of the most important books of the decade. It simply cannot be ignored. . . . it will inspire a flood of new studies, invite debate and be at the centre of intellectual discourse for the next decade. . . ." Sociobiologist E. O. Wilson likewise comments, "*Unto Others* is an important, original, and well-written book. It contains the definitive contemporary statement on higher level selection and the evolutionary origin of co-operation."

De Waal's book review of detailed studies of the nonhuman primates indicates, referring to those nearer to man, "it is entirely possible that succorant behavior and sensitivity to the needs of others are better developed in apes than in monkeys." This observation is not new. One of the

17. J. Maynard-Smith, review in *Nature* (1999).
18. I. Mysterud, review in *Trends in Ecology and Evolution* (1998).

early pioneers in this area of research, publishing in the 1920s, commented that "A certain solicitude, sympathy, and pity, as well as almost human expression and consideration, were thus manifested by these little creatures." (The reference here is to juvenile chimpanzees.)

It is in this context that we need to remember Lloyd Morgan's canon that "In no case may we interpret an action as the outcome of a higher psychical faculty if it can be interpreted as the outcome of one which stands lower in the psychological scale." In discussions of nonhuman primate behavior, anthropomorphism figures large. De Waal believes that "This use of anthropomorphism as a *means* to get at the truth, rather than as an end of itself, sets its use in science apart from use by the lay person." And he continues, "The ultimate goal of the scientist is emphatically *not* to arrive at the most satisfactory projection of human feelings onto the animal, but rather at testable ideas and replicable observations. Thus, anthropomorphism serves the same exploratory function as that of intuition in all science, from mathematics to medicine."

De Waal continues, "But what about the cherished principle of parsimony — the one great bulwark against all this liberal thinking?" And he observes that in this realm "the problem is that insofar as monkeys and apes are concerned, a profound conflict exists between *two* kinds of parsimony. The first is the traditional canon that tells us not to invoke higher capacities if the phenomenon can be explained with lower ones. This favors simple explanations, such as learned adjustment, over more complex ones, such as cognitive empathy." He continues: "The second form of parsimony considers the shared evolutionary background of humans and other primates. It posits that if closely related species act the same, the underlying process probably is the same too." Later he says, "In short, the principle of parsimony has two faces. At the same time that we are supposed to favor low level over high level cognitive explanations, we also should not create a double standard according to which shared human and ape behavior is explained differently. Such 'evolutionary parsimony' is a factor especially when both humans and apes exhibit traits not seen in monkeys, and two explanations are proposed where one may do."

De Waal has no doubt that "evolution has produced the requisites for morality: a tendency to develop social norms and enforce them, to capacities of empathy and sympathy, mutual aid and a sense of fairness, the mechanisms of conflict resolution, and so on." There is thus a good argument for the case that some aspects of self-giving and self-limiting behavior may be seen as developing over the evolutionary phyla, becoming more and more pronounced among the nonhuman primates. This reaches a point where, in the opinion of de Waal, something approaching the nature of evidence for a conscience emerges. However, as he rightly points out, the evidence from the effects of brain damage on human patients, and in particular the classical case of Phineas Gage referred to above, teaches us that conscience is not some disembodied concept that can be understood only on the basis of culture and religion. Again, to quote de Waal, "Morality is as firmly grounded in neurobiology as anything else we do or are." And he goes on: "Once thought of as purely spiritual matters, honesty, guilt, and the weighing of ethical dilemmas are traceable to specific areas of the brain. It should not surprise us, therefore, to find animal parallels. The human brain is a product of evolution. Despite its larger volume and greater complexity, it is fundamentally similar to the central nervous system of other animals." For those of us who begin from theistic presuppositions, we can thus see embedded within creation the seeds, development, and fruits of self-giving behavior. The course of creation has been such that the qualities of self-giving and self-limiting behavior, built into the neural substrate of behavior, may be traced out coming to full flower in humankind.

Kenosis, Neuroscience, Personality Traits, and Genetics

With the human genome project well advanced and frequent media reports of the discovery of "obesity" genes, a "criminal" gene, a "novelty" gene, and so on, we begin to wonder if there will soon be a kenosis gene, and will human behavior soon all be reduced to DNA? Recent reports have demonstrated how genetic manipulation may produce measurable and, according to some criteria, desirable changes in behavior. Thus, the Princeton neuroscientists[19] (Tang, Shimizu, et al.) recently reported (September 1999) how they had genetically modified mice so that by changing synaptic functions between cells in the brain they markedly improved the learning ability of their animals. The media speculated whether simi-

19. Y. P. Tang, E. Shimizu, G. R. Dube, C. Rampon, G. A. Kerchner, M. Xhuo, G. S. Liu, and J. Z. Tsien, "Genetic Enhancement of Learning and Memory in Mice," *Nature* 401, no. 6748 (1999): 63-69.

lar techniques may in due time be applied to humans, and more specifically, to children with learning difficulties as well as to those at the other end of life who develop short-term memory problems. Stephen J. Gould,[20] noting how the media boldly proclaimed the Princeton scientists as demonstrating "The I.Q. Gene," aptly remarked that the media treatment of their dramatic findings well illustrated what he called "the labeling fallacy." He pointed out that complex organisms are *not* simply the sum of their genes, nor do genes alone build particular items of anatomy or behavior by themselves. He illustrated "the labeling fallacy" by referring to the occasion in 1996 when scientists reported the discovery of a gene for novelty-seeking behavior — at the time regarded as a good thing. In 1997, another study saw a link between the *same* gene and a propensity for heroin addiction. So Gould asked the question, did the 'good' gene for enhanced exploration become the 'bad' gene for addictive tendencies? The biochemistry may be the same, but context and background matter.

Thirty years ago there was a certain fatalism about human genetics expressed in the rhetorical question, "If it's genetic then what can you do about it anyway?" In forming a genetic view of persons, the focus of the majority of the studies seeking to explore the interaction between an organism and its environment has been on identical and non-identical twins. Such studies look at correlations to provide measures of similarity between twins, from the most (1.00) to the least (0.00) similar. Such correlations are highest for structural and physiological variables, in the mid range but somewhat higher for mental ability than for personality, and fairly low for interests. When one begins to consider self-restraint or self-limiting behavior, these probably best come under the general heading of personality traits. A typical finding of the correlations for personality variables for monozygotic twins reared together (MZT) and apart (MZA) — taken from the Minnesota study of twins reared apart — shows that the correlations on personality traits at adulthood differ little, 0.50 for the twins reared apart and 0.49 for the twins reared together.

Such research on genes and personality use data based on the general agreement that there are the "big five" distinguishable personality traits normally labeled,

20. S. J. Gould, "Message from a Mouse," *The New York Times,* September 13, 1999, p. 64.

1. Extroversion, dominance
2. Agreeableness, likeability, friendliness
3. Conscientiousness, conformity, will to achieve
4. Emotional stability (with anxiety and neuroticism as opposites)
5. Culture, intellect, openness to experience.

Typical of the results of studies in this area we may consider the data for the first listed above, namely extroversion. The available data come from five large twin studies with sample sizes ranging from 475 to 12,777 pairs, an unusually large database. The results of the analyses of such studies are expressed normally in the form of correlation coefficients. The correlations for the monozygotic pairs range from 0.46 to 0.65 and for the dyzygotic same-sex pairs from 0.13 to 0.28, with the monozygotic-dyzygotic differences showing a clear genetic effect. When all the data from twins (reared together and apart) and from adoption studies are collated, genes account for 35 to 39 percent for the individual variation in extroversion. It had been assumed that environment accounts for much of the family resemblance in personality, but most of the studies showed the effect of shared environment to be close to zero.

A very recent report published in *MRC News*[21] (Spring 1999) in Britain was devoted, in part, to contemporary studies of personality. Typical of findings in this area are those reported by McGuffin.[22] In this respect human personality is much like a whole range of traits that show size, shape, and other quantitative variations in plants and animals. Further support for this general conclusion comes from the so-called Dunedin study which has been in progress for the past thirty years. The focus of this study has been to investigate the connections between childhood

21. P. McGuffin, A. Caspi, "Personality in Profile," *MRC News* (Winter/Spring 1999): 20-23, 28-33.
22. McGuffin underlined the main points made in earlier studies of monozygotic and dyzygotic twins but went on to point out an additional interesting finding to emerge from studies of normal and abnormal personality, namely that the balance between the influence of genes and environment changes over time. Although studies on criminal behavior, for example, support the general conclusion of the importance of genetic factors, they point to the fact that while genetic influences on normal personality and personality disorder certainly exist it is highly unlikely that personality traits can be linked to single genes. We should not expect to find "the gene for" neuroticism or for aggression. It is far more likely that these and other personality traits are influenced by many genes, known as quantitative trait loci (QTL's), each of which alone has only a small effect.

characteristics and a person's psychological make-up as an adult. Throughout the twentieth century, professional opinion and public advice have been swayed by claims and counterclaims about the extent of continuity and discontinuity in human development. Twenty years ago a well-known psychologist, Jerome Kagan, attacked what he saw as a misguided faith in connectiveness and suggested that early psychological characteristics and experiences have few implications for later behavior. The Dunedin study charted connections from the first few years of life — as early as age 3 — to young adulthood. Coming closer to our primary concern here, though not identical with it, we may note a study by Philip Rushton in 1986. He used questionnaires to measure, among other things, altruism and reported evidence for the heritability of this personality trait. Not surprisingly, attempts to understand the motivation for helping others have come up with a variety of explanations, including disguised self-interest. Some, such as Bates, have suggested that there are two alternative routes to helping behavior, which he labels the egoistic and the altruistic. He concludes that genuine altruism may exist.

The implications of all this for our discussions are first, that we have to consider the possibility that the capacity for self-restraint, of self-limiting behavior within any given population, may have a complex polygenetic basis. Second, that hopefully, a (kenotic) community will nurture the development and expression of kenotic behavior, though the extent or degree of expression of that behavior may depend on genetic endowment. By referring to "nurturing the development of kenotic behavior" we signal an imbalance in our presentation thus far. The approach has been essentially asking how might the properties of the neural substrate and/or genetic endowment result in this or that form of behavior, including kenotic behavior. To stop there, however, would be to limit the discussion to the "bottom-up" approach. Equally relevant, though much more important to research on kenotic behavior, is the "top-down" approach. The late Nobel Laureate, Roger Sperry,[23] constantly emphasized this. He wrote, for example, "consciousness is conceived to be a dynamic emergent property of brain activity, neither identical with nor reducible to, the neural events of which it is mainly composed," and he added, "consciousness exerts potent causal effects in the interplay of cerebral operations." This

---

23. R. W. Sperry, in *Essays in Honor of Roger W. Sperry* (Cambridge: Cambridge University Press, 1990), pp. 382-85.

theme is taken up, though with a different emphasis, by Antonio Damasio in *Descartes' Error* (1994) where, commenting on those who confine themselves to a "bottom-up" approach, he writes, "Does this mean that love, generosity, kindness, compassion, honesty, and other commendable human characteristics are *nothing but* (my italics) the result of conscious, but selfish, survival-oriented neurobiological regulation? Does this deny the possibility of altruism and *negate free-will* (my italics)? Does this mean that there is no true love, no sincere friendship, no genuine compassion? That is definitely not the case" (pp. 125-26).

In the past decade, reports have begun to appear in the neuroscience literature that begin to demonstrate what we had long suspected intuitively: namely, that what we do (and think) habitually "sculptures" the brain as well as the mind. For example, Sodate and colleagues in 1996 showed that parts of the cerebral cortex not normally dedicated to tactile processing became so in blind people highly skilled in Braille. They concluded that training and habitual use modifies the neural substrate in such a task. Other studies have confirmed this. What is more surprising is the findings of a study carried out in Italy that illustrated the possible long-term benefits of early education in warding off Alzheimer's disease. They found that the rate of Alzheimer's disease — the commonest form of senile dementia — was fourteen times greater among illiterate people with no education than among those who had had more than five years of education. That this is an artifact of a particular study carried out in Italy is unlikely, since other researchers have found the same result in other countries. Even so we certainly do not yet understand *how* education might have this effect. What is clear, however, is that "top-down" sculpturing of the brain by the mind and behavior must be seriously reckoned with even though it may be many years before we begin to understand how it comes about.

Conclusions

Exciting developments in psychology, especially neuropsychology and evolutionary psychology, reopen a number of questions concerning the nature of humankind, the limits of human freedom, and the origins and uniqueness of self-giving and self-limiting behavior. The emergence of human-like moral and ethical behavior in nonhuman species, and responsibility for the

87

expression of definable personality traits such as self-giving and self-limiting behavior, points to their polygenetic basis and indicates their possible genetic and neural substrates. A brief survey of the relevant contemporary science, it is suggested, leads to the following tentative conclusions:

1. Plausible ideas are plentiful but evidence, though accumulating, is limited. In such circumstances, unjustified extrapolations are at times offered based more on presuppositions than data.
2. Biblical notions of personhood continue to be confronted by repeated attempts to resurrect a variety of forms of substance dualism. The principal thought models within neuroscience today show convergence with the Hebrew-Christian view of persons not as *possessing* "souls" but as *being* "living souls." Equally important for our discussions of self-giving behavior is the need to recapture the biblical emphasis on the human capacity and vocation for community with God, with the human family and in relation to the cosmos.
3. While recognizing the limitations that our neurobiology places on our thoughts and actions, we equally recognize the opportunities for shaping our own behavior by the individual choices we constantly make, and this applies to self-giving and self-limiting as to other behaviors.
4. Evidence pointing to a genetic component modulating the degree of expressed self-giving and self-limiting behavior sits alongside the evidence indicating that such behavior is *not* genetically determined. Its expression is increased and multiplied by moment-to-moment, personal choices and arguably also by the catalytic effect of a kenotic community.
5. Very recent evidence of the rudiments of self-giving, self-limiting, and self-sacrificing behavior in nonhuman primates and of the variations in their cultural evolution may be interpreted as the manifestation and emergence in creation of an intrinsic property of creation. As Ellis notes (this volume) we may then see kenosis as a key to understanding one aspect of the deep nature of creation, seeing the emergence of kenosis in the biological world, of which we, as God's creatures, are part. However, constant vigilance is called for if we are to avoid slipping into sloppy thinking by assuming that similarities in overt behavior demonstrate and necessitate identical mechanisms for those behaviors.

6. Within the Christian tradition it is not necessary to deny the emergence of elements of kenotic behavior in nonhuman primates in order to defend the uniqueness of the self-giving and self-emptying of Christ. Rather, what we see of the beginnings of kenotic behavior in nonhuman primates, in individual and group human behavior, is demonstrated par excellence and uniquely in the person of Christ. Uniquely, since it is by faith that we affirm that the ultimate act of Christ's self-giving by its nature sets him and it apart from all others. He gave himself, we believe (as the Book of Common Prayer puts it), "as the one full, complete sacrifice oblation and satisfaction for the sins of the whole world." Thus while recognizing our kinship with Christ, we at the same time acknowledge his uniqueness since in that act of supreme self-giving "God was in Christ reconciling the world to himself" (2 Cor. 5:19). At the same time, while we may thankfully marvel that in creation we are given glimpses of the emergence of self-sacrificing behavior, we must feel challenged in knowing that our own attempts at following our role model are often so feeble. Like Sanday we shall remember that we still believe that Christ was more than human "by the marks which have been appealed to down the centuries in proof that in him deity and humanity were combined."

Kenotic Creation and Divine Action

JOHN POLKINGHORNE

The external constraint which love practices is often a mark of its freedom from internal limit.

Love's Endeavour, Love's Expense, p. 44

A prayer in the current Daily Office of the Church of England begins, "Eternal God and Father, you create us by your power and redeem us by your love. . . ." Although it is a much-loved prayer, its theology is open to question. We could as well speak of the God who creates us by divine love and redeems us by divine power.

Any dichotomy between creation and redemption carries with it theological dangers, and these risks are enhanced when there is an imposed correlation with different divine attributes. The act of creation, of bringing a world into being and maintaining it in being, is clearly an act of great power to which the puny powers of creatures bear no comparison. In theological discourse, only God can provide the answer to the great question, "Why is there something rather than nothing?" But that question is not solely answered by citing the divine power of radical creation out of nothing. If we may use such language, it is also necessary to consider, so to speak, what are God's motives that lie behind this great act. Pursuing that point surely involves appeal to the divine love that has willed the existence of the truly other so that, through creation, this love is also bestowed outside the perichoretic exchange between the Persons of the Holy Trinity. Creation exists because God gives to it a life and a value of its own.

The Christian hope of redemption from bondage to sin and futility, both for individual human beings and for the whole created order, is certainly founded on trust in the unfailing faithfulness of the God of love *(chesed)*. Jesus made just such a point in his dispute with the Sadducees about whether there is a destiny beyond death. He affirmed that the God of Abraham, Isaac, and Jacob cares everlastingly for the patriarchs and so is "not God of the dead, but of the living" (Mark 12:18-27). Yet the context for redemption, both human and cosmic, is the new creation. The latter is not a second creative act *ex nihilo,* for it proceeds *ex vetere* as the resurrected transformation of the old creation.[1] Differing in this respect from the initial creation, the new creation nevertheless exhibits the working of great divine power of a transcendent kind. That power has, in fact, already been manifested in the resurrection of Jesus Christ (cf. Romans 1:4).

Love without power would correspond to a God who was a compassionate but impotent spectator of the history of the world. Power without love would correspond to a God who was the Cosmic Tyrant, holding the whole of history in an unrelenting grasp. Neither would be the God and Father of our Lord Jesus Christ, for the Christian God can neither be the Creator of a divine puppet theater nor a deistic Bystander, watching the play of history unfold without any influence upon its course. Divine power and divine love must both be given their due importance. The title of this paper, juxtaposing kenosis and action, strives for the necessary balance and so poses the problem of how it is to be attained. The solution of that problem is not an easy task to achieve. All theological thinking is a precarious balancing act, seeking recourse to the coincidence of opposites in an attempt to use finite human language to discourse about the infinite reality of God. Every assertion seems to stand in need of the qualification of a counter-assertion. The warnings of apophatic theology need to be heeded, but not to the extent of a total paralysis of thought.

The need to do justice both to divine kenotic love and to divine providential power is clearly part of this theological tension. Emphasis on divine love seems to lie behind Process Theology's picture of a God who, in

1. J. C. Polkinghorne, *Science and Christian Belief/The Faith of a Physicist* (London and Princeton: SPCK/Princeton University Press, 1994), ch. 9.

A. N. Whitehead's moving phrase, is a "fellow sufferer who understands," and who acts only through the power of persuasion. It is a noble concept, but it is open to question whether deity has not been so evacuated of power that hope in God as the ground of ultimate fulfillment has been subverted. The issue is whether the presentation of the divine vision of fulfillment will be sufficient in itself to bring about its own realization, or whether creation also stands in need of the action of divine grace for this to be achieved. The matter can be put in the bluntest terms by asking whether Whitehead's God could be the One who raised Jesus from the dead.

Emphasis on divine power seems to lie behind Classical Theology's picture of a God who, through primary causality, is in total control and whose invulnerability is such that there is no reciprocal effect of creatures upon the divine nature, of the kind that a truly loving relationship would seem to imply. The scheme, as articulated by its principal exponents such as Aquinas, is intellectually impressive, but it is open to question whether its picture of the divine nature is not so remote and insulated from creation as to put in question the fundamental Christian conviction that "God is love" (1 John 4:8). There are also unresolved difficulties about the coherence of supposing that divine primary causality and creaturely secondary causality are both simultaneously at work in the world.

A great deal of creative theological thinking in the second half of the twentieth century has been concerned with a re-examination of these issues. A number of factors have encouraged this. Some of them are theological in character and we shall be content simply to indicate their general nature, since they are major concerns of other contributors to this symposium. Others arise, at least partly, from scientific insights, and we shall give them greater attention.

(1) *Incarnational Theology.* The classic kenotic text in the New Testament is Philippians 2:1-11, referring to Christ who "emptied *(ekenosen)* himself, taking the form of a servant." The self-limitation of the divine Word, in taking flesh and becoming a finite human being, is a concept that has sometimes powerfully influenced christological thinking. That was so among Lutherans in the seventeenth and early nineteenth centuries, and again among certain British theologians at the end of the nineteenth century. In the twentieth century, the application of kenotic ideas has been extended beyond a strictly christological focus to include other aspects of God's relationship with creation. Jürgen Moltmann has power-

fully laid before us the concept of the Crucified God, revealed in the Trinitarian event of the cross of Jesus Christ.[2] W. H. Vanstone has made kenotic concepts central to his exploration of the precariousness, costliness, and gift of value involved in loving acts of creativity.[3] We shall return to Incarnational insight later.

(2) *Theodicy.* The classic location for confrontation between the claims of divine love and divine power has always been the perplexities of theodicy. Divine love would seem to imply a Creator whose benevolent wish would be for the total goodness of creation. Divine power would seem to imply a Creator who can accomplish fully the divine purposes. Whence then have come the many physical ills of disease and disaster? No doubt the existence of moral beings with the freedom to choose how they act is a great good. The misuse of this gift can be seen as the origin of moral evil. However, we can no longer believe with Augustine that this abuse has also had consequences of cosmic scope for all creation, leading to the corruption of what had previously possessed paradisal perfection, so that it was the source of the physical evil in the world. Much of the problem of evil, both moral and physical, lies in its scale. In the century of the Holocaust and Hiroshima, we are only too conscious of these issues. Moltmann's work is explicitly a contribution to theology after Auschwitz, and Vanstone is concerned with the necessary precariousness of the creative process of the world. Again, these are issues to which we shall return.

(3) *Continuous Creation.* From the later eighteenth century onwards, there has been a progressive scientific unfolding of the historical character of the physical world. In terrestrial terms, it was first realized that the landscape of Earth had been subject to eons of gradual change. Some mountains had been eroded and others thrust up by subterranean process to take their place. Eventually it was discovered that the great land masses themselves had been subject to continental drift. Our impression of stasis arises simply from the shortness of human life, and of recorded history, in relation to the time scales of geological change. From a longer temporal perspective, the landscape is as much in flux as the cloudscape.

In the nineteenth century, the long-assumed fixity of species came under critical reassessment, culminating in 1859 with the publication of

2. J. Moltmann, *The Crucified God* (London: SCM Press, 1974).

3. W. H. Vanstone, *Love's Endeavour, Love's Expense* (London: Darton, Longman and Todd, 1977).

the evolutionary ideas of Charles Darwin and A. R. Wallace. The biosphere turned out to be no more static than the geosphere.

In the first decades of the twentieth century, against the ideological inclinations of many scientists (including Einstein), it was realized that the universe itself has also had a changing history. According to big bang cosmology, there was a time when there were no stars and galaxies. We live on a second-generation planet, encircling a second-generation star, which have both condensed from gas clouds and the debris of first-generation supernovae explosions.

These scientific revaluations have had their impact upon theology. The effects have been by no means without their fruitfulness. Contrary to the popular legend, still sedulously cultivated by polemicists and some sectors of the media, that Darwin met total obscurantist opposition from religious thinkers, there were Christians who, from the first, welcomed his insights and made positive theological use of them. In England, these included Charles Kingsley, Frederick Temple, and Aubrey Moore, and in the United States Darwin's Harvard friend, Asa Gray. A common theme runs through their responses. An evolutionary world is theologically to be understood as a creation allowed by its Creator "to make itself." The play of life is not the performance of a pre-determined script, but a self-improvisatory performance by the actors themselves. Although kenotic language was not explicitly used, this is a manifestly kenotic conception. God shares the unfolding course of creation with creatures, who have their divinely allowed, but not divinely dictated, roles to play in its fruitful becoming.

This understanding is in striking contrast with the accounts of creation and divine action offered by Classical Theology. From Augustine onwards, and most powerfully in the writings of Thomas Aquinas, it sought to preserve the uniqueness of divine action, and the primacy of divine power, by speaking of God's primary causality, exercised in and under the secondary causalities of creatures. Classical Theology greatly emphasized the transcendence of God and a characteristic concept was creation *ex nihilo,* the calling into being of the new at the behest of the divine creative fiat.

Of course, the distinction between a transcendent Creator, possessed of aseity, and a creation that is perpetually dependent on the will of God for its preservation from the abyss of nothingness, is a very important component in Christian theological thinking. We are right to be extremely cautious about any ideas that might put this in question. Only a God who is distinct from creation can be that creation's ground of hope beyond its eventual natural decay. However, it by no means follows that in saying this we have said all that needs to be said about the doctrine of creation. We should remember that even Augustine, reflecting on Genesis 1, vv. 11, 20, and 24, in which the earth and the waters bring forth life, believed that God had created the seeds of life from which creatures eventually developed, although, of course, he had no concept of the transformation of one species into another.

The scientific recognition of the evolutionary character of the universe has encouraged theological recognition of the immanent presence of God to creation and of the need to complement the concept of *creatio ex nihilo* by a concept of *creatio continua*. Continuous creation has been an important theme in the writings of the scientist-theologians.[4] It has a number of important theological implications.

First, in conjunction with the understanding of evolutionary process as corresponding to creation being allowed to make itself, it is clearly kenotic in its character. Its unfolding process is to be understood as being flexible and open to creaturely causality. Philip Hefner, whose theology is strongly influenced by evolutionary ideas, likes to speak of human beings as "created co-creators."[5]

Second, this kenotic sharing of power has important implications for theodicy. No longer can God be held to be totally and directly responsible for all that happens. An evolutionary world is inevitably one in which there are raggednesses and blind alleys. Death is the necessary cost of new life; environmental change can lead to extinctions; genetic mutations sometimes produce new forms of life, oftentimes malignancies. There is an unavoidable cost attached to a world allowed to make itself. Creatures will behave in accordance with their natures: lions will kill their prey; earthquakes will happen; volcanoes will erupt and rivers flood. I have called this insight "the free-process defense"[6] in relation to physical evil, in analogy with the familiar free-will defense in relation to moral evil. These defenses

4. I. G. Barbour, *Issues in Science and Religion* (London: SCM Press, 1966), ch. 12; A. R. Peacocke, *Creation and the World of Science* (Oxford: Oxford University Press, 1979), chs. 2 and 3; J. C. Polkinghorne, *Science and Creation* (London: SPCK, 1988), ch. 4.

5. P. J. Hefner, *The Human Factor* (Minneapolis: Fortress Press, 1993), *passim*.

6. J. C. Polkinghorne, *Science and Providence* (London: SPCK, 1989), pp. 66-67.

do not by any means solve all the problems of theodicy, but they temper them somewhat by removing a suspicion of divine incompetence or indifference. From this point of view, the classic confrontation between the claims of divine love and the claims of divine power is resolved by maintaining God's total benevolence but qualifying, in a kenotic way, the operation of God's power. Of course, this is a self-qualification, exercised within the divine nature and in accordance with that nature itself. It is quite different from Process Theology's conception of an external metaphysical constraint upon the power of deity, for in this case it is held that nothing imposes conditions on God from the outside. The classical theologians were right in that respect, but they had not taken adequately into account the interior 'constraints' of the self-consistency of the divine nature. Perhaps their strong emphasis on divine Unity made such a consideration inaccessible to them.

Third, if the concept of continuous creation is really to mean what it says, and to consist of more than just a pious gloss on a wholly natural process, then God's providential guiding power must surely also be part of the unfolding of evolutionary history. The kenotic Creator may not overrule creatures, but the continuous Creator must interact with creation. Thus, kenotic *creation* and divine *action* are opposite sides of the same theological coin. This is not to deny that the natural process in itself is also an expression of the Creator's will, for it corresponds to that general providence that is manifested in the divine ordinance of natural law. However, a notion of continuous creation may be expected to go beyond a deistic upholding of the universe in being, for so strong a concept seems inadequately realized in terms of the God of natural theology alone, who is simply the ground of cosmic order. Putting it another way, if, as is often said, evolutionary process is generated by the interplay between "chance" (that is, historical contingency) and "necessity" (that is, lawful regularity), its Creator must be present in the contingency as well as in the regularity. This conclusion is reinforced by considering why personal language is used in the Judeo-Christian tradition as the least misleading way of referring to God. It is surely because the God addressed as Father is one who is expected to do particular things on particular occasions and not just to function as an unchanging effect (like the law of gravity). Clearly there is a problem here which we shall have to discuss further shortly. On the one hand, we have science's account of the regularity of the processes of nature. On the other hand, we have theology's claim to speak of a God who acts in history. Can the two be reconciled with each other? I believe so, but achieving this end will call for some flexibility from both science and theology in the assessments that they initially bring to their dialogue.

(4) *Causal Nexus.* If divine providential action is an integral part of continuous creation, so that the latter is understood in some sense as being evolution in which a degree of theistic guidance and influence is present, it is necessary to consider what we know about the causal nexus of the world, with a view to seeing if it could possibly accommodate such an idea. Science has some things to say about this, but from the point of view of Classical Theology, they would not be important.

The reason is that, for Thomist thinkers, divine primary causality is considered to be of a totally different kind from the creaturely causal powers that science investigates, for it is held to be exercised in and under those manifold secondary causalities. No explanation is offered of how this happens; it is simply said to be the case. Any attempt to exhibit the "causal joint" by which the double agency of divine and creaturely causalities are related to each other is held to be impossible, or even impious. Three assertions are important consequences of this point of view.

First, the ineffability of the mode of action of primary causality has the effect of totally repudiating the possibility of any analogy between divine and human agencies. Second, God is party to every event not simply by allowing it to happen, but also by bringing it about through the exercise of the divine will. Nothing is outside God's control, an assertion that poses obvious difficulties for theodicy. The veiled and mysterious nature of primary causality can only be matched by the veiled and mysterious claim that in the end all will be seen to have been well. Third, primary causality is so divorced from the character of secondary causality that it may be believed to be active, whatever form the latter is discovered by science to take. Theology is made invulnerable to whatever may be currently understood about the process of the physical universe. However, some of us feel that the deep obscurity involved in the idea of a double agency carries with it the danger that the discussion might turn out to be no more than double talk.

What for its partisans is the strength of the notion of primary and secondary causalities is, for its critics, its greatest weakness. The strategy represents an extreme case of the "two languages" way of understanding how science and theology relate to each other. Their discourses are treated as independent, so that they talk past each other at different levels. The two disciplines may be considered as presenting two different paradigms, or involving participation in two different language games. This is a point of view that the scientist-theologians,[7] together with many others working at the interface of science and theology, are rightly emphatic in rejecting. In its place they put the affirmation of the unity of truth and knowledge — a unity ultimately guaranteed by the oneness of the Creator — with its implication that there is an active intercourse across the boundary between the two disciplines. Creation is not so distanced from its Creator that the character of its process and history offers no clues at all to the nature of God's interaction with it.

Human and divine agency both clearly fall into the category of experience that is presently well beyond our capacity for full understanding. As persons, we should not deny our basic experiences of free choice and consequent moral responsibility. As Christians, we should not deny our intuition, and the testimony of our tradition, that God acts in the world. As rational thinkers convinced of the unity of knowledge, we should not forego the attempt, however modest and tentative it must necessarily be, to see if metaphysical conjecture, arising out of modern science's understanding of physical process, might not afford us some small purchase on these problems.

Modern physics has revealed the existence of extensive *intrinsic* unpredictabilities, both in the microscopic realm of quantum physics and also in the macroscopic realm of chaotic dynamics. Such intrinsic epistemological deficiencies offer the chance, if we are bold enough to take it, of trying to turn them into ontological opportunities of openness, treating them as potential loci for the operation of additional causal principles, active in bringing about the future and going beyond and complementing the causal principle of the exchange of energy between constituents that has been the conventional description used by physics. The complete set of all causal principles, including human and divine agency, will then be what brings about the future state of the world.

Such a move is metaphysical in character; it can neither be affirmed nor denied on the basis of science alone. Since scientists are instinctive realists, such an attempt, which amounts essentially to aligning epistemology (unpredictability) and ontology (new causal principles) as closely as possible to each other, is a natural strategy for them to pursue. In the

7. See J. C. Polkinghorne, *Scientists as Theologians* (London: SPCK, 1996), ch. 1.

case of quantum theory, this has been the almost universal tactic, with Heisenberg's uncertainty principle (which originally related to the episte-mological issue of what can be measured) being interpreted ontologically as a principle of indeterminacy, and not just a principle of ignorance. The alternative ideas of David Bohm, yielding a deterministic interpretation of quantum theory,[8] make it clear that this is a metaphysical choice and not a logically forced move. Some of us have sought to pursue a similar tactic in relation to chaotic dynamics.[9]

Study of complex systems has served to emphasize that our descrip-tion of physical process must have a dual character, involving not only en-ergy, but also what one might call 'pattern'. The future behavior of a cha-otic system is not totally haphazard. It displays a kind of orderly disorder. What will happen is not predictable but it is confined within a large but restricted range of possibilities that technically is called a "strange attrac-tor." This consists of a portfolio of possible future patterns of motion, all of equal energy but differing in the ways in which they unfold. There are a number of executive toys, consisting of jointed rods and weights which, when released from apparently the same configuration, execute a bewil-dering and unpredictable variety of subsequent motions. Playing with one of these toys is an exploration of its strange attractor. The openness that a chaotic system is interpreted as possessing corresponds to the mul-tiplicity of possibilities contained within its strange attractor, and any motion actually executed can be understood as corresponding to an input of information that specifies its detailed structure ("this way, then that way, etc."). The hypothesized new causal principles would then be such as to complement energetic causality with a pattern-forming informational causality. One sees here a revival in modern form of an old idea, for infor-mational causality bears some kinship with Aristotle's concept of formal cause, interpreted in a dynamical sense.

A second feature of chaotic systems is that they are intrinsically un-isolatable. Because they are so sensitive to circumstance, they cannot be insulated from the effects of their environment. They must, therefore, be treated holistically, in their total context. Thus it turns out that the causal

8. D. Bohm and B. J. Hiley, *The Undivided Universe* (London: Routledge, 1993).

9. I. Prigogine, *The End of Certainty* (New York: The Free Press, 1996); J. C. Polkinghorne, *Reason and Reality* (London: SPCK, 1991), ch. 3; *Belief in God in an Age of Science* (New Haven: Yale University Press, 1998), ch. 3.

99

nexus of the world is exceedingly complex, with un-isolatability implying a considerable degree of mutual entanglement and feedback between systems whose spatial separation might naively have led one to believe that they could be treated separately. (A similar entanglement is also present at the microlevel of quantum physics, where the celebrated non-locality of the "EPR effect" implies a breakdown of separability.)[10]

Putting these two features of pattern-formation and non-locality together, we can see that, in an ontological approach to the metaphysical interpretation of chaos theory, one would expect there to be additional causal principles of a holistic and pattern-forming kind. One might call such causality "active information" and denote its holistic character by the phrase "top-down causality," meaning by that an influence of the whole on its parts. This idea offers a *glimmer* of a hope of beginning to describe agency, both human and divine, which may also be held to have this character of holistic action.

The discussion given above will have made it plain that the nature of causality is ultimately a metaphysical question. Scientific accounts of the process of the physical world are inputs to that discussion but they do not, of themselves, determine what its outcome will be. The debate about whether quantum theory is to be interpreted indeterministically (Bohr) or deterministically (Bohm) perfectly illustrates the point. All metaphysical proposals are open to contest and they have to defend themselves on metaphysical grounds, appealing to such qualities as comprehensiveness, economy, and adequacy to human experience. The metaphysical picture espoused above bases itself on two fundamental considerations. One is the realist desire to align epistemology and ontology as closely as possible. The other is the attraction of a scheme that offers, however tentatively and conjecturally, the prospect of accommodating our human experiences of willed action and our religious intuitions of God's providential care.

Notice, that if there is an element of truth in this picture of the nature of divine action, it is exercised within the open grain of natural process and not in a way contrary to that process. God may properly be said to interact with creation, but the word 'intervene', with its connotations of arbitrary interruption, would not be appropriate. It is important to rec-

10. See, for example, J. C. Polkinghorne, *The Quantum World* (London and Princeton: Longman/Princeton University Press, 1984/85), ch. 7.

ognize that the causal entanglement we have identified implies that an itemization of what is happening — allocating this event to natural process, that event to human agency, and a third event to divine providence — is impossible. The cloudiness of unpredictability veils us from being able to make such a decomposition.

Theological consideration of divine action, whatever form it may take, will always wish to preserve a necessary degree of uniqueness associated with deity. In relation to general providence (God's holding the universe in being and ordaining the lawful regularities that undergird its process), that uniqueness is clear enough. Here are exercised powers of absolute Being to which no created being could pretend. In relation to special providence (God's particular interactions with the unfolding course of creation's history), and in particular in relation to a special providence exercised in a kenotic mode, the issues are more perplexing. We are back with the tension, noted at the beginning, between the demands of an adequate understanding of divine love and an adequate understanding of divine power. It is time to consider what composition can be made between the twin themes of the title. I shall do so by first briefly discussing the position I have held up till now and then going on to suggest a significant modification of it. The latter will arise in the course of considering the variety of forms that a divine kenosis in creation might take.

My principal strategy for preserving the unique character of deity in the exercise of special providence has been to locate the Creator/creature distinction in the contrast between God's acting through *pure* information input, while creaturely acts involve a mixture of energetic and informational causalities, corresponding to the embodied status of creatures. This idea could be the prosaic translation of theology's poetic insight that God's action is the working of pure Spirit. Such a distinction is tenable because, while passive information storage of the kind discussed by communication theory does exact an irreducible energetic tariff for the recording of bits of information, the same is not true for the kind of active information being discussed.[11] Thus the concept of pure informational causality, unmixed with energetic causality, is a coherent one.

The purpose of this form of the proposal, with its emphasis on pure information input, was to try to absolve it from the charge that it had re-

---

11. Cf. Bohm and Hiley, *The Undivided Universe*, pp. 31-38.

duced God to the role of a mere cause among other competing causalities. The Creator, it was supposed, was more fittingly to be thought of as the director of the great cosmic improvisatory play, than as an invisible actor on the stage of the universe. It was not possible, however, to remove all unease about how successful the strategy actually is in this regard. The scientist-theologian is in a Catch-22 situation. The more explicit the talk is about the causal joint by which God acts in the world, the greater the possibility that special providence becomes just one form of causality among other causes. Yet without some such attempt at explication, special providence is at risk of remaining too mysterious for any discussion beyond fideistic assertion.

I have recently come to reconsider whether the theological objection one is trying to meet is actually as forceful as is commonly supposed. What has caused this revaluation is trying to take the kenotic nature of God's creative action as seriously as possible. To carry this further, it will be helpful to disentangle different aspects of kenosis that may be involved in the Creator's loving relationship with creation. I suggest that a fourfold discrimination is possible:

(1) *Kenosis of omnipotence.* This centers on the fundamental divine allowing of the created other to be and to act, so that, while all that happens is permitted by God's general providence, not all that happens is in accordance with God's will or brought about by divine special providence. Such an understanding is basic to the interpretation of evolutionary history as creation's making of itself. Such an understanding is also basic to theodicy's disclaimer that God does not will the act of a murderer or the destructive force of an earthquake, but allows both to happen in a world in which divine power is deliberately self-limited to allow causal space for creatures. This qualification of omnipotence is the most widely recognized and accepted aspect of divine kenosis.

(2) *Kenosis of simple eternity.* By bringing into being a temporal creation, whose nature is expressed and realized in its unfolding history, the Creator has granted a reality and a significance to time. Since Augustine, theologians have understood the created nature of time, so that the universe came into being *cum tempore,* not *in tempore.* The modern scientific insights of general relativity, linking together space, time, and matter, have given endorsement to this view, some fifteen centuries after Augustine. This has led many twentieth-century theologians to believe that time is a reality for the Creator as well as for creation. We may suppose

that God knows things as they really are and so, if time is real and events are successive, surely God will know them temporally in their succession, and not merely that they are successive. In other words we are led to believe that, while God has not set aside the timeless and eternal nature of divine Being, there has been 'added' to that (so to speak) a temporal pole of divinity that corresponds to the Creator's true engagement with created time. While there must be in the divine essence that which is wholly free from the possibility of variation, so that God's loving mercy is eternally unchangeable, there must also surely be that which corresponds to the changing but perfectly appropriate relationship to the varying circumstances of a temporal creation. God would have related to the universe immediately following the big bang, when it was simply a ball of energy, in a way different from that in which God relates to a world containing sinful human beings.

This divine acceptance of the temporal may fittingly be called a kenosis, since the Eternal has freely embraced the experience of time. Many contemporary theologians have consequently wished to speak of the dipolar God of eternity/time. It has been particularly characteristic of process theologians to do so. They are owed a special debt in this respect, but it is a concept that has been accepted much more widely than that. The scientist-theologians have all espoused this point of view.[12]

Of course, the idea has not won universal acceptance. It runs quite counter to the insights of Classical Theology, in which God is wholly outside time. However, the Incarnation involves so drastic a divine involvement with temporal reality that it might be held natural for Christian theology to expect that time is not wholly foreign to the divine nature in itself. On this view, Philippians 2 offers insight into the nature of God as well as into the nature of Christ, for the Incarnation was the historical enactment of what is eternally true of the nature of God.

(3) *Kenosis of omniscience.* The metaphysical picture with which we are working is that of a world of true becoming, open to a future that is brought about by intertwined causal principles, such as natural law, human agency, and special providence. Such a world is radically temporal.[13] The future does not yet exist and this leads to the belief that even God

12. See Polkinghorne, *Scientists as Theologians,* p. 41.
13. See J. C. Polkinghorne, "Natural Science, Temporality and Divine Action," in *Theology Today* 55 (1998): 329-43.

does not yet know it. In other words, creation has involved a kenosis of divine omniscience. God knows all that can be known, and so possesses a current omniscience, but the divine engagement with the reality of time implies that God does not yet know all that will eventually be knowable, and so does not possess an absolute omniscience.

This is, of course, a contested view. It is in total contrast with Classical Theology's understanding that the atemporal God knows all of temporal history "at once" *(totum simul).* Yet, the kenosis of omniscience has been a quite widely accepted aspect of twentieth-century theological thinking.[14] It by no means implies that God is unprepared for the future (so that God sees how history is moving and can warn Jeremiah that Egypt will not rescue Judah and that Babylon will prevail), but God does not see that unformed future in all its detail (exactly how Jerusalem will fall to the invaders). Current omniscience represents a limitation on God, but one that has been embraced within the divine nature and not imposed from without.

(4) *Kenosis of causal status.* Here is the new proposal which, if accepted, would modify significantly my previous position. I have come to believe that *the Creator's kenotic love includes allowing divine special providence to act as a cause among causes.* Of course, nothing could reduce talk about the Creator to terms that bear a valid analogy to creaturely discourse, other than that the divine condescension had allowed this to be so. We return to the central Christian kenotic paradox of the Incarnation, which centers on just such an act of divine self-limitation as God's nature is manifested in the plainest and most accessible creaturely terms, by the Word's assumption of our nature and consequent participation in human life and human death in Jesus Christ. The invisible God took our flesh and became a visible actor on the stage of creation. In the Incarnation we see that, in first-century Palestine, God submitted in the most drastic way to becoming a cause among causes. Of course, that was not all that God was doing in that period. Christian theology has never simply equated Jesus with God or supposed that the historic episode of the Incarnation implied any attenuation of the divine governance of the universe. The Incarnation, however, does suggest what character that governance might, at all times, be expected to take. It shows us that God is willing to share with creatures to an extent not adequately reflected in Classical Theology's pic-

14. For the scientist-theologians, see note 12.

ture of the God who, through primary causality, is always in total ineffable control.

We have repeatedly emphasized that God allows creatures their part in bringing about the future. There must, then, be an interweaving of providential and creaturely causalities. According to the metaphysical conjecture that has been presented, this interweaving is located within the cloudiness of intrinsic unpredictabilities, so that unfolding history cannot be itemized. Such a picture of undisentangleability corresponds to God's loving choice to be, in the evolving history of creation, a present cause among causes. If this idea is accepted it would become possible to conceive that this kenotic providential causality is also exercised energetically as well as informationally. However, there is theological attraction in identifying the working of the Spirit with pure information input.

There is a final form of kenosis that might be considered but which I do *not* accept. That would be a kenosis of novelty, the idea that God is self-restricted to act in the future only as God has acted in the past. Of course, God could not be whimsically capricious about deciding to do something unprecedented, as if engaging in an act of divine showing off. Yet it is perfectly coherent to believe that in new circumstances ("the fullness of time") God will do new things. This realization is the basis of accepting the possibility of the miraculous, in particular the central Christian miracle of the resurrection of Jesus Christ, seen as the seminal event from which the great divine act of the new creation has begun to grow. The theological credibility of miracle depends upon being able to exhibit the divine consistency that underlies the novelty, for there is certainly no theological reason to suppose that God must always be boringly restricted to doing nothing new.[15]

No writer on divine action can fail to be aware of the hubris involved in appearing to wax confident in talk about the Creator and the Creator's acts. There is a real sense in which all theology is "humility theology," as we confess our limitation and ignorance in the face of the divine Mystery. The Infinite will not be caught in the finite meshes of our rational nets. Yet I believe we know enough to say that God is indeed loving and cares not just for creation in general, but for individual creatures in particular. We know also, however faint and perplexing our perceptions may be at times,

15. See Polkinghorne, *Science and Providence*, ch. 4.

that God is at work in the created world. We know also that we have been given the kind of minds and powers that make science possible for us and so we have been able to understand many things about the physical process of the universe. All these are privileges for which we should be grateful and which yield us insights that we should take with the greatest seriousness. Sometimes this may lead us to what may initially seem strange conclusions. To think of God's providence as acting as a cause among causes may be one of these. Kenotic theology is inevitably paradoxical theology, for it is founded on the concept of the humility of God.

Kenosis as a Unifying Theme for Life and Cosmology

GEORGE F. R. ELLIS

We know only that God is love.

Love's Endeavour, Love's Expense, p. 67

Synopsis

This paper tries to demonstrate the virtues of kenosis as a unifying theme in the understanding of both human life and cosmology. After introducing the basic idea, it briefly presents a view of the kenosis of Christ's life (the interpretive key). It then considers the implications of this first for our way of action (ethics), and second for the nature of God's action as creator (providing the missing metaphysics of cosmology). The kinds of evidence that can support this view are outlined, before finishing with a consideration of implications and issues arising, the most important being the need to develop a viable criterion for determining how a kenotic approach to action should be implemented.

A. Kenosis as a Unifying Theme

In my view, kenosis is a key theme in many aspects of human life — in particular in personal and group psychology, in learning and art, and in properly understood ethics and social action. This is fully coherent with the concept of a kenotic creator God, as proposed inter alia by William Temple,[1] Jürgen Moltmann,[2] and Arthur Peacocke,[3] implying a consequent self-sacrificial view of religious and social life. (See, for example, W. H. Vanstone[4] and K. M. Cronin.[5]) This can all be integrated into a kenotic cosmological-theological-ethical view,[6] providing a consistent picture which is in principle capable of uniting the sciences and humanities in an overarching worldview (a *consilience,* in the terminology reintroduced by E. O. Wilson[7]).

On this viewpoint, kenosis is understood not just as letting go or giving up, but as being prepared to do so in a creative and positive way for a positive purpose in tune with the nature of God. Thus it is seen, when given a theological grounding, as follows:

> *Kenosis:* a joyous, kind, and loving attitude that is willing to give up selfish desires and to make sacrifices on behalf of others for the common good and the glory of God, doing this in a generous and creative way, avoiding the pitfall of pride, and guided and inspired by the love of God and the gift of grace.

This concept is then seen as the key to understanding the deep nature of creation, in the sense that it provides the metaphysical underpinnings of cosmology as well as ethics. The basis for this view is understood here to be theological: it reflects an essential part of the nature of

---

1. William Temple, *Readings in St John's Gospel* (London: Macmillan, 1961).

2. Jürgen Moltmann, *The Crucified God: The Cross of Christ as the Foundation and Criticism of Christian Theology* (New York: Harper and Row, 1974).

3. Arthur Peacocke, *Theology for a Scientific Age: Being and Becoming: Natural, Divine, and Human* (Minneapolis: Fortress Press, 1993).

4. William H. Vanstone, *Love's Endeavour, Love's Expense* (London: Darton, Longman and Todd, 1977).

5. Kevin Cronin, *Kenosis: Emptying Self and the Path of Christian Service* (Rockport, Mass.: Element, 1992).

6. George F. R. Ellis, "The Theology of the Anthropic Principle," in *Quantum Cosmology and the Laws of Nature,* ed. R. Russell et al. (Vatican Observatory/CTNS, 1993), hereafter *QCLN;* George F. R. Ellis, "God and the Universe: Kenosis as the Foundation of Being," *Bulletin of the CTNS* 14, nos. 1-14 (1994); Nancey Murphy and George F. R. Ellis, *On the Moral Nature of the Universe* (Minneapolis: Fortress Press, 1997), hereafter *MNU.*

7. Edward O. Wilson, *Consilience* (New York: Knopf, 1998).

God.[8] Its centrality to some Christian understandings of the life of Christ (including my own) derives from many sections in the New Testament, including Philippians 2:5-11 and much of the Sermon on the Mount. It is central to the resolution of the temptations in the desert, as is very clearly demonstrated in William Temple's book *Readings in St. John's Gospel.* This is not a claim that this is the total nature of God, but rather that this is a fundamentally important aspect of God's nature, which then shapes in a crucial way our true relationship to God. This view rejects the religious traditions and churches that are militaristic, monarchical, or tyrannical, and accepts at least provisionally those that are genuinely loving, freedom-based, and with a strong element of self-sacrifice as an essential ingredient. This group includes, but is not restricted to, a major strand of the Christian tradition; it probably occurs as a strand in almost all religious traditions.[9] This view is compatible with those religious strands capable of seeing the search for truth in other religions, and rejects those that dogmatically claim a sole access to truth (representing the idolatry of infallibility, as against the kenotic virtue of giving up certainty).

Given its central nature in allowing us to undertake truly creative and effective action, the question is: What is the aim of kenosis? To what purpose will it be used? The answer is given by Keith Ward:[10] theosis, or covenant with God. Because God loves humanity and his creation, this in turn implies that our lives should be tuned to the welfare of others and of the world, as well as for the praise of God. Thus those creeds that demand self-sacrifice on behalf of domination of others are not seen as kenotic, even though they do indeed contain the element of self-sacrifice. The additional key element is that this is to be used for the good of others, indeed to help give them true freedom, and not to dominate them or place them in subjection. On this view, ethical behavior should be shaped along kenotic

8. Lucien Richard, O.M.I., *A Kenotic Christology, in the Humanity of Jesus the Christ, the Compassion of our God* (Washington, D.C.: University Press of America, 1982); Geddes MacGregor, "He Who Lets Us Be: A Theology of Love," *The Ecumenist* (1974): 17-21.

9. John B. Cobb and Christopher Ives, eds., *The Emptying God: A Buddhist-Jewish-Christian Conversation* (Maryknoll, N.Y.: Orbis Books, 1991); Keiji Nishitani, *Religion and Nothingness* (Berkeley: University of California Press, 1982); Sir John Templeton, *Agape Love* (Templeton Foundation Press, 1999).

10. Keith Ward, Chapter 9 this volume.

lines in order to be consonant with the deep nature of reality, expressing a fundamental aspect of the nature of God, and so of the underpinning of the created universe. The idea can be distorted and become a self-defeating or self-denying vision, where one's own self is not valued. But this is not the nature of the true idea, which is life affirming and joyous, because it affirms the other *as well as* the self. It is also the foundation of a profound path of social and political action, as evidenced in Martin Luther King's political life,[11] and in the writings and life of Mahatma Gandhi.[12] It will indeed in the end lead to a better life for oneself as well, but that is not the ultimate reason for adopting it. Enlightened self-interest will suggest this way to some extent, but in the end will not justify it.

Holmes Rolston suggests one might adopt a broader definition that is not so self-consciously religious, thus including humans who act selflessly but are not consciously religious about it. In my view, although one must certainly recognize the merit of those actions, that step would preclude one from framing the broader integration which is the aim of this paper. Thus I propose keeping the definition here, while recognizing such acts as partaking of a kenotic nature but without being able to realize the full depth of what is intended here. Holmes Rolston also comments that one could use the word 'altruism' instead, which is more current and widespread in use. In my view, while that word has similar connotations, it does not have the hard edge that 'kenosis' does — it is a partial step in the right direction, but not the same thing. And in the end that is related to the previous point: kenosis attains its full power when seen as being fully related to the nature of God. Most of the current debate on altruism is aimed precisely at avoiding making this connection; and that is why it deals with a somewhat weaker concept, in effect the sophisticated self-interest of 'virtue ethics'. The suggestion is that kenosis is deeper than that.

B. The Kenosis of Christ's Life

Given the omnipotence of God as creator and sustainer of all that is, the question arises as to what use God makes of this omnipotence. On the

11. J. Ansbro, *Martin Luther King Jr: The Making of a Mind* (Maryknoll, N.Y.: Orbis Books, 1984).

12. R. Duncan, *The Writings of Gandhi* (New York: Fontana, 1983).

viewpoint put here, the answer is, in a completely loving and sacrificial way, in full consonance with the idea of kenosis. It is this that is clarified by the gospel message conveyed through the life of Jesus. Considering in the desert the options of using his power to satisfy the creature wants of himself and his human brethren, of winning the kingdoms of the world by establishing an earthly monarchy, or of providing irresistible evidence of his divine mission so that doubt would be impossible, he comes to the key insight described here by William Temple:

> Every one of these conceptions contained truth. Yet if any or all of these are taken as fully representative of the Kingdom, they have one fatal defect. They all represent ways of securing the outward obedience of men apart from inner loyalty; they are ways of controlling conduct, but not ways of winning hearts and wills. He might bribe men by promise of good things; he might coerce men to obey by threat of penalty; he might offer irresistible proof; [but] all these rejected methods are essentially appeals to self-interest; and the kingdom of God, who is love, cannot be established that way. . . . The new conception which takes the place of those rejected is that the Son of Man must suffer. For the manifestation of love, by which it wins its response, is sacrifice. The principle of sacrifice is that we choose to do or suffer what apart from our love we should not choose to do or suffer. . . . The progress of the Kingdom consists in the uprising within the hearts of men of a love and trust which answer to the Love which shines from the Cross and is, for this world, the Glory of God.[13]

This then is what was made manifest during the rest of Christ's ministry, both through his preaching and by the way he lived and died.[14] Underlying this view is the claim that the New Testament replaces the Old: the God who coercively destroys Sodom and Gomorrah is an Old Testament vision, while Christ on the Cross is the core vision of the New Testament.

One characterization of the way demonstrated is that it always tran-

---

13. William Temple, *Readings in St. John's Gospel*, pp. xxix-xxxii.
14. I am of course aware of the claim that a few of Jesus' actions are not of this nature, and specifically that this applies to the cleansing of the Temple. A detailed response to this claim is given in *MNU*.

scends the immediate problem by changing to a context of self-giving loving, thus moving to a higher plane where love and forgiveness are the basic elements. This change of perspective and context has the possibility of transforming the situation. The fundamental importance of this revelation is twofold: in terms of ethics, and in terms of the metaphysics of cosmology.

C. Our Way of Action: Kenosis in Our Lives

First, it shows us the way we should act if we are to be true to a Christian calling. The choice for the kingdom is the choice for generosity and the forgiving spirit of the kingdom. This does not mean compromising truth; it does mean creating hope of reconciliation, in that all activities can be forgiven, so that anybody can be redeemed. Our acts and spirit of forgiveness should demonstrate this, if necessary, through loving sacrifice. It means being willing to love the enemy rather than giving in to hate, which has the power to transform us into a hateful kind of person. Thus it is a refusal to give in to the hatred embodied in the enemy image. And here is the hardest part. It is easy to see that respect for 'that of God' in a person enables one to help and support those oppressed. But the point is that this theme applies to the oppressors too. They too are human; they too have the light of God in them.

If in our pursuit of the rights of one group, we turn in fury on their oppressors and kill them or torture them because of what they have done, then we too have fallen into the fatal trap: the infection of hate will have taken hold of us too, and made us behave as the oppressors did. True respect for every person does not excuse or condone evil, but also does not deny the humanity and spark of vital life and the possibility for change in even those persons who are carrying out the foulest deeds. That is the real test and the real foundation. It does not lead to political impotence, as the lives of Mahatma Gandhi and Martin Luther King have shown; rather it is the basis of that transforming spirit which is the basis of social and political miracles. The attempt to follow this way is incredibly difficult. It will be much easier if we are able to practice the presence of God, and particularly an awareness of the light of Christ within every person.[15] In-

15. J. Pickvance, *The Light of Christ in the Writings of George Fox* (New Foundation Publications, 1948).

deed the two are inexorably linked, for if we are aware of that Presence and its loving nature, we will see the present problems in this profound context, and this will transform its nature for us.

Thus this view disputes the standing model of the social sciences in most fields, which often moves from observing that people in many cases act in self-interest in the political, social, and economic spheres, to imputing that they ought to do so. That step is of course illegitimate in terms of moral justification, but is often made without drawing attention to what is going on. This issue is discussed in depth in my book *On the Moral Nature of the Universe* (hereafter *MNU*), and I will not address it further here. Overall, this approach entails learning to give up what we desire to cling to, accepting the implied loss as the basis of greater good; this leads to a profound view of how to live at all levels of life. According to Robert Bellah,

> The deepest truth I have discovered is that if one accepts the loss, if one gives up clinging to what is irretrievably gone, then the nothing which is left is not barren but is enormously fruitful. Everything that one has lost comes flooding back out of the darkness, and one's relation to it is new — free and unclinging. But the richness of the nothing contains far more, it is the all-possible, it is the spring of freedom.[16]

This applies to understanding and belief as well as to moral action in the world. The point is that this gives an overall guide as to how one can hope to behave both in the individual and the group context. However, many doubt that it can be taken seriously when facing real-world situations, and this view is expressed in many of the comments on this paper by other participants. In contrast, I suggest it can be made a reality to a large degree, and can always be the aim. I will return to this point after considering the cosmological context.

---

16. R. Bellah, *Beyond Belief: Essays on Religion in a Post-traditional World* (New York: Harper and Row, 1976).

D. The Nature of God's Action:
Cosmology and Kenosis

The second point about the kenotic revelation given by Christ is that it shows the nature of God's creative action in the world. Given the established natural order, created and sustained by God, God's action in human life is through images of love and truth, not through any form of coercion. This mode of action is a voluntary choice on the part of the Creator, made because it is the only mode of attaining the goal of eliciting a free response of love and sacrifice from individuals endowed with free will. It implies total restraint in the use of God's omnipotent power, for otherwise a free response to God's actions is not possible. This can then guide us in the interpretation of the nature of creation, giving a metaphysical basis for cosmology. (See "The Theology of the Anthropic Principle," in *Quantum Cosmology and the Laws of Nature* [hereafter *QCLN*] and *MNU*.)

The key idea is that the *fundamental aim of loving action shapes the nature of creation and of transcendence in practice*, setting their meaning, implications, and limitations. Thus we take seriously the concept that the purpose of the universe is precisely to make this kind of sacrificial response possible, and pursue the implications. The meaning of the phrase "in practice" is that the Creator could have ordered things differently, but has voluntarily and specifically restricted the nature of creation to that required for this purpose. This states the metaphysical basis underlying cosmology and hence determining the nature of physics. Science cannot provide such a metaphysical basis. Given this basic aim, we can examine its implications for the creation process to be compatible with it.

1. The Ordered Universe

First, there is a need for the creation of a universe where ordered patterns of behavior exist, for without this, free will (if it can be attained) cannot function sensibly. If there were no rules or reliable patterns of behavior governing the activity of natural phenomena, it would not be possible to have a meaningful moral response to the happenings around one. Thus the material world, through which sentient beings are to be realized, needs to be governed by repeatable and understandable patterns of struc-

114

ture. Thus we envisage the Creator at all times maintaining the nature of the physical world so that a chosen set of laws of physics govern its evolution. Once this choice has been made, then the manner of action of laws will be seen by us as absolute and as rigorously determining the behavior of matter. One can then act freely within the confines of the laws, but the laws themselves cannot be altered by any action of humanity.

2. The Anthropic Universe: Free Will

We require further that these laws and regularities allow the existence of intelligent human beings, who can sense and react in a conscious way, and who have effective free will. The word 'effective' here means that whatever the underlying mechanisms governing human life, there must be a meaningful freedom of choice that can be exercised in a responsible way (for without this, the concept of ethics is meaningless). This implies accepting the conclusions resulting from Anthropic Principle discussions:[17] fine-tuned laws of physics are required, leading to the self-creative power of matter in the expanding universe leading to the spontaneous growth of complex structures[18] and eventually the emergence of intelligent life. Thus here we see the underpinning both of the physics of the Hot Big Bang, and the structuring of matter in such a way that physics can underlie chemistry, biochemistry, and a biology that allows the emergence of intelligent life, on this Earth and almost certainly on a vast number of other planets throughout the universe. There will exist numerous habitats that are not hospitable to life; the remarkable thing is that there are any at all that do allow life to exist. Creating conditions (laws of physics, boundary conditions to the universe) that allow such life anywhere is the truly remarkable feature.

However, more is implied, for we need to ensure the conditions required in order to attain free will. We do not know what these conditions are, except of course that they are compatible with the laws of physics and

17. John Barrow and Frank Tipler, *The Cosmological Anthropic Principle* (Oxford: Oxford University Press, 1984).

18. Joe Silk, *A Brief History of the Universe* (San Francisco: W. H. Freeman, 1997); George F. R. Ellis, *Before the Beginning: Cosmology Explained* (Bowerdean/Boyars, 1993); Martin Rees, *Just Six Numbers: The Deep Forces That Shape the Universe* (London: Weidenfeld and Nicholson, 1999).

chemistry as we experience them. Nevertheless it seems probable that fixed laws of behavior of matter, independent of interference by a Creator or any other agency, is a requisite basis for existence of independent beings able to exercise free will; for they make possible meaningful complex organized activity without outside interference. Thus we envisage the Creator choosing such a framework for the universe, thus giving up all the other possibilities allowed by the power available to the Creator, for example the power to directly intervene in events in a forceful way from time to time. One can then suppose the Creator rejoices both in the universe itself — the galaxies, stars, planets, etc. — and in all the abundance of life that is thus enabled.

A fundamental question is, Are the features of pain and evil implied in every universe that allows free will, as outlined here? Almost certainly, the answer is Yes — because of the very nature of free will; for any restrictions on the natural order that prevented that self-centered and selfish use of will which is the foundation of evil action, would simultaneously destroy the possibility of free response and loving action which is the aim of the whole. God then shares in the resulting suffering — thus transforming it.

3. The Provident Universe

Given the existence of creatures with free will, one can still imagine universes arranged so that this will is constrained in an essentially unfree way, contrary to the spirit set forth in the last section. In the temptations, Christ rejected the use of force to establish men's allegiance, and the offer to them of a good (material) time conditional on obedience. The same essential nature needs to be built into the creation of the universe, for otherwise a free response would not be possible. This is achieved by the impartial operation of the laws of physics, chemistry, and biology, offering to each person alike the bounty of nature irrespective of their beliefs or moral condition (actually humankind could not evolve were this not so). The rain falls alike on believer and unbeliever, and makes their existence possible.

4. The Hidden Nature

A further requirement must be satisfied, to enable the free response envisaged in Jesus' response to the temptations: that the created world not be dominated by God himself, striding the world and demanding obedience on pain of punishment (as in the myths of some other religions), or alternatively dominated by explicit marks of God's activity so that belief in God's existence and nature would be forced on everyone — they could not deny it, and the resulting demand on their ways of behavior. Thus the further requirement is that the nature of God and his creative activity be largely hidden, so that doubt is possible. This again is satisfied through the nature of creation as we see it, governed by impartial physical laws, which nevertheless allow a free and open response to those hints as to God's true nature that are given us. Sufficient evidence is given for knowledge of God's existence and an outline of his will, but this evidence is not overbearing. The ability to see the truth is dependent on readiness to listen and openness to the message (John 3:3).

5. The Possibility of Revelation

This leads to the final requirement: that despite the hidden nature of the underlying reality, it still be open to those who wish to discern this nature (indeed, on the view taken here, it is the wish of God that they should do so) and to receive encouragement to follow the true way. The feature I will assume is that there is indeed a channel for visions of ultimate reality, available to those open to them: allowing the nature of that transcendent reality to partially shine through into the immanent reality of the world, making available to us new patterns of understanding, and providing encouragement and strength to follow these visions.[19]

The whole represents exactly what is described by William Temple: *"What we find is power in complete subordination to love"*; for the possible exercise of creative power by the Creator is voluntarily restricted to that which enables a universe where a free and loving response by humankind

---

19. G. S. Wakefield, *A Dictionary of Christian Spirituality* (London: SCM Press, 1983). How this can be achieved is discussed in the Vatican/CTNS volume on *Neuroscience and the Person,* ed. R. J. Russell et al.

is possible, despite the costs and sacrifice entailed, specifically ordaining things so that humans with free will can act as they will. Thus in this view of God as the transcendent creator, we see kenosis centrally embodied in the creative act that underlies physical cosmology.

E. Evidence

The view put forward so far seems coherent as a combination of both religious and scientific concerns. The further question is what evidence there is to support it. The relation to the Christian view of creation and incarnation has already been discussed above. In my view kenosis is central to a deep understanding of Christianity with strong historical roots. It is characterized on the personal side by the theme of grace and acting as a channel for God, as particularly expressed in St. Francis's prayer *("make me an instrument of thy grace"),* which requires setting one's own wishes aside in order to act as a channel for God's will. This is of course one of the central themes in a developed devotional life, which must always be aware of the danger of pride and the need for humility, which in the end is essentially a demand for a kenotic outlook in terms of one's own importance and abilities.

In interfaith terms, as mentioned above, this kind of view is encompassed in many religions as well as Christianity; for example, it is powerfully embodied in Gandhi's vision of *ahimsa* and *satyagraha.* The issue of how specifically this may be true is a fruitful source for research. I suspect that it is more deeply contained in the core concept of Christianity — the incarnate God who voluntarily suffers and dies — than in other religions, but this remains to be tested. It is certainly not *embodied* more powerfully in the practice of Christianity than other religions; indeed major sections of Christianity reject it and are based on power and coercion, and the historical record of Christianity is in many ways abysmal, incorporating numerous instances of extreme intolerance and cruelty of a breathtaking order, not just as occasional wayward outliers of behavior, but rather as the center of doctrine and practice in many cases over many centuries. However, here I reverse the argument: I regard degree of alignment with kenosis as a key test of religious authenticity.[20]

20. A partial justification for this view is that one can judge religious institutions by the extent to which they fulfill the viewpoints of their founders, as well as by their fruits;

There is a much wider range of evidence supporting the importance of kenosis as a general principle in human life and in morality in particular. At a certain level, evidence is provided by the basic theme of mother and child in animal and human life — the willingness to protect the child at whatever cost, letting go of one's own life in the process. This kind of theme has been developed in depth by proponents of sociobiology; indeed, the process of giving up individual desires in favor of the common good is the underlying essential element in creating a society or community out of individuals with diverse interests and wishes. However, this does not encompass the full depth of the kenotic idea, for it does not extend to one's enemies (as exhorted in the Sermon on the Mount). There is an understanding of this deeper concept in various communities who have experienced the moral power of forgiving and sacrifice.[21] One can also look at the converse: the ongoing pain and suffering in those conflict-torn communities that refuse to take the major step of forgiveness — Northern Ireland might suffice as an example. Forgiveness has important kenotic aspects, for it involves giving up revenge in favor of the common interests of peace, and placing reconciliation with the opponent before justice;[22] it is a central element in the growing restorative justice movement.[23]

In a different but centrally important context, a basic element in individual and community learning is the willingness to give up previous certainty in order to be able to understand and learn. This is, for example, made explicit in a large literature on physics education,[24] where a prime barrier to understanding modern physics, or even in properly learning

and as indicated above, the position taken here is that kenosis is a core feature of Christ's life. I assume other religions are visions of the same fundamental reality, but based in different histories and cultural viewpoints. I believe there are sufficient strands of kenosis in the other religious traditions to justify this as a viable view.

21. The way this has worked out in the South African context is outlined in *MNU*.

22. Donald W. Shriver, *An Ethic for Enemies* (New York: Oxford University Press, 1995); Martha Minow, *Between Vengeance and Forgiveness: Facing History after Genocide and Mass Murder* (Boston: Beacon Press, 1998); Desmond Tutu, *No Future Without Forgiveness* (London: Rider, 1999); E. L. Worthington, *Dimensions of Forgiveness: Psychological Research and Theological Perspectives* (Templeton Foundation Press, 1999).

23. Jim Consedine, *Restorative Justice: Healing the Effects of Crime* (Lyttleton: Ploughshares Publications, 1995); P. McCold, ed., *Restorative Justice: An Annotated Bibliography* (Willow Tree Press, 1997).

24. L. C. McDermott and E. F. Redish: "Resource Letter: PER-1: Physics Education Research," *American Journal of Physics* 67 (1999): 755-67.

Newtonian theory, is that the learners hang on to previous worldviews. These are what they really believe in, despite strong evidence presented for the new viewpoint; the learner refuses to let go of the familiar ideas. Physics teaching techniques need to take this into account. More generally, in all fields the arrogance involved in knowing the answer with absolute certainty is the ultimate barrier to learning the way things really are, and so successfully adapting to them. Thus, being willing to let go of previous knowledge in order to look at the world afresh is a key to learning. Similarly a process of giving up one's own controlling status is central to all great art, as is discussed for example in Vanstone's book *Love's Endeavour, Love's Expense.* The author of an artwork of any kind must, in order to attain real depth, eventually give up directing the way it develops according to his or her own preconceived wishes, and rather respond to the integrity of its own developing identity. There are interesting analogies here with the process of God's activity in creating the world, including beings in it who have free will and their own inner integrity.

There are some wider analogies that support the view presented here. The theme of new life being enabled by death of earlier generations occurs in the biological world,[25] enabling more complex life forms to arise from simpler ones, with the same set of chemical elements being circulated over and over again in the biosphere. Indeed, we are made of materials that are lent to us for the period of our lives, incorporating in our bodies atoms that have been utilized by many thousands of living beings before us, and that will be utilized again by many thousands more after our death. And kenosis can be seen in biological sexual reproduction, for a central feature in the higher orders is in fact unselfish genes giving up their unique identities in order to create new genes with new coding patterns, thus creating new phenotypes, and so powering the Darwinian process of evolution by natural selection.

Taken together, this wide range of evidence from the religious through social to analogues in the natural sciences provides backing for the broad picture suggested here of kenosis as a central theme in much of creation. It does not of course give proof it is correct, for such proof is unattainable.

---

25. Holmes Rolston, III, "Does Nature Need to Be Redeemed?" *Zygon* 29 (1994): 205-29.

F. Implications and Issues

Clearly the overall view set out here has solid implications as to how one should live one's life, in a moral and religious sense: it suggests that God desires our voluntarily choosing good and following the vision outlined above; but we need grace to liberate the will to do so. Because of the paradoxical nature of the concept *("he who would save his life shall lose it . . ."),* the answers will often not be obvious; the practice of kenosis leaves great room for creativity. It cannot be captured in a set of behavioral rules, but can be illuminated by studies of those who have been its great practitioners in personal and public life, and studies of communities built on this idea.[26] Some comments on this are given in *MNU,* particularly pointing out that in each of the legal, economic, and political spheres, there do indeed already exist a number of examples of successful real-world implementations of kenotic practice, which can usefully be studied and emulated. For example, in the economic sphere, the Scott-Bader Commonwealth and the Van Leer Foundation provide examples of commercial companies with explicitly ethical bases of a kenotic nature; and as Peter Drucker has remarked,[27] many organizations (the Scouts, the Salvation Army, numerous charities) form a significant part of the economy that is not profit-motivated.

I will conclude with some comments on the key issue of kenosis and practicality. The question is as follows: clearly kenotic action is a great ideal that can be very inspiring, but can it in fact be a practical guide to personal and social action? Is it an idealistic but impractical idea, which cannot be applied in real situations? There is sufficient evidence that it can work some of the time to make it a worthy, indeed highly desirable, mode of action; could it be viable in all, or at least many, circumstances?

Two preliminary remarks are needed to set the scene. First, the concept of kenosis presented at the start of this paper did not state that this mode of action demands *acting in a sacrificial way at all times;* what it proposed was that *at all times one would be willing to do so.* This makes a crucial difference. What that implies is that in any specific situation, one should be prepared to first — as a conscious act — set one's own interests

---

26. See, for example, Daisy Newman, *A Procession of Friends* (Friends United Press); Elfrida Vipont, *Quakerism: A Faith to Live By* (London: Bannisdale Press).

27. Peter Drucker, *Innovation and Enterprise* (New York: Pan Books, 1985).

aside, letting go of them; and then look both dispassionately and passionately at the problem facing one (that is, both with analytic clarity and with a resolve to take whatever action is needed), and decide what action to take that would further the overall kenotic goals advocated here. That action might or might not be of a sacrificial nature, but it would always be framed in such a way as to attempt to regard all involved as Children of God,[28] as far as possible furthering each person's interests in a win-win way. Thus you love your neighbor as yourself, and indeed love your enemies; but this does not preclude acting in your own interests.

Given the resolve to act this way, one then needs decision aids as to when in fact sacrificial kinds of acts are called for, and when not. It is not possible to give specific rules in this regard that are universally applicable, for an essential part of such acts is their creative nature. However, the key point is that *they are appropriate when they have the potential to transform the nature of the situation to a higher level,* as has been discussed above. One indicator of when this is not the case, is any situation when this kind of action is *taken for granted by the opponent;* for then sacrificial actions cannot have the transformative power that is their goal, reaching out and changing the hardened heart. When this is the case, some form of standing up to the opponent — which also demands courage and indeed perhaps sacrifices — may be indicated (and this may be the situation many women find themselves in, in their domestic lives). It is the kenotic spirit that should be preserved — aiming to transform rather than destroy the opponent. Of course if that spirit truly exists, one would indeed expect to see it from time to time expressed in actions of a sacrificial kind; if someone claims to embody that spirit but never actually acts sacrificially, one would have to regard their claims with skepticism.

The second point is that in any specific situation of conflict, action of a kenotic type has to try to take into account the needs and natures of the different parties involved, and this cannot be done by treating them all in the same way, even if one's mode of action aims at imputing equal intrinsic value to them. Indeed, in many cases some parties may be clearly identifiable as aggressors or perpetrators of deeds of an evil nature, with others

28. This kind of phraseology can of course sound highly simplistic. Nevertheless I use it because I believe it can have power in real political situations, as demonstrated for example by Desmond Tutu; and part of Christ's message was that we should indeed in some ways be childlike.

being victims of these acts. In particular this applies if crimes against humanity are being carried out such as genocide or massacres, where human life is clearly held as of no value. There must then be a societal ability to restrain such acts, in order to set the stage where minimal respect for life exists and can be a basis for building further. Standing up to such acts on behalf of the victim may call for defensive coercive action against one group in order to protect another group, and this may arguably be considered sometimes to be a consequence of a kenotic view. It leads to the need for policing by armed forces, for those engaged in such acts will inevitably be armed. Undertaking this can be a sacrificial act, for it will often place one's own life in danger.

Here there is a splitting of opinion amongst those advocating a kenotic worldview. The logic just expressed leads to attempts to adopt some kind of just-war theory with an explicit kenotic slant — envisaging policing or warlike action undertaken with minimal use of force, and that at all times offers the other a way out, and takes their humanity and needs into account. But this is the start of the slippery slope. It sounds fine as an idea, but almost inevitably in practice results in expedience and can be used to justify whatever it is you want to do; indeed in many wars *both sides* invoke a just-war theory, explicitly or implicitly — making clear its expedient nature in practice. It is the path that leads from the Holocaust to Dresden, responding to evil with evil, and indeed is the dangerous road easily leading to the 'untermensch', torture, and retaliatory genocide. This is expressed explicitly for example in the development, deployment, and use of napalm — a deliberate instrument of torture, to be used as part of the war policy of terrorizing the 'enemy' populace, as in Vietnam. We can always find excuses to use coercion at the cost of the other's freedom and in the end at the cost of our own humanity — and this may be inevitable in a war situation. Consequently some adopt a pacifist position: the refusal to bear arms against others in any circumstances. The pacifist case is argued in *MNU;* it will continue to be a source of controversy and debate.

Given this background, in an attempt to focus the question of when a kenotic approach is viable, one can consider the possibilities expressed in Table 1 on page 124.

There are four options shown here. First, **Case SS:** maybe it is desirable as a course of action for some people some of the time. This implies there are some people who should never be expected to act this way. This is a lowest view of human nature, which I suggest should be resisted as de-

When	Who	
	Some People	All People
Some of the time	SS	AS
All the time	SA	AA

Table 1. The options for kenotic action

meaning and a self-fulfilling negative prophecy; it is the view that some people are irredeemable.

A much more positive position is **Case AS**: it is desirable for all people some of the time. This is much better in suggesting that all have the capacity to act this way; but avoids regarding it as always appropriate. But then how do you decide when it is appropriate and when not? When should self-interest take precedence over more kenotic behavior (noting that self-interest is in many cases compatible with a kenotic moral approach — the question is when it supersedes it?). You need some kind of selection rules for when a kenotic approach will be used, and when not, based on an assessment of the nature of the situation and the likelihood of succeeding.[29] A major question then is what is designated as 'success'; how this is defined — in terms of one's own welfare only, or the welfare of all concerned — is crucial to whether one will try the kenotic route or not in a particular situation. But the key point is that once one has decided to deliberately not act kenotically in circumstance X, this will with high probability be extended soon to include circumstances Y and Z, and so on, until it is never attempted. Occasional exclusions tend to become the norm, because that is the easy road.

This is why **Case AA** can be strongly supported as the ideal, and what indeed should be attempted as far as possible: the aim should be kenotic action by all people all the time. If this happened, life would be transformed. Now human selfishness prevents this happening fully, but it can

29. Note that this is not the same as deciding when sacrificial action is appropriate. That issue needs consideration after one has adopted a kenotic overall position, cf. the discussion above.

still be the aim, and the attempt to move this way could be implemented in many ways in both personal and public life; even a little success in this way would make a big difference. The major problem is the claim that this cannot be countenanced in the face of real evil, for example genocide, mass murder, or premeditated rape and murder, which have to be stopped with lethal force, so public policy has to deviate strongly from this ideal. One can argue, as above, that this is not necessarily always in contradiction to a kenotic attitude. But another possible response is that the strong kenotic position of pacifism is the only truly profound way to deal with real evil, and its supposed lack of success is quite misleading: the true situation being that it is almost never tried, and if it were, things would often be radically different; the problem is that we do not have the courage and strength to try it, for it is an extremely costly road to go. If we regard the other persons involved as always human and open to generosity invoked by sacrificial behavior, we will be taking the high road and imitating the true nature of God, thus opening the way to true transformation. In contrast, the use of force is a way of responding to like with like; it does not have the power to transform the situation.

However, in the end the real problem with *Case AA* as a proposal, in either its weak or its strong form, is that *one cannot impose the will to act kenotically on other people,* by whatever method, for the attempt to do so violates the very nature of kenosis. When one tries to impose it by force, as has happened on various occasions (e.g., in Communist China), worse evil results than from not trying at all. Thus the attempt to make this case come about must inevitably fail. All one can do is persuade, and this will never fully succeed.

Thus realistically the best we can hope for is not *Case AA,* desirable as that is, but *a combination of Case AS together with* **Case SA**: there will be some people who will act this way all the time, indeed often adopting the strong kenotic position of pacifism. They will be regarded as hopeless idealists by many, but they will succeed in transforming some parts of society, and can hope to make that part gradually larger over the years as they steadfastly act this way. Some will accuse them of hiding behind others who are prepared to do the dirty work of society, and they will have to attempt to make sure this criticism is not true by being prepared to take action to help in those desperate areas too (as for example in the Quaker ambulance crews in the two world wars of the twentieth century). And meanwhile they would be trying all the while to influence the nature of society at large as much as possible in a fully kenotic direction — for example, encouraging kenotic action in as wide a range of circumstances as possible, and ensuring that when force is used, there is always an underlying intention to use it only as a last resort and continually allowing the opponent a way out, instead of trying to destroy them.

They would try to exemplify this outlook and way of life themselves, and to extend it to as great a part of society as possible by example and persuasion. In particular they would continually experiment with ways of extending its ambit in public life, as discussed in *MNU,* and developing selection rules for the whole range of options for wider public policy in a graded way that at all times chooses the most kenotic-like option. But their own lives will in some cases fully reject the option of coercion, being steadfastly kenotic in intent and action as far as they are able, and providing a faith community within wider society where this is the continuing aim.

G. Conclusion

The basic view put forward here is presented in *QCLN,* and is laid out in much more detail in *MNU,* which also outlines some of its relations to the social sciences. In the end it is fundamental that *kenosis has a paradoxical nature* — when truly successful *it represents a transition to a higher plane of action and meaning that transforms the nature of what is happening and how it is seen.* It rejects a zero sum mentality as against one of sharing and true transformation, which is only possible when heart and mind are persuaded rather than coerced. This result cannot be attained by other means.[30] It is a practical way of action in many cases. The case is strong for aligning oneself both theoretically and practically with those who try to implement it all of the time.[31]

---

30. See *Christian Faith and Practice in the Life of the Society of Friends* (London: London Yearly Meeting, many editions) for various examples of this attitude and how it can be implemented.

31. I thank the participants in the meeting that gave rise to this book, particularly Holmes Rolston for his helpful comments and Graham Cotter for a copy of his notes on kenosis, "Our God Is the Die That Is Cast."

Romantic Love, Covenantal Love, Kenotic Love

MICHAEL WELKER

If creation is seen as the work of love, then no normal man can be indifferent to that response of creation on which depends the triumph or the tragedy of love.

Love's Endeavour, Love's Expense, p. 78

Whoever does not love abides in death.

1 John 3:14b

I. The So-Called "Romantic Love" and the Problem of Gaining a Perspective on Love as the Ultimate Nature of Reality[1]

The fact that love is a creative power and even has to do with the "ultimate nature of reality" is not easily conveyed to people in the Western industrialized nations at the beginning of the twenty-first century. Human life together, without love — that is certainly unimaginable. There is no way around love for the establishment of relationships and marriage on

1. I am grateful for many helpful comments on my contributions to the consultation on "Love as the Ultimate Nature of Reality: Cosmology, Freedom, and the Theology of Kenosis" by its participants, especially John Polkinghorne, Keith Ward, and Ian Barbour.

the basis of the free choice of a partner. Nor can we imagine the living together of a family without love. Yet at the same time sociologists and theorists of culture advise us to reduce exaggerated expectations in love and to historicize them — to date them back to the early nineteenth century.

The hope that love, along with art, could become a protective agent "against the dominant characteristics of modern society . . . , against the economic necessity of work and exploitation, against regulations by the state, against research with its drive towards technology," this hope has turned out to be a failure. The hope was: "The threatened I saves himself/herself by turning to love, he/she regenerates in the family and finds ways of expression in art." Reality, however, is different: "The passion of love becomes the pathology of family life which cannot be dissolved into a chain of proofs of love to be expected and given; and if art represents the world of the bourgeois, then it does so in forms which reach from mild irony to sarcastic parody."[2]

Thus a strange tension remains of extremely high expectations centered on "love" and a normality of endless disappointments, a tension that provides one of the most important ingredients for entertainment and popular music, from "All you need is love" and "I worship the power of love *(Ich bete an die Macht der Liebe)*" to "Love grows colder when love grows older" and "Love mostly begins with red roses, but what comes then? *(Mit roten Rosen fängt die Liebe meistens an, doch was kommt dann . . .)*"

Common sense and literature, but also theology and philosophy have let themselves be captivated by this cultural fixation on "love" *in the mutual emotionally affected communication between two partners* which is often termed "romantic love." Christian theology has all too often not moved beyond this "relation," "mutuality," and "I-Thou-constellation" in its numerous efforts to illustrate and to reflect on "love." The few seminal differentiations that were reached immediately became "classics," such as the differentiation into "eros and agape."[3] More recently the intricate relation between self-reference and selflessness has been at the center of

---

2. Niklas Luhmann, *Die Gesellschaft der Gesellschaft* (Frankfurt: Suhrkamp, 1997), pp. 987f.; cf. N. Luhmann, *Liebe als Passion. Zur Codierung von Intimität* (Frankfurt: Suhrkamp, 1982) [Love as Passion: The Codification of Intimacy, (Cambridge, Mass.: Harvard University Press, 1986)].

3. Thus the title of the much cited book by Anders Nygren: *Eros und Agape. Gestaltwandlungen der christlichen Liebe,* 2 vols. (Gütersloh: Bertelsmann, 1930 and 1937).

thought. The suggestions offered are rather vague or even rhetorical: "In ever so great self-reference still greater selflessness."[4]

It has seldom become clear that along with this concentration on the romantic "love relation" an enormous reduction was made that even omitted the structural wealth of family love relations,[5] not to speak of more complex or even religious conceptions of love. This inability to find orientation is probably one of the main reasons for the difficulties that current Western industrialized nations have in their attempts to privilege an ethos based on the family over against an ethos centered only on partnership, e.g., the many heated and helpless debates about marriage between homosexual partners. Despite the fact that disclosures about "love" were amazingly scarce and poor, the paradigmatic concentration on the affective person-to-person relation was maintained. The subject of the meeting that gave rise to this book, "Love and the Ultimate Nature of Reality: Cosmology, Freedom, and the Theology of Kenosis," may be seen as a suggestion to move out of this captivity of thought.

For myself, at least, I should like to read the subject as a suggestion to regain a deepened understanding of the power of love on the basis of religious sources. I should like to emphasize the fact that such an understanding could be made fruitful in the context of personal and family relations. Thus the aim is not an abstract opposition of love as a social, cultural, or even cosmic power to love within the limits of an I-Thou relationship.[6]

---

4. Cf. Eberhard Jüngel, *Gott als Geheimnis der Welt. Zur Begründung der Theologie des Gekreuzigten im Streit zwischen Theismus und Atheismus* (Tübingen: Mohr, 1977), pp. 430ff.

5. For the fixation on 'partnership' and the subject of dominance and subjection, see Karl Barth, *Kirchliche Dogmatik* (Zurich, 1932-67), III/1, esp. pp. 347ff.; III/4, esp. pp. 244ff.; Alfred North Whitehead, *Adventures of Ideas* (New York: The Free Press, 1967), pp. 288ff., offers an instructive opposition in the concentration on the caring love towards the child.

6. Like many other conceptual and cultural achievements of modernity, romantic love within the boundaries of the I-Thou relationship was a powerful form to support abstract equality and freedom. Sarah Coakley rightly emphasized this in our consultation. Today we see the price that was paid for the disembodied and de-contextualized self of modernity which is the 'reference point' of this kind of love. We gradually become aware of the dynamics of the self-secularization and self-banalization of religious communication connected with an empty faith (the mere relation to a transcendent 'inner other'), that was compatible with the modern concept of the self. And we also see the lack of bind-

II. Accesses to Love as a Creative Power
on the Basis of the Biblical Traditions

If we take the time to compare the numerous statements about love in the biblical traditions we are first struck by the multitude of "relations" that cause them to speak of "love." From the Pentateuch to the Song of Songs, numerous references to family and certainly also to person-to-person forms of love are present, some of which come close to the romantic form. More conspicuous, however, as is well known, is the more general love of the neighbor, the love of the stranger, the love of the enemy, and — particularly extensive in the texts of the New Testament letters — the "brotherly" love or rather the fraternal love that thematizes more complex social relationships.

Furthermore, the love of God is dealt with in detail — the love of God's name, of God's word, the love of God's justice, God's instruction, commandments, and law. There is strong attention to God's love of the people of Israel, of the world, of the city of Jerusalem, of law and justice, etc. Even if some of these "relations" should be nothing but rhetorical analogies, as perhaps the love of darkness or of injustice[7] that are occasionally mentioned, a rich supply of forms and contents remain, and they need a closer examination.

Apart from the great variety of "love relations" in the biblical traditions it is striking that *for centuries the love of God is strictly connected to the respect for and "attention to the commandments" or to the "holding fast to God's word."*[8] Correspondingly, "to love God's name" and "to serve God" (Isaiah 56:6) can be connected. Surely the relation between the "love of God" and acting according to God's intention and order becomes particularly clear in Jesus' relation to the Creator and is represented in detail in the Johannine writings (John 14:31). The *"Love of God," however, quite*

---

ing and nurturing power in the romantic mutuality of two transcendental egos. Most of us lost the trust in speculations that, with the young Hegel and other philosophers, see this kind of love as the ultimate "dialectical unity of unity and difference" of two egos.

7. The biblical talk of love should be taken seriously in relations definitely characterized as negative ('love of this world', love of 'the respect among people', cf. also the opposition of love of God and of 'mammon'), and the relationship of love to instances not directly personal (justice, wisdom, goodness, and faithfulness) should not be ignored.

8. Exod. 20:6; Deut. 7:9; Luke 11:42; John 14:15-21ff.; John 15:9; 1 John 5:3 and more often.

obviously also means to take up and pursue God's intentions as they pertain to the good order and the well-being of creation in general.

These interests of God in the good order and the thriving of creation are best and most perfectly served in the love of neighbors, but also of strangers and even of enemies. *For this very reason the fulfillment of the love of God does mean that this love cannot be grasped merely in terms of a reciprocal one-to-one relation.* It includes, and even opens up, law-abiding and loving relationships to the world, to fellow human beings, and even to other fellow creatures, according to God's intentions. The so-called "double commandment of love"[9] should thus not be regarded as a combination of two different basic relations, but as a strict connection that says something important about the biblical understanding of love in general. If love is globally termed the "fulfillment of the law" (Rom. 13:8; Gal. 5:14), then the loving relation to God must not be left out of consideration, even in places where it is less clearly detailed than in most of the New Testament traditions.

The love relation to God that is concretized and materialized in the fulfillment of the law or in love of fellow creatures is not a mere "moral motivating power," nor is it a continuous impulse to selflessly outgrow oneself and to outgrow the merely reciprocal and symmetrical love relations: "If you love those who love you, what credit is that to you? For even sinners love those who love them" (Luke 6:32; cf. 6:33ff. and Matt. 5:46f.). The Johannine writings present this in detail when they strictly connect love of visible fellow human beings and love of the invisible God (cf. 1 John 4:12-20). The love between the Father and the Son is a love that does *not* just mean "abstract reciprocity," in which human beings can only somehow "mystically" gain participation.

Rather, it is a love connected with the making known of the Father or his name (John 17:26), or with the revelation of the Son and his dwelling among his witnesses (John 14:21ff.). The love God loves with and wants to be loved with is thus revealed to human beings, and God is revealed in this love. In this love, *God's identity and power are made known.* In the same way the Creator entrusts Jesus Christ with divine power via the love relation, human beings are also to become familiar with God and gain participation in God's power through love.[10]

9. Mark 12:30f.; Matt. 22:37-39; Luke 10:27; cf. Deut. 6:4-31 and Lev. 19:18.
10. Cf. John 3:25; 14:21ff.; 17:26ff.; 21:15 and more often.

Paul describes this giving of participation in God's power by saying that God's love has been poured into our hearts through the Holy Spirit (Rom. 5:5).[11] At the same time Paul repeatedly describes a process not easily grasped, a process of *growth* in those who let themselves be seized and stamped by God's love and by love for God. *They enter into a relationship to the living God that transforms them.* For in love, they cannot be satisfied with a relationship to God the knowledge of which is distanced and objectivizing. They must try to obtain that knowledge "face to face." "Then I will know fully even as I have been fully known" (1 Cor. 13:12; cf. 1 Cor. 8:1ff.).

At this point the complex love relation to God threatens to collapse into a clueless mystical relation in which the meaning of the imperative: "Pursue love!" (1 Cor. 14:1), growing in love (1 Thess. 3:12), increase of knowledge in love (cf. Phil. 1:8-9), and particularly the creative power of love, simply cannot be seen anymore. But the living and loving relationship to the invisible God is no *unio mystica*. It is certainly no romantic love between God and human being in which God and human exchange their personal emotions on the basis of abstract equality. The living and loving relationship to God, which takes shape in the forms of love among the creatures and grants participation in God's power, sets free a *process of growth*.

The different New Testament traditions describe this process of growth with striking similarity. In love, human beings participate in God's identity and truth in a way that God's identity and truth gain shape and reality in themselves, in their bodies and their lives.

- Paul describes this when he says that "Christ's love" actually urges human beings to know: God's creative activity invites us in Christ to participate in Christ and to become "a new creation" (2 Cor. 5:14-17).
- The Letter to the Colossians emphasizes that in the *union of love* we "have all the riches of assured understanding and have the knowledge

---

11. Cf. also the talk of love as the most important fruit or gift of the Spirit in the First Letter to the Corinthians. For the figure of the 'pouring of the Spirit', see M. Welker, *God the Spirit* (Philadelphia: Fortress Press, 1994), pp. 134ff. and 228ff.; M. Welker, "'And Also Upon the Menservants and the Maidservants in Those Days Will I Pour My Spirit,' On Pluralism and the Promise of the Spirit," in *Soundings* 78, no. 1 (1995): 49-67.

of God's mystery, that is Christ himself in whom are hidden all the treasures of wisdom and knowledge" (Col. 2:2f.).

- According to the Letter to the Ephesians, Christ's love which "surpasses all knowledge" is not only known through the rooting in love and is based on it, but also the loving persons receive an ever increasing participation in God's strength and being, "so that you may be filled with the fullness of God" (Eph. 3:11; cf. 17ff.).

III. Covenantal Love and Kenotic Love

If we explore this rich texture and structure of divine love and of love directed to God, the *covenantal form of love* becomes clear. John Polkinghorne differentiated it into "the mandatory aspect, the revelatory aspect and the transforming aspect: 'you will be my people and I will be your God'."[12] The covenantal love bestows a great dignity on human beings. They are dignified to take up and pursue God's intentions in relation to creation, God's interests in the well-being of creation. They are dignified to reveal God's will and God's plans for creation. And they are dignified to work toward the fulfillment of the divine creative, sustaining, and transforming agency. No less is expressed in the notion of the *imago Dei*.[13]

The covenantal form of love discloses the *weight of love,* its communicative and creative powers. On the other hand, it can appear as a challenge and as a burden that makes God's love absolutely inaccessible to human beings. For who could claim that he or she could respond to this calling and take care of God's intentions for the creation? Who could claim to participate in God's strength and being? And even if we found such (and even found ourselves among them), who would be ready to claim all this on the basis of the covenantal love, for the covenantal form would seem to restrict the universality of God's love.[14] Even if we escaped a superficial understanding of God's relation to creation and to human beings framed in terms of romantic love — the notion of covenantal love

12. John Polkinghorne in a response to a first draft of this text.

13. Cf. M. Welker, "Creation, the Image of God, and the Mandate of Dominion," in *Creation and Reality* (Philadelphia: Fortress Press, 1999), pp. 60ff.

14. Keith Ward has pointed out this problem to me: Does the covenant in Judaism not set apart the Jewish People? Does the New Covenant not set apart the Church?

could come as a threat of turning love into a living law that it would be beyond our capacity to live up to.

The kenotic love of God revealed in Christ and recursively visible in God's creation does not give up the dignifying weight of covenantal love. But it reveals that God turns lovingly to those who in themselves do *not* have any potential to take care of God's intentions for creation, who in themselves do *not* have any potential to reveal the goodness of God in their ministry, and who in themselves do *not* have any potential to help transform the world according to God's will. In kenotic love God unconditionally turns to creatures in order to liberate them out of the depths of confusion, lostness, and sin, to win them for the coming reign of God, and to ennoble them to the experience and enactment of God's love, something they can only experience and enact as a new creation.

In this kenotic love, God really gives space for the individuality and depth of creatures. They are not measured by a rod stretching beyond their possibilities. Out of their depths God rescues them and re-creates them for the divine purpose.[15] In kenotic love God reveals a burning passion for creatures — not just for their suitability to the divine plan for the world. On the other hand, this interest is not just an erratic longing for an erratic contact with an erratic existence; it is the willingness to meet creatures at their greatest distance from God and even in their attempts to seclude and shield themselves from God, so that they may finally "share in bliss and become vehicles of the truly creative freedom of the divine nature."[16]

A passionate interest in the otherness of the other, a passionate interest in letting the other unfold himself/herself in freedom, a passionate interest to pave ways for the unfolding of his/her life, all are characteristic of kenotic love. But at the same time, it is *love* that is directed to the other — not just curiosity. This love does not come without the element that I would now like to term "covenantal promise" and "covenantal challenge." It respects the depth and the mystery and the freedom of the loved one; it even keeps this depth and mystery and freedom alive and holds it open.[17] But it seeks to win the other for a new life in a new creation. The kenotic love of God seeks a *new* covenantal relationship — without boundaries,

15. Cf. Ian Barbour's plea for "reconceptualizing divine power as empowerment rather than overpowering control," Chapter 1 in this volume.

16. Keith Ward, Chapter 9 in this volume. Holmes Rolston, Chapter 3 in this volume, rightly speaks of a "second birth."

17. Cf. 1 Cor. 12, particularly 12:7.

without exclusion, but with the divine purpose to win the beloved one for a participation in the divine life and in the divine plans for creation. The life of Christ offers guidance to help us become familiar with these plans. And his unconditional love for the world, which secluded itself from God and turned life-supporting powers against God, time and again wins us over for the loving communion with God in which we become restored to the *imago Dei* and to membership in the new creation.

No other New Testament text describes this intention in greater detail than the first letter of John. In love, human beings become "children of God." Even if their participation in God's identity waits for further revelation, their belonging to God is certain, because it is based on their love and the fulfillment of Christ's commandment connected with it (cf. 1 John 3). "Everyone who loves is born of God and knows God" (1 John 4:7). The first letter of John connects this living in God's love and living as a loving being with a "new life." A person who does not love, however, remains in death. But a person who loves has passed from death to life in the new creation (cf. 1 John 3:14).

This whole process, again, is not just a one-to-one event between God and a beloved creature. Although the uniqueness and depth of the individual creature is of utmost importance to God, and should be of utmost importance to the whole creation, the manifestation of love and the transformation of the creation *ex vetere* into *creatio nova*[18] is of utmost importance to the rest of creation. Here we can learn of Paul's burning interest in raising faith, love, and hope in a community (in fact: in different concrete communities with individual profiles of faith, love, and hope), in sharing and rejoicing in it — in the common expectation of eschatological fulfillment and in growth toward it. According to Romans 8 this development and growth are not just of importance for fellow Christians. The lives of those who live in God's kenotic love are of the greatest importance because they point the expectation of the whole creation to nothing less than the full revelation of God's intentions for the world. For this reason "the creation waits with eager longing for the revealing of the children of God" (Rom. 8:19).

God's kenotic love, which gives to creation an unconditional share in itself and in that power of new life — which it is — time and again directs

18. Cf. John Polkinghorne, Chapter 5 in this volume; also *The Faith of a Physicist* (Princeton: Princeton University Press, 1994), ch. 9.

us towards God and a fuller revelation.[19] The power of God's kenotic love, revealed in Christ's love and bestowed on creatures by the working of the Holy Spirit, draws human lives into the creative love that makes them bearers of God's presence and the incarnation of the new creation.

19. John Polkinghorne and Michael Welker, *The End of the World and the Ends of God: Science and Theology on Eschatology* (Harrisburg, Pa.: Trinity Press, 2000).

God's Kenosis in the Creation and Consummation of the World

JÜRGEN MOLTMANN

> *. . . faith in [love's] triumph is neither more nor less than faith in the Creator Himself—faith that He will not cease from His handiwork nor abandon the object of His love.*
>
> Love's Endeavour, Love's Expense, p. 63

As a theologian, I should like to begin this contribution with an account of Christian and Jewish kenotic theology, and shall then go on to ask about its possible relevance for an understanding of God's presence and activity in the cosmos. A theological doctrine of creation is not a religious cosmology that enters the lists in competition with the cosmologies of physics. But it has to be compatible with physical cosmologies.[1] The theological account of experiences of God is different from the scientific account of experiences of nature. But if we bring them into dialogue with each other, two things soon emerge. First, theologians have a particular preference for the 'great scientific narratives', with their unique and unrepeatable histories, because these narratives correspond to their own histories with God. The one narrative is the development of the expanding cosmos since the 'Big Bang'; the other the evolution of life in 'the phylogenetic tree'. Sec-

---

1. My attempt at a doctrine of creation that is compatible with the natural sciences may be found in *God in Creation: An Ecological Doctrine of Creation* (Gifford Lectures 1984-85), trans. Margaret Kohl (London, 1985).

137

ond, theologians have a particular interest in a natural phenomenon for which scientists have no great liking: 'contingency'. We know from the unpredictable fortuities in human life and in our own personal biographies that these can put paid to our plans, for both good and ill. Sociologists such as Jürgen Habermas and Hermann Lübbe therefore actually see the very function of religion as being "the mastery of contingency." So in developing a theology of nature, we ask about God's presence in the history of nature and in the chance events that herald a future which cannot be extrapolated from the past and present of the cosmos. We shall see whether here Christian and Jewish kenotic theology can sharpen our insight.

1. Christian Theology of the Kenosis of Christ

Christian experience of God springs from perception of the presence of God in Jesus Christ and his history. According to the hymn that Paul quotes in Philippians 2:5-11, Christ's history was understood as a kenosis for the sake of the redemption of God-forsaken men and women:

> Have this mind among yourselves, which is also in Christ Jesus;
> who, though he was in the form of God,
> did not count equality with God a thing to be grasped,
> but *emptied himself,* taking the form of a servant,
> being born like another.
> And being found in human form
> he humbled himself and became obedient unto death,
> even death on the cross. Therefore God has highly exalted him. . . .

The history of Christ which the first part of this hymn describes begins with the 'divine form' of the Son of God in heaven and ends with the 'form of a servant' on the cross at Golgotha. The becoming-human of Christ presupposes his 'self-emptying' of his divine form and results in his 'humbling of himself', his self-humiliation. God's Son becomes human and mortal. He becomes the servant of human beings and dies on the cross. He does all this out of 'obedience' to God the Father. I shall not go here into the many individual exegetical problems,[2] but shall turn directly to the theological ones.

2. For the exegetical questions I may point to the excellent study by O. Hofius, *Der*

1. *Early Lutheran theology* tried to understand this kenosis of the Son of God in the light of the christological doctrine of Christ's two natures.[3] Christ's kenosis means that in becoming human Christ renounces the attributes of divine majesty, so that he is not almighty, omnipresent, and omniscient, but becomes 'like another human being', which is to say a limited being, who encounters other human beings in a human way. But it was only in respect of his human nature that he 'renounced' (as the Gießen theologians said) these divine attributes, or 'concealed' them (as the seventeenth-century Tübingen theologians explained). Neither group was prepared to talk about a kenosis of the *divinity* of the eternal Logos. They merely wished to make room for the true and real humanity of Christ's life on earth.

In the nineteenth century the Lutheran 'kenotics' (Sartorius, Liebner, Hofmann, Thomasius, Frank, and Geß) initiated a new approach and, following patristic theology, took as subject of Philippians 2 not the Christ-who-has-become-human, but the Christ-in-his-becoming-human. His kenosis does not relate only to the attributes of majesty inherent in his divine nature; it already appertains to the divine being of the eternal Logos itself. Out of a self-limitation of the divine proceeds, as Thomasius taught, the Son of God-human being. His human form, which is the form of a servant, takes the place of his original divine form. But if nothing divine encounters other human beings in the incarnate Son of God, how could they then recognize him as the Christ of God? The kenotics replied — though admittedly with some degree of embarrassment — by postulating a dichotomy in the divine attributes: the incarnate Son of God 'renounces' the divine attributes of majesty related to the world, but retains the inward attributes that constitute God's essential nature: truth, holiness, love. For the act of kenosis is an act of God's free love for men and women.

To split the attributes of the Godhead in this way, as presupposition for the incarnation and the kenosis of the Son of God, remained so unsatisfactory that the nineteenth-century Lutheran kenotics found no successors. But they had detected a problem, for all that. The attributes of deity

---

Christushymnus Phil 2,6-11. Untersuchungen zur Gestalt und Aussage eines urchristlichen Psalms (Tübingen, 1976).

3. I should also like to recommend here P. Althaus's article "Kenosis," in RGG[3], III, pp. 1244-46, which is brief but very informative.

related to the world (omnipotence, omnipresence, omniscience, immortality, impassibility, and immutability) derive from Aristotle's general metaphysics. They have little to do with God's attributes according to the history of God to which the Bible testifies. So they cannot, either, be the attributes of the God in whom people believe 'for Christ's sake', and whom they therefore call 'the Father of Jesus Christ'. For that God 'was in Christ', according to Paul (2 Cor. 5:19), 'dwells' in Christ, according to the Gospel of John (14:11), and is 'worshiped' in the Son.

This brings us to the other attempt at understanding Christ's kenosis.

2. *Hans Urs von Balthasar* interprets the kenosis, not in the framework of the christological doctrine of the two natures, but in the context of the doctrine of the Trinity.[4] It is the essential nature of the eternal Son of the eternal Father to be 'obedient' in complete love and self-surrender, just as it is the essential nature of the eternal Father to communicate himself to the Son in complete love. If the incarnate Son becomes 'obedient' to the will of the eternal Father to the point of death on the cross, then what he does on earth is no different from what he does in heaven, and what he does in time is no different from what he does in eternity. So in 'the form of a servant' he is not denying his divine form, nor does he conceal it or renounce it; he reveals it. In his obedience he realizes on earth his eternal relationship to the Father. By virtue of the love for the Father which is intrinsic to his nature, in his obedience to the point of death on the cross he is completely one with the Father. For it is not just that he 'empties' himself 'to' the human being, and in the human being to the being of a servant, and in human mortality to the cruel death on the cross; in these things he 'empties' himself in obedience to the will of his divine Father in heaven. So kenosis is not a self-limitation and not a self-renunciation on God's part; it is the self-realization of the self-surrender of the Son to the Father in the trinitarian life of God. By virtue of limitless love, the inner life of the Trinity takes its impress from the reciprocal kenosis of the divine persons in relation to one another. The Son by virtue of his self-surrender exists wholly in the Father, the Father wholly in the Son, the Spirit wholly in the Father and the Son. Kenotic self-surrender is God's trinitarian nature, and is

4. H. Urs von Balthasar, *Mysterium Paschale* in *Mysterium Salutis,* III, 2 (Einsiedeln, 1964), pp. 133-326. I should also like to draw attention to the fruitfulness of the kenosis idea for Christian-Buddhist dialogue. See J. Cobb, Jr., ed., *The Emptying God: A Buddhist-Jewish-Christian Conversation* (New York, 1990). My dialogue with Masao Abe may also be found in this volume.

therefore the mark of all his works 'outwards' (the creation, reconciliation, and redemption of all things).

The inner-trinitarian kenosis is part of the inner-trinitarian *perichoresis,* in Latin: *circuminsessio.* The theological tradition used this concept to interpret the unity of God the Father and Jesus the Son of God as a unity, without mixing and without separating. The one is *in* the other, as the Gospel of John says of Jesus: "I am in the Father, and the Father is in me" (14:11). They are not one subject or one substance, but one community by their mutual indwelling in each other. Each person of the Trinity is in ecstasy out of itself in the other. "The Father is totally in the Son and totally in the Spirit. The Son is totally in the Father and totally in the Spirit. The Holy Spirit is totally in the Father, totally in the Son," says the Council of Florence (1438-1445). Seen from the other side, one may say that the divine persons of the Trinity become habitable for each other in their mutual perichoresis, giving each other open life-space for their mutual indwelling. Each trinitarian person is then not only subject of itself but also room for the other. In the perichoresis of the eternal Trinity we find therefore not only three persons but also three "broad rooms." It is not by chance that one of the secret names of God according to the Jewish tradition is MAKOM, "broad place" (see also Job 36:16; Psalm 18:19; 31:9).

This attempt to explain the kenosis of Christ as it is described in Philippians 2 by drawing on trinitarian doctrine goes beyond the interpretations of the nineteenth-century kenotics and is the next logical step. But it completely dispenses with the attributes of God that are related to the world and understood metaphysically, and uses solely the mutual inner-trinitarian relations of the Son to the Father and of the Father to the Son, as seen in the second part of the hymn. This premises that the world of human beings and death does not exist outside God, but that from the very beginning it lies within the mystery of the Trinity: the Father creates the world out of love for the Son — the Son redeems the world from sin and death though his emptying of himself out of love for the Father. If conversely we wanted to see the world outside the triune God, we should have to conjoin these inner-trinitarian relationships with God's relationships to the world; and then either go back, after all, to talking about the metaphysical attributes (omnipotence, immutability, etc.) or, alternatively, reform these world-related divine attributes in a biblical and christological sense. We have the kenotics to thank for at last having made the contradiction plain: the God who is metaphysically described in negative terms cannot suffer and cannot change; the God of the biblical history, in contrast, is 'faithful', but he can also 'repent' — 'be sorry' — be full of passion and mercy. And for that reason he is able to love and to suffer.[5]

We shall come back at the end of this essay to a new formulation of the divine attributes in relation to the world, and I shall offer some suggestions.

2. Jewish Theology of God's Shekinah

In the idea of the Shekinah — God's 'indwelling' — we find the Old Testament presupposition for the Christian idea of Christ's kenosis, and its Jewish equivalent.[6]

God's promise, "I will dwell in the midst of the Israelites," is already implicit in the covenant made with the chosen people: "I will be your God and you shall be my people."[7] The eternal, infinite God whom even the heavens cannot contain "comes down" (Exod. 3:8), so as "to dwell" among his powerless little people. Israel's history tells about this indwelling of God in vivid and pictorial terms. God led his people out of slavery in Egypt into the liberty of the promised land, and went ahead of them in "the pillar of cloud by day" and "the pillar of fire" by night. He dwelled in the Ark of the Covenant (the transportable altar of God's wandering people) until David brought the Ark to Mount Zion, where King Solomon then built the Temple for it. In the Holy of Holies of the Temple, the "indwelling" of God among the Israelites was present.

But what happened to the Shekinah when in 587 B.C. the Babylonians destroyed city and Temple? Did God withdraw his earthly indwell-

---

5. I have described the transformation of the metaphysically determined attribute of *immutabilitas Dei* into the biblically based faithfulness of God in my book *Theology of Hope,* trans. J. W. Leitch (London, 1967), and the transformation of the metaphysically determined attribute of the *impassibilitas Dei* into the passibility of love in *The Crucified God,* trans. R. A. Wilson and J. Bowden (London, 1974).

6. The standard work is A. M. Goldberg, *Untersuchungen über die Vorstellung von der Schechinah in der frühen rabbinischen Literatur* (Berlin, 1969).

7. B. Janowski, "'Ich will in eurer Mitte wohnen' Struktur und Genese der exilischen *Shekina*-Theologie," in *Gottes Gegenwart in Israel. Beiträge zur Theologie des Alten Testaments* (Neukirchen, 1993), pp. 119-47.

ing to his eternal presence in heaven? That would have been the end of his covenant, and the death of the people of Israel. Or did his Shekinah go into Babylonian exile with the captured people, remaining "in the midst of the Israelites" even though it was now homeless, humiliated, exiled, and exposed to the persecutions of the powerful nations? This second answer has kept Israel's faith in God alive in destruction and exile down to the present day. Ever since, God's Shekinah has been the comrade on the way and the companion in suffering of the homeless Israelites. The people suffer persecution and exile, and God's indwelling suffers with them. "In all their afflictions he was afflicted" (Isa. 63:9). Out of these Israelite experiences of God's Shekinah in its shared suffering later rabbinic literature conceived the theology of God's self-humiliation.[8] This theology led to the hope that at the end, with the redemption of the people from its suffering, God's Shekinah itself will be redeemed from the suffering it endures with the people, and with them will return to its eternal home.

This brings us to the theological interpretations of Israel's experiences of the Shekinah.

1. In his theology of Israel's prophets, *Abraham Heschel* developed out of Israel's experience of the Shekinah and its Sh'ma prayer to the One God a 'bipolar concept' of that One God. In history, God exists in a twofold presence: in heaven and in his exiled people, unlimited and limited, infinite and finite, free from suffering and death, while at the same time suffering and dying with his people.[9]

2. *Franz Rosenzweig* interpreted Israel's experience of the Shekinah with the help of Hegel's dialectic as a "self-differentiation in God": "God himself cuts himself off from himself, he gives himself away to his people, he suffers with their sufferings, he goes with them into the misery of the foreign land, he wanders with their wanderings."[10] He talked about a "divine suffering" on the part of "the banished God," who makes himself in need of redemption in fellowship with his people. This "redemption of God" is the homecoming of the departed Shekinah to the fullness of the

---

8. P. Kuhn, *Gottes Selbsterniedrigung in der Theologie der Rabbinen* (Munich, 1968). God carries Israel with its guilt "like a servant" (p. 84).

9. A. Heschel, *The Prophets* (New York, 1962), ch. 18: "Religion of Sympathy," pp. 307-13.

10. F. Rosenzweig, *Der Stern der Erlösung*, 3rd ed. (Heidelberg, 1954), II, 3, pp. 192-94 (*The Star of Redemption*, trans. W. W. Hallo [London, 1971]). The quotation is translated directly from the German.

One God. Something of this takes place in every Sh'ma Israel prayer, for in the acknowledgment of the One God, God himself is "united," according to Rosenzweig. God will be finally redeemed and united when the One God becomes the All-One God, and is "all in all," as he says with 1 Corinthians 15:28. Then heaven and earth will become God's dwelling place and all created being will participate in the indwelling livingness and glory. Max Jammer quotes a Jewish midrash that says: "We do not know whether God is the space of his world, or whether his world is his space."[11] The Christian answer is to draw on the idea of perichoresis — that is to say, mutual interpenetration: just as the person "who abides in love abides in God and God in him" (1 John 4:16), so in the consummation God will find space in the finite world in a divine way, and the finite world will find space in God in a 'worldly' way. That is a reciprocal interpenetration, in which the differences are not intermingled but where the distances are gathered up and ended.

3. Is the Creation of the World Linked with an Act of Kenosis on God's Part?

In the next two sections we shall turn to the creation of the world and the history of creation, asking about the possible interpretation and meaning of the kenosis idea for the presence of God and his future in creation and in the preservation of the world.

In our hymns we find two verses in which the Creator and sustainer of the world is conceived of in "the form of a servant" which Christ assumes. Luther writes:

Er äußert sich all seiner G'walt,
wird niedrig und gering,
und nimmt an sich ein's Knecht's Gestalt,
der Schöpfer aller Ding.

And W. H. Vanstone:

11. Quoted by Max Jammer in *Concepts of Space* (Cambridge, Mass., 1954; Oxford, 1955).

Thou art God, no monarch Thou
thron'd in easy state to reign.
Thou art God, whose arms of love
aching, spent, the world sustain.

In his Christmas hymn Luther sees in "the self-emptying Christ" the
Creator of the world, while Vanstone sees in the sustainer of the world
"the crucified God." With these figures of speech, both writers express the
conviction that the creation and sustaining of the world are not simply
works of the almighty God, but that in them God gives and communi-
cates himself, and is thus himself present in his works.

a. Is creation an act of *divine self-definition?* If in his freedom God re-
solves to create a being who is not divine, who can co-exist with his own
divine being, then this resolve does not affect the created being only; it
touches God's own being too. He determines himself to be the Creator
who lets a creation co-exist with himself.[12] Logically speaking, God's self-
determination to be the Creator precedes the act of creation. God determines himself before he determines the world. It is therefore correct to see
God's self-determination to be the Creator of a non-divine world as already a self-limitation on God's part: (1) out of his infinite possibilities
God realizes this particular one, and renounces all others; (2) God's determination to be Creator is linked with the consideration for his creation
that allows it space and time and its own movement, so that it is not
crushed by the divine reality or totally absorbed by it. By differentiating
himself as Creator from a created world, God creates a reality that is not
divine but is not Nothing either, and preserves it by distancing himself
from it. How can a finite world co-exist with the infinite God? Does it set a
limit to the limitless God, or does God limit himself? If this limit or frontier between infinity and finitude is already 'fore-given' to God, then God
is not infinite. If God is in his very essence infinite, then any such limit or
frontier exists only through his self-limitation. That makes it possible for a
finite world to co-exist with God. This self-limitation of God's which is
given with the differentiation between Creator and creation is viewed in
theology as the first act of grace. For the limitation of his infinity and omnipresence is itself an act of his omnipotence. Only God can limit God.

b. Is creation an act of *divine self-contraction?* Before God went out of

12. K. Barth, *Church Dogmatics*, III, 1, section 42 (Edinburgh, 1960), pp. 330ff.

himself in order to create a non-divine world, he withdrew himself into himself in order to make room for the world and to concede it a space. That was Isaac Luria's idea. He called it *zimzum*. According to the Kabbala, the infinite Holy One, the One whose light primordially filled the whole universe, withdrew his light and concentrated it wholly on his own substance, thereby creating empty space.[13] God withdrew his omnipresence in order to concede space for the presence of the creation. In this way creation comes into being in the space of God's kenosis. In the dispute between Newton, with his idea about absolute space, and Leibniz, with his notion of relative spaces, Henry More introduced into the discussion this Jewish-kabbalistic idea of *makom-kadosh,* though without perceiving the possibility it offered for solving this dispute about the concept of space.[14] Gershom Scholem took up Luria's *zimzum* idea, using it to provide new explanatory grounds for the Jewish-Christian concept of the *creatio ex nihilo:* "Where God withdraws himself from himself to himself, he can call something forth which is not of divine essence or divine being."[15] Speaking metaphorically, when God contracts himself in order creatively to go out of himself, then in his self-contraction he gathers together his creative energies. It may be noted in passing that in interpreting the 'Big Bang' *(Urknall),* similar metaphors are used scientifically to explain the primal impetus *(Urschwung).*

c. Is creation an act of *divine self-humiliation?* Many Christian theologians from Nicholas of Cusa down to Emil Brunner have seen in the fact that God commits himself to this finite and fragile creation a first act of self-humiliation on God's part, an act continued in his descent to his people Israel and reaching its nadir in Christ's self-surrender to death on the cross.[16] "The Lamb slain from the foundation of the world" (Rev. 18:8) is

13. G. Scholem, "Schöpfung aus Nichts und Selbstverschränkung Gottes," in *Eranos Jahrbuch* 25 (1956): 87-119.

14. For more detail see J. Moltmann, *God in Creation,* ch. 6: "The Space of Creation," pp. 140-57, esp. 153-57.

15. G. Scholem, "Schöpfung aus Nichts," p. 117; see also his *Major Trends in Jewish Mysticism* (New York, 1954; London, 1955).

16. E. Brunner, *Dogmatics,* vol. 2, trans. O. Wyon (London, 1952), p. 20: "This, however, means that God does not wish to occupy the whole of space Himself, but that He wills to make room for other forms of existence. In so doing He limits Himself. . . . The *kenosis* which reaches its paradoxical climax in the cross of Christ, began with the Creation of the world."

a symbol to show that there was aleady a cross in the heart of God before the world was created and before Christ was crucified on Golgotha. From the creation, by way of reconciliation, right down to the redemption, God's self-humiliation and self-emptying deepen and unfold. Why? Because the creation proceeds from God's love, and this love respects the particular existence of all things, and the freedom of the human beings who have been created. A love that gives the beloved space, allows them time, and expects and demands of them freedom is the power of lovers who can withdraw in order to allow the beloved to grow and to come. Consequently it is not just self-giving that belongs to creative love; it is self-limitation too; not only affection, but respect for the unique nature of the others as well. If we apply this perception to the Creator's relation to those he has created, what follows is a restriction of God's omnipotence, omnipresence, and omniscience for the sake of conceding room to live to those he has created.

Hans Jonas took up the *zimzum* idea early on, linking it first with the evolutionary world picture, and later also with experiences of death in Auschwitz.[17] For him 'omnipotence' is a meaningless concept, because almighty power is power without an object, and would therefore be a powerless power. "Power is a relational term," and links a dominating subject with a dominated object. God's creative power therefore includes a "self-renunciation of unlimited power" for the sake of created beings. If God as Creator commits himself to this world, he at the same time delivers himself up to this "world-in-its-becoming." Whatever happens to it, happens to God too. As Creator, God becomes part of the fate of the world. Hans Jonas calls this fate "the odyssey of the universe." God becomes dependent on the world, as the world is dependent on him. They share a common history.

Kierkegaard detected similar lines of thought in Hegel's idea of world

---

17. H. Jonas, *Zwischen Nichts und Ewigkeit. Zur Lehre vom Menschen* (Göttingen, 1963), pp. 55-62 (with reference to the doctrine of evolution); F. Stern and H. Jonas, *Reflexionen finsterer Zeit* (Tübingen, 1984), pp. 63-86: Der Gottesbegriff nach Auschwitz: "So that the world might be, and might exist for itself, God renounced his own being; he divested himself of his divinity in order to receive it again from the odyssey of time, laden with the fortuitous harvest of unforeseeable temporal experience, transfigured, or perhaps also distorted by them. . . . Only with creation out of nothing do we have the *unity* of the divine principle together with its *self*-restriction, which gives *space* for the existence and autonomy of a world" (pp. 68, 83).

history as "God's biography," and maintained in opposition that only almighty power can limit itself, can give itself and withdraw itself, in order to make the recipient independent; so that in the divine act of self-humiliation we also have to respect an act of God's omnipotence. We might put it epigrammatically and say that God never appears mightier than in the act of his self-limitation, and never greater than in the act of his self-humiliation.

What is true of the self-limitation of omnipotence in God's love for those he has created can also be said about the other metaphysical attributes of his divinity: omnipresence, omniscience, inviolability, and self-sufficiency. God does not know everything in advance because he does not will to know everything in advance. He waits for the response of those he has created, and lets their future come. God is not incapable of suffering; he opens himself in his Shekinah for the sufferings of his people, and in the incarnation of the Son for the sufferings of the love which is to redeem the world. In a certain way God thus becomes dependent on the response of his beloved creatures. In Christian theology one would not go so far as to declare God "in need of redemption" together with his people Israel; but nevertheless, God has laid the sanctification of his Name and the doing of his will in the hands of human beings, and thus also, in its way, the coming of his kingdom. It must be viewed as part of God's self-humiliation that God does not desire to be without those he has created and loves, and therefore waits for them to repent and turn back, leaving them time, so that he may come to his kingdom together with them.

4. The Preservation and Consummation of Creation Through God's Patience and the Driving Energies of His Spirit

If the creation of a world not divine is already linked with a kenotic self-limitation on God's part, how much more can this then be said about its preservation for its consummation! In his relation to the world, God is not almighty in the sense that as *causa prima* he effects everything in everything through the *causae secundae* — good and evil, becoming and passing away, genesis and dissolution. The person who assumes that this is the way in which God "so wondrously reigneth" ends up with the unanswerable theodicy question: If God is almighty, why evil? Either he is omnipotent and effects everything, in which case he is not good; or he is good, but then he cannot be almighty. If we start from God's kenosis, we discover his almighty power in his almighty suffering patience, as Russian Orthodox theology says. It is not God's power that is almighty. What is almighty is his love, about which Paul says: "Love is long-suffering and kind. . . . It bears all things, believes all things, hopes all things, endures all things" (1 Cor. 13:4, 7). In this eulogy of love, Paul heaps up the words invoking the 'all'. Through the power of his patience God sustains this world with its contradictions and conflicts. As we know from human history, patience is the most powerful action because it has time, whereas acts of violence never have time and can therefore win only short-term victories. Patience is superior to violence. God does not sustain and rule the world like an autocrat or a dictator, who permits no freedom; he is more like a suffering servant who bears the world with its guilt and its griefs as Atlas carries the world on his shoulders. (Cf. Exod. 19:4; Num. 11:12; Deut. 1:31; Isa. 66:12; 53:4; Matt. 8:17; Heb. 1:3. God's conservation of the creation is in biblical language again and again expressed by God's carrying of the world. As God's creation, the world doesn't exist per se, but per Deum.) To put it without these metaphors: God acts in the history of nature and human beings through his patient and silent presence, by way of which he gives those he has created space to unfold, time to develop, and power for their own movement. We look in vain for God in the history of nature or in human history if what we are looking for are special divine interventions. Is it not much more that God waits and awaits, that — as process theology rightly says — he 'experiences' the history of the world and human beings, that he is "patient and of great goodness," as Psalm 103:8 puts it? Israel's psalms never tire of praising God's great goodness and patience. It is because of his steadfast goodness that "we are not consumed" (Lam. 3:22 AV) — "not yet cut off," to follow Luther's translation. "Waiting" is never disinterested passivity, but the highest form of interest in the other. Waiting means expecting, expecting means inviting, inviting means attracting, alluring, and enticing. By doing this, the waiting and awaiting one keeps an open space for the other, gives the other time, and creates possibilities of life for the other. This is what the theological tradition called *creatio continua* and what differentiates the ongoing creation from the *creatio originalis* in the beginning and from the *creatio nova* in the end.

But why should God bear and endure the world with its contradictions and conflicts and catastrophes? According to Aristotelian metaphysics, which have been taken over by Christian theology down to the present day, God is the supreme reality *(summum ens)* and pure act *(actus purus)*. All reality derives from, and is caused by, the highest reality, which is God, and therefore points towards this divine reality. Consequently God must also be the power who is all-efficacious in everything. It was only with Kierkegaard and Heidegger that a new idea began to take shape: "higher than actuality stands *possibility*."[18] And all actuality is nothing other than 'realized possibility'. Possibility can become actuality, but actuality never again becomes possibility.

If we put these two modalities of being together with the two modes of time, future and past, then future is the sphere of possibilities but past the realm of actuality. So the future is 'higher' than the past, because in history the future turns into irreversible past, whereas the past never again becomes future. If we switch over from the metaphysics of reality to a metaphysics of possibility, we can then view divine Being as the supreme possibility, as the source of possibilities, and as the transcendental making-possible of the possible. In the theology of time, what corresponds is the future as the transcendent source of time, as Georg Picht has shown, following Heidegger.[19]

If we apply this to our problem, it means that the God who in patience bears and endures the history of nature and human beings, allows time and gives time, and in so doing makes possible ever-new possibilities, which are either realized or not realized, and can be used for further development but also for annihilation. All systems of matter and life are complex systems with a fixed actuality/past and, in each case, a specifically open scope of future/possibility. Their present is the interface between the two times in which more complex structures of reality can be built up. With them there also grow in each case the scope of possibilities. But there can be negative realizations of possibilities too, through which these open systems destroy themselves.

It is in the gift of future and the stream of new possibilities that we have to perceive God's activity in the history of open systems of matter

18. M. Heidegger, *Being and Time,* trans. J. Macquarrie and E. Robinson (London, 1962), p. 63; cf. also p. 378: "The primary phenomenon of primordial and authentic temporality is the future."

19. G. Picht, "Die Zeit und die Modalitäten," in *Hier und Jetzt: Philosophieren nach Auschwitz und Hiroshima,* vol. 1 (Stuttgart, 1980), pp. 362-74.

and life — and it is out of these open systems that the world we know exists. This means, not least, that all open systems point beyond themselves to the sphere of what they can be, and are read theologically as true symbols of that future in which they are in God and God is in them, when they will participate unhindered in God's indwelling fullness of possibility without being destroyed by it, and become that for which God has destined them. The goal of God's kenosis in the creation and preservation of the world is that *future* which we describe with the symbols of the kingdom of God and the new creation, or 'world without end'.

Cosmos and Kenosis

KEITH WARD

[In the progress of love] each step is a precarious step into the unknown, in which each triumph contains new potential for tragedy, and each tragedy can be redeemed into a wider triumph.

Love's Endeavour, Love's Expense, p. 63

The theology of kenosis is associated primarily with the work of some Lutheran theologians in Germany and with Charles Gore in England. In a way that has not always been noticed, it posed a radical challenge to the traditional concept of God, which had been developed by a long line of Christian theologians, most notably perhaps Augustine, Anselm, and Aquinas.

The traditional concept of God in Christianity is that God is eternal, in the sense of being timeless — that is, without temporal relation to anything in time, and without internal relations of a temporal nature. It follows from this that God is strictly immutable. Whatever happens in the created cosmos makes no difference to God, and does not change God in any way. The cosmos is created by a non-temporal act, and God creates every moment of time, from first to last, in one and the same act of intentional causation.

This in turn entails that the incarnation of the second hypostasis of the Triune being of God is effected by God in the very same non-temporal act by which God also creates and consummates the created order. The in-

152

carnation causes no change in God, but lies in a particular relation of the created nature of Jesus to the creator. It is not literally true that "the Word became flesh" (John 1:14), since the eternal Word cannot become anything. It must always remain timelessly and changelessly what it is. The situation is rather that the human nature of Jesus has a unique relation to the eternal Word, a relation of enosis,[1] unity, by which it expresses in time the nature of the Word and manifests in a uniquely direct way the salvific intentions of the Triune God. The human nature is said to be 'assumed' by the divine person of the Word, but exactly what that assumption consists in remains a mystery of faith. While it can be imagined as a possibility, the human mind cannot gain a clear comprehension of it.

Important points for the traditional account are that the incarnation causes no change in the nature of God, and that it is not a new idea which occurred to God subsequently to his creating the universe. It is part of the one creative divine act, and thus may rightly be said to have been willed from the beginning of creation.

The nineteenth-century Lutheran idea[2] of kenosis radically challenged this traditional account. Basing their theology of incarnation on Philippians 2:7 ("Christ Jesus, though he was in the form of God . . . emptied himself, taking the form of a servant"), kenotic theologians held that the incarnation brought about a radical change in the eternal Word. The Word, being in the form of God, is properly omnipotent, omniscient, and perfectly good. When the Word becomes flesh, however, he empties himself of some of these divine attributes. Generally speaking, when the Word takes the form of a man, he gives up omnipotence and omniscience. He actually renounces those divine properties, though he receives them back from the Father after the ascension.

It may seem that Jesus would at least retain the divine property of perfect goodness, and many kenotic theologians held that the Word retains the 'moral attributes' of God. But even that is doubtful. For divine goodness is such that God is incapable of sin, not subject to obligation and not subject to temptation. But even the greatest human goodness is capable of sin, even if it never actually sins. It is subject to obligation and

---

1. I am using the Anglicized term, as it occurs in the Oxford English Dictionary, of the Greek *henosis*.

2. Jürgen Moltmann says something about earlier Lutheran theologians in this volume.

it can be tempted, as Jesus apparently was. In that case, Jesus as the incarnate Word would not even retain the property of divine goodness. He might possess perfect human goodness, but that would be different in kind from the divine goodness, which is not capable of sin or obligation. In the same way, Jesus might possess the greatest possible human power and knowledge, but this would not be divine omnipotence and omniscience, which are outside the reach of human nature.

So it was held that if God is truly to become man, he must set aside or radically curtail his divine properties. Such properties are retained, however, by the Father and by the Holy Spirit, and can be restored to Christ at the proper time. Such a kenotic view entails that there is change in God, and therefore that there is time, which alone makes change possible, in God. If the Word really became a human being, it also entails that there is suffering in God, so that God is passible, changed by what happens in the created cosmos.

For the traditional view, the divine nature does not suffer, though it can be said that 'God suffers', in the sense that the human nature which is assumed by the Word suffers. For the kenotic view, it is not the case that a human nature is assumed by an eternal Word. The Word really changes and limits himself to become human, and so really suffers and dies as human, before taking up his divine properties again (if, indeed, he can ever really do that so long as he remains in human form).

Why did the Lutheran theologians make this change in the concept of God? Part of the impetus for a kenotic christology lies in the desire to preserve the sense that God enters fully into the human situation, understands it from the inside, and shares the human condition. Many people have the feeling that if a changeless God simply assumes a human nature to the divine nature, the sense in which God shares in human suffering is purely verbal, and that something of the pathos and depth of the incarnation is lost. Luther's strong sense of the importance of the passion and the cross in Christianity led him to an insistence that the divine nature of the Word must truly share in suffering, and thus enter fully into the human situation.

Another reason for adopting a kenotic christology is, to put it in the broadest theological terms, the rejection of a Platonic concept of God. In Platonic philosophy the timeless is superior to the temporal, the changeless to the changing, and the intelligible and universal is superior to the material and particular. The classical Christian concept of God was constructed

154

on Platonic lines, so that God was seen as timeless, changeless, intelligible, and universal (a subsistent Form). In modern times Platonism has been generally rejected as a worldview. Since the rise of the sciences, especially, the material and particular have been seen as the truly 'real', while the universal is an abstraction. So time and change, aspects of the material, become important aspects of reality, not simply illusory or merely apparent.

Interestingly, there has been a partial reversal of this change in modern cosmology. Quantum cosmologists are apt to talk of time and space as just four dimensions of a multidimensional reality in which time does not 'flow', and timelessness becomes again the ultimate reality, of which the 'arrow of time' is a phenomenal appearance. This remains a highly controversial topic, but it must be noted that these quasi-Platonic speculations do not usually find much use for the notion of God, positing instead a myth of self-existent mathematical structures (quantum fluctuations) without intrinsic value or purpose. It is Platonism without 'the Good', and therefore of little theological help. In the early modern period, however (in Newtonian physics, for example), the existence of particulars in an objectively existing time was widely accepted as characterizing ultimate reality. Partly in accordance with such views, some Protestant, especially Lutheran, theologians developed a much more personalist view of God, which would be free of Platonic influences.

This is associated also with a greater stress, since the Renaissance, on human freedom, creativity, and individuality. Individuals are seen as having an ultimate moral freedom, a uniqueness that cannot be dissolved into some greater cosmic unity, and a genuine creativity that can change the world, either for better or for worse. In the light of such changes in worldview, God is reconceived as the most creative, free, changing, and individual reality, rather than being seen as a timeless pure Form.

All these changes worked together to produce a kenotic view of God and of the incarnation, particularly in Lutheran theology. In that tradition, two main views developed, after the initial systematic presentation by Thomasius (1802-1875). The Tübingen school held that the incarnate Word possesses the divine attributes but does not use them. Such possession without manifestation is sometimes called krypsis (hiding). The Giessen theologians held, more radically, that the Logos incarnate emptied himself of the divine attributes — that is, kenosis.

Against the kenotic view, traditional theologians feel that for God, even for the second hypostasis of a Triune God, to lose some essential divine properties, even temporarily, is simply for God to cease to be God, and to change into something else, so that proper worship for the divine Word, which is due to him even in his incarnate state, is undermined. The krypsis view is not subject to this criticism, though it is widely rejected on the ground that it involves some form of change in God.

What is at stake in this dispute? I would be hesitant to draw immediate links between such theories and Christian practice. Yet some link might be drawn between an ideal of God as an impassible changeless being and a Christian practice that seeks the cultivation of an attitude of impassibility and disconnection from temporal things as ideals of human life. And a link might be drawn between the ideal of God as a relational, passionate being and a Christian practice that seeks to be involved creatively in worldly action with others, and that sees change in terms of positive possibility.

In any case I think that kenotic theologians are right in thinking that God truly shares in the human condition, and so feels the suffering of every suffering creature, as well as sharing the joy of every finite happiness. But if that is so, one might well think that the divine sharing in finite experience and action cannot be confined to just one case on the planet earth, the case of Jesus. God must share in all finite experience, wherever in the universe it is. Such sharing does not require incarnation as its necessary condition. What it requires is that God truly feels, by a direct and empathetic apprehension, every experience that creatures have. One may feel such a thing is involved in the possession of true omniscience — not merely a factual registering by God that something is the case, but God's acquaintance with what each experience is like.

For classical notions of divine omniscience, God's knowledge consists of a sort of intellectual knowledge of every true proposition. It is quasi-propositional knowledge, and excludes feeling or passion, which were regarded as defects in a perfect being. Nevertheless, God was said to exist in a state of perfect bliss, and so some analogy to feeling existed in God. It just was not considered to be of cognitive significance, and it was certainly not dependent upon the world in any way.

It may well be thought, however, that no being is truly omniscient if it lacks knowledge of what it feels like to experience suffering or happiness. If I know that the proposition 'You are in pain' is true, but I do not know what it feels like for you to be in pain, then there is something I do not know — and that something, you may well think, is the most important thing of all. If that is so, then any omniscient being must know what it feels like for creatures to feel as they do. That may be called affective knowledge, a much more involving and intense thing than propositional knowledge.

The classical theist may say that it is just not possible for God to know what pains feel like (at least in the divine nature). God can only have propositional, not affective, knowledge. It is noteworthy that classical theologians do place restrictions on what is possible for God at this point. Omniscience, even for the classical theologian, must be interpreted to mean: knowledge of everything that it is logically possible for a being with the divine nature to know. There is no such thing as logically unqualified omniscience. We all place restrictions on divine possibilities at some point (that will become important when considering divine omnipotence). But are there really good reasons for denying the possibility of divine affective knowledge? I think the main reason offered is that it would be a defect for a maximally valuable being to feel pain, even by empathetic knowledge. But that is precisely what has been strongly questioned in post–nineteenth-century theology.

The crucial nature of the change is this: in classical theories, God is considered in isolation, as it were, as a being of completely self-contained perfection. Perfection is a state of God, whatever else exists or occurs, and it cannot suffer diminution or change in any way. God is exclusively infinite and perfect. All that is finite or imperfect lies outside of God, and does not affect God in any way. For post-classical theories (and Hegel is perhaps the major influence here), God is inclusively infinite, and the divine perfection must include relationship to whatever other realities exist. So God relates to finite creatures in ways which make the divine reality different than it would have been had there been no such creatures. For such a more relational or participative view of God, it would be an imperfection not to know affectively what creaturely experiences are like. Any being that co-exists with suffering creatures would be less perfect if it failed to have affective knowledge of what those creatures experience. If one takes that seriously, then one may say that not just the incarnation, but the creation of conscious and rational beings itself is a kenotic act on God's part. For it will involve a giving up of pure divine bliss, and accepting many experiences of pain and suffering. It will involve a giving up of complete control, and accepting the freedom of created beings to make their own decisions, however misdirected. It will involve giving up complete knowledge, and accepting that much about the future must be unknown until it is determined by the actions of creatures. These are real limitations, and this may be thought of as a sort of kenosis, a giving up of some great goods, in order that free creatures may exist in independence, community, and creativity.

This is not, however, kenosis in the sense of giving up divine properties in order just to allow others to possess the values of freedom and community. It is also a way of adding new and distinctive values to the divine being itself. For the creation of finite agents with a real degree of autonomy adds to God himself the possibility of cooperating with them in creative action, of delighting in their existence and in the values they bring into being, and of bringing the cosmic process to a final consummation in which all the values it has brought forth in the long course of its existence will be conserved and apprehended in God forever.

In other words, this sort of kenosis is not just a self-giving. It is also, and equally importantly, a self-realization, a way in which God realizes possibilities that are eternally present in the divine being, and comes to experience new forms of value that otherwise would never have been actualized. When God gives up pure bliss, he obtains in return many new sorts of values that could only be actualized in a cosmic process from which finite agents emerge. When God gives up total control, he obtains relationship in community with creatures. When God gives up full knowledge of the future, he obtains the possibility of genuinely new creativity, undetermined even by his own previous nature.

By self-limitation, God obtains many new sorts of values that would not otherwise be obtainable. Of course, these values are mixed with many sorts of disvalues. Along with the values finite agents create are all the forms of suffering they endure. Along with the positive cooperation God can experience with finite agents, are the many forms of obstruction to the divine will that such agents realize. Along with new creativity go possibilities for destruction and conflict within the cosmos. Nevertheless, theists are committed to believing that the good will far outweigh the bad, and that the bad can itself in some way be redeemed, both in the experience of God and, ultimately, for the creatures God can unite to the divine experience.

God, on this view, does not just limit the divine being in order that free finite agents might exist. God realizes, makes actual, aspects of the divine being that otherwise would have remained potential. Entering into relationship and communion, and cooperating in realizing new forms of finite value, are realizations of great values in and for the divine nature it-self. Perhaps some such realization is essential to the divine nature, so that God necessarily creates other personal agents. If one thinks that 'God is love' (1 John 4:16), that love is an essential property of the divine nature, and that love can only be properly exercised in relation to others who are free to reciprocate love or not, then the creation of some universe contain-ing free finite agents seems to be an implication of the divine nature. However, trying to say what is or is not essential to the divine nature is a rather presumptuous exercise, and perhaps the most one can do here is to draw attention to a range of implications that follow from various inter-pretations of the idea of God.

Some would hold that God could have remained in unchanging bliss, all-determining power, and unrestricted knowledge, but freely chose not to do so in order to create a universe of finite persons. Some would hold that God can realize love adequately in the inner relationships of the per-sons of the Trinity, but chooses to realize a different form of love in rela-tion to creatures. And some would hold that a truly loving God must cre-ate a universe of genuinely other persons in order to realize the essential divine nature. It is hard to know how to decide what is essential to the di-vine nature. Perhaps we could be content to say that God certainly has the greatest possible power and knowledge that any being could have, and has in fact chosen to realize it in the creation of a universe of free persons, which entails certain restrictions on those powers — restrictions that are necessary to enable genuinely free finite persons to exist.

Those restrictions are such that some actual and much possible suf-fering is necessarily entailed in creation. The type and extent of suffering will depend largely on the choices free creatures make, though some ele-ment of suffering seems inevitable in any universe in which there is an evolutionary emergence of potentially self-aware and self-directing agents. Having very little knowledge of the inner structure of the physical cosmos, and even less knowledge of the essential nature of God, we are quite unable to say just what those necessities are that cause conflict and suffering to arise in the world. We view them as necessities because it is unacceptable to say that God would positively intend suffering to exist, and yet all suffering must arise from the divine nature as its only ultimate source. We are thus logically compelled to say that while all suffering arises from God, it must do so, not as intended by God, but as necessarily implied in the sort of universe God has created — a universe in which many great goods exist that otherwise could not have existed, and in which all evil will ultimately be overcome by divine goodness, which is what God positively intends.

For Christians, this is not simply a piece of abstract metaphysics. It is a view based firmly on the disclosure of the nature of God in the person of Jesus. As Canon Vanstone has powerfully shown, that nature is revealed in the cross and resurrection of Jesus as one of unrestricted love, and as one that does not simply eliminate suffering, but shares in and overcomes suffering by the patience of love.

If one asks, "Why did God not just create the good things?" the answer is that even God could not just create the sort of morally responsible, creative beings we are in a wholly good universe, without any actual or possible conflict or suffering in it. In a way not discernible in detail by us, evil arises from the divine nature, though in an unintended way, and in a way that is always opposed by, and that ultimately can be overcome by, goodness, a goodness that God intends.

This picture involves a double reversal of the classical view that God is wholly immutable. God limits the divine properties in order that a cosmos of free finite agents should exist. But God thereby realizes new aspects of the divine nature as God enters into real relationship with creatures. God not only suffers new things. God also enjoys and delights in new things. And in the end all those good things are to be conserved in God, and perhaps shared with creatures, for ever. There is an addition to the divine being as well as a limitation of it, and the two are essentially bound together. So if we can speak of a kenosis in God, a renunciation of his absolute and unmixed perfection, we must also speak of a pleroma, or fulfillment, in God, by which new forms of perfection are added by creatures to the divine being.

This is in accordance with the continuation of the passage in Philippians 2:5-11, which says that, because of Christ's self-emptying, "God has highly exalted him." The moment of self-emptying is followed by the moment of divine exaltation, in which the whole of creation is ultimately to be included (Eph. 1:10).

This form of kenosis is not a loss of such essential divine properties as omnipotence and omniscience. Indeed, it is the way in which they are exercised. There is nothing wrong with speaking of 'kenosis', as long as it is understood to mean a self-limitation that makes possible new forms of divine glory. It may seem that God could exist in perfect bliss, but in fact

God has affective knowledge of a world in which pain and suffering exist. It may seem that God could control all things unilaterally, but in fact God acts in such a way as to make creaturely freedom possible. It may seem that God could know the future completely and in every detail, but in fact God renounces such knowledge in order to let creaturely creativity exist. There are necessities of the divine nature which mean that God cannot exist in a state of unmixed bliss, of all-determining power and unrestricted knowledge, if there is to be a world of free and creative personal agents.

God wills to realize the divine nature in creation, relationship, and cooperation. Without such a willed self-realization God would not be the God known to be revealed in Jesus. Whether or not there was a real alternative to some such creation, we have no way of telling. Even if there was not, one can reasonably say that God truly wills creation. For 'willing' does not need to imply some alternative that might have been willed instead. Such willing may itself be, as the classical tradition affirmed, an essential part of the divine nature, which is necessarily what it is. Thus God may will kenosis, not as something that might not have been willed, but as something that truly expresses the divine nature as love.

It may be held that such a view of kenosis, not as divine loss but as divinely willed restraint, is a more accurate reflection of the passage in Philippians. For what that passage says is not that Jesus gave up some of his divine or human attributes, but that he did not insist on status and power. Instead, he became a servant, and "humbled himself." That is a matter, not primarily of what attributes one has, but of how one exercises them. Jesus could perhaps have claimed instant obedience, and ordered the apostles to serve him. Instead, he washed their feet and gave his life for them. The New Testament scholar James Dunn has proposed an influential interpretation of the Philippians passage which denies that it refers to some decision of a pre-existing Christ, deciding to become incarnate on earth. Rather, he argues, it speaks only of the human Jesus who, like the first Adam, had the form of God by being a perfect image of God. The passage then would be asserting that Jesus did not take advantage of his superiority over virtually all other humans in status and ability. Instead, he showed what the image of God truly is by serving others, by healing, forgiving, and submitting in love to the power of evil.

The lesson of kenosis is a moral one. It does not speak of a renunciation of ontological powers, but of a way of exercising those powers in love rather than in pride. This is how Jesus' human life was lived, and it gives a true picture of the nature of the God who seeks to help humans in love rather than to dominate them. Whether one accepts Dunn's interpretation or the more traditional view that the Philippians passage is about the eternal Word becoming flesh, the important point remains that one is not speaking so much of a literal renunciation of certain divine powers, but of the choice of a way of exercising those powers that empowers creatures to enter into conscious relationship with God. This is a sort of self-limitation, but one that I have suggested might be seen as both divinely willed and as necessarily implicit in the divine nature.

If this is a true picture of God, one might say that God does not compel all rational creatures to obey him, but seeks by the persuasion of love to draw them to himself. Kenosis, then, belongs to the creation of rational creatures even before it belongs to incarnation. And because rational creatures are integral parts of the physical universe, that universe must from the first possess an autonomy and openness that will prepare an appropriate environment in which free and rational creatures can emerge. One can thus see a form of kenosis in the creation of the universe, inasmuch as God restrains the divine power to allow an autonomous universe to develop. There is a cosmological self-limitation of infinite divine power, which makes possible the existence of an autonomous cosmos wherein freedom and creativity can in due course emerge and flourish, but in which they can also be impeded by the existence of communities of finite created agents.

The incarnation is not a necessary condition of cosmic kenosis. God can will to cooperate with creatures, share in their experiences, and inspire their new and creative actions, whether or not there is an incarnation. The Christian belief, however, is that God the Word did become incarnate as man, and that incarnation is an eminently appropriate form of divine self-revelation. The life of Jesus is important because it shows the nature of what God always and everywhere is. It is the revelation of the nature of God in a human person. The life of Jesus is not the only place where God acts in persuasive, self-giving love to draw creatures to the divine. It is the place where God's universal salvific action is disclosed in a paradigmatic way to human beings.

For this to be true, the life of Jesus must be plausibly seen to be completely informed and freely directed by the Spirit of God. There is here a sort of double kenosis — the kenosis of Jesus is that he empties himself of pride and egoism, so that he may be filled with the Spirit of God. The kenosis of God is that the divine being is emptied of perfect bliss and all-determining power, so that the passion of Jesus and the creative action of Jesus can become true expressions of the divine nature in time. Neither form of kenosis is a loss of essential human or divine attributes. In this mutual self-limitation one human life and the divine life are bound together in an intimate and inexpressible way, so that they may be said to be one: Jesus is the Christ, the eternal Word of God in time.

This is not what has been usually called a kenotic christology, for the Word does not change into a man. In some ways it is more like the traditional christology, for which the Word assumes to itself a human nature. Yet what is different from the traditional view is that the Word is a passionate, related, and therefore temporal hypostasis of the divine being. In the life of Jesus, the Word obtains a clear and full expression within history. The kenosis of Jesus makes possible the manifestation at a particular point of earthly history of that cosmic kenosis of the divine being which makes creation itself possible.

The incarnation is also a specific act of God that accomplishes in a human person the saving destiny God wills for all. In Jesus there may be seen a threefold manifestation of the nature and activity of God in relation to the created universe. The first moment of this divine activity is kenosis, the self-limiting expression of divine power that brings it into relation with a universe containing finite moral agents. In this relation, God does not order all things by divine fiat, but seeks to help and empower moral agents to formulate and attain their own objectives, insofar as they promise to realize good. This means that God will have affective knowledge of forms of suffering and evil, which constitutes a real renunciation of unmixed divine bliss. It means that God will constitute the divine being in relation to others who may to some extent frustrate the divine will. This is a real form of self-limitation, even though it is a true expression and self-manifestation of the divine nature, not a renunciation of that nature.

Jesus' life of healing the sick, forgiving the guilt-ridden, befriending social outcasts, and undermining hypocrisy, is a very good image of the compassionate and persuasive love of God. Because of this disclosure, God can be worshiped not only as the all-powerful source and sustainer of all beings, but as a Father (or indeed a Mother) who cares for finite persons as his children, and wishes them to become fully conscious of his

163

loving presence. In the moment of kenosis, God relates the divine being to creatures who have a proper autonomy and otherness, which it is the divine will not to infringe.

The second moment of the divine relation to the cosmos is that of enosis, a mysterious but intimate uniting of divine personhood and finite personhood, so that finite lives can become true images of the divine nature and mediators of divine power, so that divine and creaturely persons become one. It is through the activity of the Holy Spirit that God acts on this planet within human persons to transform them into transparent images and effective instruments of the divine being. In this relation, creatures do not remain as beings separate and distinct from their heavenly Father, however closely related to him they are in love and respect. Their lives are interpenetrated by the divine Spirit, so that they may, at their best, say with St. Paul, "Not I live, but Christ lives in me" (Gal. 2:20). The Spirit that found exemplary fulfillment in Jesus Christ can also be in the lives of his disciples, to the extent that a person may find it almost impossible to distinguish what she does and what the Spirit does in her. The inward unity between divine and human was fully realized in the life of Jesus, but it is part of Christian faith to hope that it will be partly realized, at least, in the lives of all believers. God not only limits divine power to relate to finite persons as if he were a person (so Christians believe that God relates to us in and through the person of the risen Christ). God also actively empowers finite persons, so as to give them a share in the divine reconciling and redeeming activity in the creation. In the moment of enosis, exemplified supremely in the person of Jesus, God enters into the being of those who freely consent to such mediating action, and acts in and through them to make them living sacraments of the divine presence.

The third moment of the cosmic divine activity is theosis, that unity with or sharing in the divine life (2 Peter 1:4) which is the final purpose of God for creation. As the Spirit unites with human nature to effect the divine purposes in creation, so human nature is ultimately raised to find its final destiny in sharing in the glory of God. The Christian tradition embodies the view that the whole of creation is in some way to be consummated in a 'new creation'. It is not to be merely relegated to a forgotten and transcended past. It is not to be continued in the same entropic way. It is to be taken into the eternal life of God, and there transfigured into a new life. Paul describes that life as like wheat blossoming in the light of the sun, after its birth in the darkness of earth (1 Cor. 15). On that analogy, this cosmos is the soil in which the seeds of eternal life are sown. Its future will be unlike its present, and yet causally related to it — a consummation and not a cancellation of history.

It is extremely difficult for anyone to envisage such ultimate possibilities. But I can think of nothing more important for Christian faith in our day than to recover the truly cosmic sense of redemption that was characteristic both of the biblical writings and of the Church Fathers. Redemption will not be seen as the saving of a few human beings from the destruction of one small planet. It will be seen as a reconstituting of the whole cosmos in the presence of God, in a more glorious form. When Jesus proclaimed that the kingdom (the rule) of God was at hand, present and active in his own person, one way of understanding this is as an attempt to evoke a vision of each present moment as standing before the possibility of its own eternalization in God. For any theist, it is true that God knows each present moment in the most intimate way. But as each finite moment is taken into the divine experience, it is transformed so that its negative qualities are mitigated and its positive qualities enhanced by the wider context of the divine experience. God's experience is of the world seen in the light of eternity, and so God knows things as no other being is able to know them.

Belief in theosis is belief that finite agents will be given a share in God's experience, so far as that is possible for them. They too will see temporal things in the light of eternity, and so see the events of history as having a purpose and pattern that is largely hidden in via. But this may still sound too much like a purely personal experience. It must be remembered that Christian belief is in the 'resurrection of the body'. It is not some form of disembodied experience of God that finite agents have. The forms of time and space themselves will be reiterated, but in a transformed way, free of decay and suffering. When the whole universe is so transformed that it manifests in an unrestricted way the beauty and goodness of God, and when personal beings, including human beings, are able to give conscious expression to this transformation, then the cosmos may indeed be said to share in the life of God.

For a Christian view, history is important. The resurrection world is not one that could just have been created perfect, without all the struggle and suffering that formed part of cosmic history. The resurrection world is precisely a world formed out of struggle and conflict, a world perfected and not simply a world created perfect.

165

It may not be the case, as some Indian traditions hold, that the cosmos is the body of God. It is perhaps too autonomous and its conscious agencies too self-willed for that. Yet its destiny is to be the body of God. For those who have lived and died with Christ will be raised in Christ (Col. 2:12). All things will be united in Christ (Eph. 1:10). Thus at that stage God will be all in all (1 Cor. 15:28), and there will no longer be a distinction between the church and the world. There will be no church, and no separated world. The cosmos will be fully integrated into the life of God, as the vehicle of divine action and the manifestation of divine glory. In the moment of theosis, the cosmos is transfigured to become the unrestricted manifestation of God's glory, and all rational creatures become the instruments of his praise.

God in Jesus foreshadows in one human person the divine purpose for all creation. But that purpose is to be gradually worked out in the history of this planet, by the inclusion of many persons within that divine-human unity. The Holy Spirit, forming the new community of the church, works in a new way, a way that is explicitly patterned on the life of Jesus, and incorporates people into 'the body of Christ'. Thus the new way of redemption that God begins in the incarnation is continued through the Holy Spirit in the life of the church. Even though the incarnation was not perhaps necessary for the realization of God's purpose, it is in fact the way, and a richly appropriate way, in which God is carrying out that purpose on this planet. Kenosis is one important aspect of the realization of that purpose. It gives a special and distinctive vision of the character of the creator, as one who leaves us free, shares in our freedom, and will fulfill that freedom in conscious loving relationship to the divine. It also gives a powerful moral insight into the way in which creatures should seek to implement the divine purpose in their own lives.

There is a very definite cosmic vision implicit in a Christian view of creation as a kenotic and pleromal process. As the beginning of creation is kenosis, so the end or consummation of creation is theosis. God shares in the pain and permits the wayward freedom of creatures in order that, finally, creatures should share in the bliss and become vehicles of the truly creative freedom of the divine nature. It is that cosmic movement from divine self-emptying to creaturely fulfillment in God which is the sacred history of the cosmos, and, it seems to me, the deepest meaning of the Christian gospel for this planet in the middle of its journey through the mystery of time.

166

Creation Out of Love

PAUL S. FIDDES

The activity of God in creation must be vulnerable.

Love's Endeavour, Love's Expense, p. 66

God creates out of love. This seems a simple enough statement, equally suitable for liturgy as for academic theology, as likely to be found in prayers and hymns as in seminars and journals. But when its implications are taken seriously, we find that it conceals a whole bundle of conceptual traps for the unwary, as well as offering us a key model for understanding the nature of the cosmos and God. The claim that love is at the heart of the universe is both problematic and immensely illuminating, as I hope to show in this essay. It is an assertion, I suggest, that may not even be out of place in the institutes of science, as well as being thoroughly at home in the church and departments of theology.

As soon as we say anything about God we must, of course, 'unsay' it. There will always be a crisis of representation in attempting to speak of God as "that than which nothing greater can be thought."[1] However, while no human words about God can be a literal description of who and what God is, I take the view that metaphors can still point to the reality of God. This is not the occasion for a thorough defense of the use of analogy in talking about God, but before considering the image of God as a loving

---

1. Anselm, *Proslogion*, 2.11.

creator I should make two preliminary points. First, while all analogies affirm both *likeness* and *unlikeness* between their terms of reference, I shall be claiming quite a high degree of correspondence between human and divine love. Second, my strategy in doing so is to begin from what we seem to be required to say from religious experience, especially from those heightened moments of awareness that we might identify as the effect of the self-revealing of God, and most especially from the story of Jesus whom Christians find to be the final manifestation of the nature of God. We have already acquired, as believers, a concern to speak of a creator who makes loving relationships; if we test this concern for inner coherence, and for its power to explain the world around us, we may be able to discover some of the scope and limits of this key analogy of love.

The shape of my argument here is thus to offer a basic proposal, to explore a conceptual problem arising from it, and then to see how one way of answering the problem might throw light on the action of God in a world where natural processes have a considerable amount of self-creativity.

1. The Needs of Love

To say that God creates the world 'out of love' is to offer a reason for creation, and reasons are dangerous things. Those theologians who believe that the world is totally unnecessary to God, wholly superfluous to the divine perfection, think it safer to assign 'no reason whatever' to the decision of God to create.[2] The argument runs that as soon as we begin to offer explanations as to why God might have made the world — for example, to enjoy loving fellowship with personal beings outside God's self — then we infringe the absoluteness of the will of God by ascribing motives to it. It is better simply to regard creation as an act that demonstrates the divine goodness insofar as it is entirely (according to this way of thinking) to our benefit alone. But I am commending a more dangerous kind of theology than this, into which we are invited by God's own hazardous self-giving to us. We can indeed affirm that the reason for creation is love, as long as we are prepared to accept the consequences that follow from it.

2. E.g., Eric Mascall, *He Who Is: A Study in Traditional Theism* (London: Longmans, Green & Co., 1945, repr. 1958), pp. 103-4.

One major implication may seem to some Christians to be theologically outrageous, but I believe that it opens up the issues at the heart of a doctrine of creation. I propose that a God who creates 'out of love' has needs to be satisfied. A loving God needs response from some kind of created world, and especially from personal beings who are outside the internal life of God. Later we must see how this implies no deficiency in God, and constitutes no restriction at all on divine freedom; but we might well set the tone of the debate with a reflection from the seventeenth-century poet and mystic Thomas Traherne:

> [42] This is very strange that God should Want, for in Him is the Fulness of all Blessedness. . . . He is from Eternity full of Want: or els He would not be full of Treasure, Infinit Want is the very Ground and Caus of infinit Treasure. It is Incredible, yet very plain: Want is the Fountain of all his Fulness. Want in God is a treasure to us. For had there been no Need He would not hav Created the World, nor Made us, nor Manifested his Wisdom, nor Exercised his Power, nor Beautified Eternity, nor prepared the Joys of Heaven. But he Wanted Angels and Men, Images, Companions. And these He had from all Eternitie. [43] Infinit Wants Satisfied Produce infinit Joys.[3]

The word 'want' here means 'need', something required which is otherwise missing, rather than 'wish' or 'desire' (a somewhat later usage of the word than the time of Traherne). However, Traherne adds immediately that since God has these needs, "He did Desire infinitly" for them to be satisfied. Traherne is maintaining that God's needs ('wants') do not affect his perfection because they are also eternally fully satisfied, and I intend to take issue with this view of the essential immutability of God; there are other ways of reconciling 'wants' with perfection. However, Traherne is also making the important point that the joy of God, divine 'felicity', springs from the meeting of needs and the satisfying of desires through a loving companionship with creation. Similarly he is urging his readers to learn how to have needs as God does, rather than to adopt the Platonic stance of pretending that we need nothing; while the ancient philosophies

---

3. Thomas Traherne, *Poems, Centuries and Three Thanksgivings*, ed. Anne Ridler (Oxford: Oxford University Press, 1966), *The First Century*, 42-43.

taught that "the Gods needed nothing at all," Traherne believes the Christian message to be that "God made us to Want like Gods, that like Gods, we might be satisfied." His plea is for us to enjoy the natural world and each other as God does, and this involves recognizing our needs. Until we learn what our 'wants' are, he reflects, we will never be happy.

So a modern theologian, Vincent Brümmer, claims a place for the satisfying of "need-love" in healthy relationships with others, and finds an analogy in God:

> We long for the love of others because as persons we necessarily need to be loved. But can we say the same of God? . . . If, as we have argued, God desires our love, it would seem to follow that he also needs our love, for this desire to be fulfilled.[4]

The 'need' or 'want' of God might be understood from two angles, first from a general comparison between God's love and the dynamics of love as we experience them, and second from the particular situation of a creator who is full of love. From the first perspective we can discern several reasons why any true act of love involves allowing others to satisfy our needs at the same time as seeking to meet theirs, and we shall consider some of these factors shortly. The second perspective is opened up with unique reference to a creator God: if infinite love is a part of God's character as creator,[5] it seems that God will be overflowing with an excess of love that cannot be satisfied within God's own self, even in the communion of the Trinity, but which needs free, responsive beings capable of loving relationships.

These perspectives interact with each other, as we shall see, and both depend on an analogy with our human experience of what it means to love others. Much of the Christian tradition has, however, taken a sharply different turn at this point, firmly denying that God has any needs to be satisfied. Two kinds of argument are employed in support of this claim, one based on a certain reading of the human analogy of love, and the other stressing a radical discontinuity with the analogy of love. The first

4. Vincent Brümmer, *The Model of Love* (Cambridge: Cambridge University Press, 1993), p. 236.

5. I have a reason for preferring the term 'character' to 'essence', as will become clear in section 3.

approach urges that the very best examples of human love show us that divine love must be totally self-giving and have no trace of self-fulfillment within it. In terms of a classical Protestant debate, it is said that God's love must be purely *agape* with no hint of *eros;* the two loves are driven apart as opposites.[6] *Eros* is self-affirming and self-realizing love, in which an object of love brings satisfaction to a person's own being; by contrast, *agape* is defined as a totally self-spending love, in which someone sacrifices herself for another without any benefit to herself. It is argued that the best kind of human love approaches the heights of divine *agape;* correspondingly, a God who found self-fulfillment in creation would be making creation into a selfish act.

This moral point has been supplemented by the second kind of argument, one based in the metaphysical assumptions of scholastic thinking (and in particular the thought of Aquinas).[7] It is presumed that God's *aseity* (self-existence) would be infringed if the being of God owed anything to any other reality outside itself; God, it is asserted, can only be the origin and primary cause of all contingent realities if God's own being is totally unconditioned by the world. There has to be one uncaused cause of all. Moreover, if perfection means lacking nothing, then a perfect God cannot have desires and certainly will not need our love. In the more technical language of philosophy, it is asserted that God has no potentialities that remain unactualized: God is *actus purus* — pure act — in the sense that all potentials are eternally realized, leaving no room for desire.

However, despite this powerful critique from both morals and philosophy, there are several good reasons to think that divine self-fulfillment through love is a thoroughly coherent concept.

(a) Receptive Love

In the first place, if we pursue the analogy of the best kind of human love, we find that true lovers do not in fact assume a rigid stance of refusing to receive anything from those they love. *Eros* (need-love) is always mixed

---

6. This was maintained strongly by Anders Nygren, *Agape and Eros,* trans. P. Watson (London: SPCK, 1953); by contrast, Daniel Day Williams urges the integration of agape and eros in *The Spirit and the Forms of Love* (Welwyn: Nisbet, 1968).

7. Aquinas, *Summa Theologiae,* 1a.2.3; 3.1; 9.1.

with *agape* (gift-love); the attempt at a purely self-giving attitude which insists "I can do everything for you but you cannot do anything for me" is at best a cold kind of do-gooding, and at the worst a kind of tyranny.[8] Lovers will affirm the identity of those they love by receiving gladly the other's contribution to the relationship. In so doing they will receive new values brought about by the other, as well as becoming more truly personal through the very act of making another personal. As Eberhard Jüngel puts it, with the analogy of God as love in view:

> Lovers are always alien to themselves and yet, in coming close to each other they come close to themselves in a new way.[9]

This self-realization is not selfish, since it is not the aim but the mysterious by-product of losing ourselves in love for another. In the words of the Gospel text, "the one who loses his life will gain it."

If we apply this analogy to God's love, receptive to us, it need not come into conflict with careful ('philosophical') talk about God. For God to experience a "still greater self-relatedness" (Jüngel's phrase) through self-giving does not deny the *aseity* of God, if we distinguish self-existence from 'self-sufficiency'. Traditionally the two have been identified, and so for God to be the one reality that exists *a se* was thought to mean that God must be *totally* unconditioned by anything else. But there is no reason why a God who depends upon nothing else for existence itself should not choose to depend on others for some aspects of the *mode* of existence. A God who is self-sufficient with regard to the very fact of existence is not thereby prohibited from electing not to be self-sufficient as far as the ongoing richness and value of divine life is concerned.[10] Here we begin to enter upon the idea of kenosis or the freely chosen self-limitation of God, and to this I intend to return.

8. So John MacMurray, *Persons in Relation* (London: Faber and Faber, 1961), pp. 189-90: "the worst kind of tyranny."

9. Eberhard Jüngel, *God as the Mystery of the World,* trans. D. L. Guder (Edinburgh: T. & T. Clark, 1983), p. 318.

10. I develop this distinction in Paul S. Fiddes, *The Creative Suffering of God* (Oxford: Clarendon Press, 1988), pp. 65-67.

(b) Suffering Love

In the case of God's love, *agape* and *eros* come together strongly in the dimension of suffering. When we continue to explore the human analogy of love, we find that if love is to be more than beneficence or cold charity, then it must involve suffering with those who are loved. This is a vulnerability that arises from several quarters; there is, for instance, the painfulness of empathy with the loved one's own experience of pain, and there is the hurt that comes from being rejected or misunderstood by others. Love as we experience it involves a sharing of feelings, and to suffer like this means in turn to be *changed* by the other. As Aquinas saw clearly, suffering and being changed are bound together, which is why he denied both states in God.[11]

But the analogy of love seems to fail altogether if there is nothing corresponding to this fundamental quality of love in God. Moreover, the story of the cross of Jesus and the perception — indeed, revelation — that God is identified with the suffering Christ prompts us to affirm that God suffers in creating out of love. This is surely *agape,* self-giving and self-sacrificing love. Yet there is a paradox here, involving *eros.* Suffering involves being changed by others, but God cannot suffer the kind of change which is a degradation of being; God cannot change to become less God, or less than "that than which nothing greater can be thought." We can say that in the transforming power of love God uses even suffering to fulfill God's own being, becoming more truly who and what God is. In suffering through desire to bring many sons and daughters to glory, God completes the divine glory as well. *Agape* and *eros* are truly integrated in the suffering of divine love.

Of course, there is no question of supposing that God therefore desires to suffer. This would be a divine masochism, with the most destructive consequences for a spirituality of the imitation of God. The point is that if God desires fellowship with created beings, this implicates God in suffering, and through this self-sacrifice *(agape)* God becomes more fully satisfied in love *(eros).* Briefly, suffering love achieves something for God as well as for us. We can meet the philosophical critique about the perfection of God which this view raises, if we do not confuse perfection with completion. The ancient objection to the notion of a God whose being

11. Aquinas, *Summa Theologiae,* 1a.9.2, 1a.20.1.

gains anything (first voiced by Plato, it seems) was that a perfect God cannot increase his perfection, and that if he could he would have been less than perfect in the first place. But this assumes that 'perfection' is a kind of fixed maximum.[12] If we understand perfection to be the perfect relation of God to all the reality there is at any one point, then we will have a dynamic view of perfection; God can constantly exceed or grow in perfection as the purposes of creation move towards greater and greater completion. The perfection of a creator's relationship to the universe when it was a cosmic 'soup' immediately following the 'Big-Bang' will certainly be different from a perfect relationship to the present world containing conscious and moral beings.[13]

(c) Creative Love

Christian reflection upon the desire of God is at least as early as the Lady Julian of Norwich, who finds that "as truly as there is a property of compassion and pity in God, so there is as truly a property of thirst and longing in God."[14] So far we have been considering this desire as a movement towards satisfaction in personal relationships, but at the same time it can be understood as a momentum that drives creativity. If God did not just create once upon a time, but is continuously creative, then God is constantly imagining and realizing new forms of what is good. Later we shall need to ask *how* we can conceive of a God of love as working continually within the developing processes of the cosmos, but for the moment it is enough to say that God will desire the existence of new things before they are actualized.[15] Such a "thirst and longing" in God means that not all the potentialities in God's creativity can be actualized at once, and we have already seen that this runs contrary to the scholastic understanding of God as *actus purus*. But continuous realizing of desire does not deny either the power or wisdom of God. With regard to the first attribute, a God who is

12. Charles Hartshorne argues for a God who can exceed his own maximum: *The Divine Relativity* (New Haven: Yale, repr. 1976), pp. 76-82.
13. I owe this illustration to John Polkinghorne, made in discussion of the paper.
14. Julian of Norwich, *Revelations of Divine Love*, trans. E. Spearing (Harmondsworth: Penguin Books, 1998), ch. 31, p. 84.
15. This point is made by Keith Ward, *Religion and Creation* (Oxford: Oxford University Press, 1996), p. 185.

engaged in ongoing creativity hardly seems less powerful than a God who has created once for all. With regard to the wisdom of God, for God to be omniscient does not require that God knows all potentials *as already actualized;* it simply means that God must on the one hand know all the possibilities there are, and on the other know all the actualities there are.

Indeed, several modern philosophers have pointed out that a God who knows all the details of the future can hardly be committed to the process of time; some have denied that such a God can even act in the world and history.[16] God will still be omniscient if God knows all that there is to be known; possibilities which have not yet been actualized can only be known as possibilities, and so for God not to know them as actual is not a deficiency in knowledge. Moreover, when they *are* actualized, created beings will bring to them something new that accords with the reciprocity of love I have already described. To take a mundane example, a Christian pastor may set out to create a community with a fairly clear vision in her mind as to all the possibilities there might be in a community of loving, interdependent yet free persons; but the reality of that community, say in a local congregation, will depend upon the contribution that each makes to it, sometimes bringing an unexpected value, or sometimes failing in what might well have been expected.

2. Needs and Relationships

We have been teasing out a major implication of the statement that "God creates out of love," namely that creative love includes — as one dimension — the satisfying of needs. If God desires the good of created beings (whether they are potential or actual), then God desires what is their greatest good, which is for them to love and enjoy God; the creator therefore desires mutual relations with them, and all our human experience tells us that mutuality includes allowing others to satisfy our needs. A God of love, then, will gain much both in delight and in the values produced by creation, through drawing created persons into the fellowship of divine life.

It may be protested, however, that it would be far better to avoid the

16. So Richard Swinburne, *The Coherence of Theism* (Oxford: Clarendon Press, 1997), p. 221.

language of 'the needs of love' altogether, and keep ourselves to the language of 'desire' which I have also been using. Surely, it might be urged, it would be more appropriate to speak only of the fulfilling of God's desire, and to avoid any talk of the satisfying of need. This critique might come especially from Christian practitioners of science, who are used in their disciplines to placing talk about 'needs' at a low level of biological function.[17] Within their framework of discourse, it is customary to locate 'willing', 'choosing', and 'desiring' at the higher level of cognitive function, while 'needing' belongs among the lower instincts and drives of the mind and psyche. In terms of brain function, talk of a need might arise, for instance, as something generated through some biochemical depletion in the neural substrate. From an evolutionary point of view it can be argued that the areas of the brain that deal with 'needs' develop early on, whereas those dealing with higher-level cognitive functions such as choosing and desiring appear later. This leads reductionist thinkers such as Richard Dawkins to identify a 'selfish gene', a metaphorical way of referring to an inherited basic drive for survival, a self-centered quest for the meeting of our needs that marks our evolutionary progress and provides a kind of motor for natural selection.[18] Surely, it may be argued, we should see the Christian hope for individuals and society in replacing these need-driven urges by the true relationality of love. The violence of nature in its need for survival can be transformed into self-sacrificial love. In such a context, it might seem regressive to speak of divine needs.

Of course, the blend of *agape* and *eros* I have been commending recognizes the unhealthiness of relationships based on one person's attempt to satisfy their own needs at the expense of others. Nor, in our relationship to God, should we regard the satisfying of our needs for security and self-esteem as being any kind of reward that we merit; the meaning of 'justification by faith' is that our value as persons is bestowed on us as a free gift of love. So in our relations to others we do not love in the expectation of *earning* a response that affirms us in our being. Love is offered without any calculation as to gains that might be achieved, and with the humility of knowing that we might be rejected. But for all that, the 'needs

17. The following section is, in fact, a response to this critique raised by several scientists in the consultation. I am particularly indebted here to the verbal contribution of Professor Malcolm Jeeves.

18. Richard Dawkins, *The Selfish Gene* (Oxford: Oxford University Press, 1977).

of love' do belong among the higher functions of the psyche, as they concern the nature of reciprocal relationships and interpersonal communication: we need to be valued for who we are, to be confirmed in our personal identity, and these needs are satisfied as an unmerited gift precisely as we bestow value on others by our unconditional love of them. While there can be no exact transfer to the love in which God lives and acts, there is some analogy insofar as our response to God gives God praise and glory, adding the particular kind of value to God's life that only a created world can produce.

A theological dialogue with science on the concept of need is not then simply a question of clarifying that the true needs of love are neither biochemical deficiencies nor brute instincts. Rather, it should be an exploration of both continuity and discontinuity between 'low level' and 'high level' functions of need. Instead of driving a wedge between 'needs' and 'love', we may be able to begin to trace the path taken by the creative Spirit of God in luring created beings along the evolutionary trail, until the needs for survival are not canceled by something 'higher', but *transformed* into a means of making truly personal identity. A need that emerges from something 'missing' in the context of physical brain structure (for example, a chemical or electrochemical depletion) becomes an altogether different 'lack' in the personal realm (for example, the assurance that we are valued). Correspondingly, a handling of needs properly at the 'higher' levels of consciousness could have a 'top-down' effect on needs embedded in the substrate of the brain. Then it is appropriate that God too should know needs; in the words of Traherne, we learn to "need All Things as God doth that we may receive them with Joy, and lov in His Image."[19] Talk of needs requires us to look at the human being as an integrated whole, both material body and personality that transcends it, while it also sharpens up the implications of a God who has desires for the making of relations.

The Christian image of God as Trinity affirms that love is relational and not simply attitudinal; the God who is love exists eternally in the relationships of Father, Son, and Spirit. But this very model of God has been appealed to in order to deny that a loving God needs a created world in which to exercise love. It has been proposed that God could have loved 'others' without a finite world since there are 'other persons' in the imma-

19. Traherne, *First Century,* 40.17-18.

nent Trinity. In making this argument, Augustine also finds an 'eros' character in the divine love, as God desires and enjoys God's own self in triune communion.[20] In agreement with many theologians today, I do not find this a convincing picture of divine love; among other reasons, the image of God as Trinity has been developed from experience of God's salvific action in the world, and so already includes human beings within the story of the divine relationships. The sending forth of the Son by the Father in eternal generation, for example, cannot be torn apart from the sending of the Son on mission into time and history. An immanent Trinity detached from the *oikonomia* of God in the world is a mere speculation.[21]

My proposition that a loving God is in need of response from some creation of free beings has thus enabled us to open up various aspects of God as ultimate reality. But it also raises a sharp problem.

3. The Freedom of Love

The problem is that of freedom. If, as I have been suggesting, the God who is made known to us is one who needs some created world, how can either God or the world be truly free? If God's love requires a world, how can this be anything other than an inevitable emanation from the being of God, and so threaten the freedom of both creator and created? For the question is not only how in such a case God can be sovereign; if the universe is a necessary outflow from the divine being, how can it be truly contingent? That is, how can there be a world in which things could be otherwise than they are — a world in which, for instance, there is more than one way for Leonardo to paint the smile on the face of the Mona Lisa? We seem here to be involved in a conundrum about love: on the one hand, God's love requires a world of free, responsive beings, while on the other if such a world is required it seems to be no longer able to respond freely.

(a) One answer to this problem is to accept that God is indeed subject to some external necessity, some ultimate metaphysical principle,

---

20. Augustine, *De Trinitate*, 14.3.

21. This is the point of Karl Rahner's phrase, "the immanent Trinity is the economic Trinity"; see Rahner, *The Trinity*, trans. J. Donceel (London: Burns & Oates, 1970), pp. 21-22.

which demands both a creating God and a created world. This seems to be the solution of some forms[22] of process theology, in which the process of creativity requires a material world and a God as the source of stability and novelty within it. Each has its part to play in the drama; each has its need of the other. This is simply the nature of the creative advance from disorder to order, from simplicity to complexity; there is no question of God's *choosing* to limit God's self in giving freedom to creation, or in suffering in the world. Neither can we properly speak of the kenosis or voluntary self-emptying of God. Those who take this view then work hard to show that God and the world are nevertheless relatively free in this situation, each having their own appropriate power of creativity. As far as God is concerned, it may be said that while God depends to some extent on the world, the world is far more dependent on God, or that while God is one cause among others, he is the most significant cause. It may even be suggested that the 'metaphysical necessity' referred to is both external and internal to God at the same time, since it only amounts to saying that God had no options to be anything else than a loving creator.

Process theology offers many insights that, in my view, enrich any attempt to speak of the relation between God and the world; among them are God's empathetic suffering with finite entities, and the persuasive power of this involvement.[23] But I suggest that the metaphysic underlying process thought cannot really reflect the dynamics of love. Self-giving is always set here in the wider framework of a necessary process, so that it fails the test of love as memorably expressed by Marie de Champagne in the twelfth century — that "lovers give each other everything freely, under no compulsion of necessity."[24]

(b) Another answer to this problem roots loving creativity more clearly in the essential properties of God's own nature, but distinguishes

22. The formative process thinker, A. N. Whitehead, refers to God as "the creature of creativity" in *Process and Reality* (New York: Macmillan, 1929; repr. 1967), p. 129; cf. p. 529. John Cobb, however, attempts to deny that God is subject to creativity, along the lines that creativity — unlike God — is a principle and not an agency: see his *A Christian Natural Theology* (London: Lutterworth, 1966), pp. 211-14.

23. I am also indebted, in this essay, to the process distinction between God's knowledge of potentialities and actualities: see Charles Hartshorne, *A Natural Theology for Our Time* (La Salle, Ill.: Open Court, 1967), pp. 20-21.

24. Quoted by Vincent Brümmer, *The Model of Love* (Cambridge: Cambridge University Press, 1993), p. 91.

this general inclination from the creation of any *particular* world. A more technical way of putting this is to distinguish between 'essential' and 'contingent' properties in God.[25] Thus it may be supposed that the disposition to create and to enter into loving fellowship with created beings is as much an attribute of God's 'necessary being' as is God's goodness, wisdom, or everlastingness. God being what God is, this outward-directed love and creativity *must* be actualized at some particular time and place. The divine freedom is, however, claimed to be preserved insofar as God freely chooses a particular world in which to actualize this potential for relationship with created beings. Moreover, we may also say that God freely chooses to affirm the essential divine quality of loving creativity, just as God affirms goodness over against evil.[26]

This is an attractive solution to the problem of necessity and freedom, and certainly represents a coherent attempt to speak about the being of a God who must finally elude all human speech. However, I am uneasy about some of the implications that flow from it. We are bound to say, for instance, that while some created universe is 'necessary' to satisfy God's ecstatic love, we ourselves in this particular world are not necessary. This drives apart the two aspects of the 'needs' of divine love I began with, the necessity of creation for a loving creator and the needs that arise within actual relationships. It is not possible to say that 'God needs us', but only 'God needs some creatures somewhere', and this severely disrupts the analogy of love we have been exploring. It is also not possible to speak of 'kenotic' love exercised in the very act of creation, since the making of a world of free, responsive beings over against God represents no divine self-limitation or self-emptying; it is simply something that a loving creator will be bound to do at some point since it belongs to God's essential being. It may well still be possible to use the concept of kenosis in speaking of God's suffering with creation, but this is then torn apart from the divine activity in continuously creating. A further point is harder to put one's finger on, but arises from the place of trust and risk within relationships of love; as Vincent Brümmer expresses it, if God remains faith-

25. So Keith Ward, *Religion and Creation*, pp. 186-91, and also earlier: *Rational Theology and the Creativity of God* (Oxford: Blackwell, 1982), pp. 140-46. This has some similarity with a dipolar view of God in process theism; see, e.g., Hartshorne, *Natural Theology*, pp. 27, 44.

26. Ward suggests that the creator God affirms this property as something that he "would have chosen" if he could: *Religion and Creation*, p. 163.

ful to us because this is his essential nature rather than his free decision, "we need not trust God not to let us down, since we can rest assured that he lacks the ability to do so."[27]

Despite the unease I have expressed, it may be that this solution to the conundrum of a necessary creation is the best we can do, but it is worth considering another approach that begins from a different point. Instead of thinking of an essential divine nature that sets the boundaries for contingent choices, we might approach the ancient problem of the relation between nature and will in God from the other end.

(c) A third answer thus begins from the perspective of the divine will, which is "the ultimate standard of goodness,"[28] and concepts of divine nature are to be seen as subsequent to God's acts of free will. The divine nature, in this sense, is something like God's 'identity', which emerges from God's acts. According to this way of thinking, God freely determines the kind of God that God wills to be. As Karl Barth puts it, "God's being is . . . his willed decision."[29] Building on Barth's thought, we might then regard creation as being part of God's self-definition, an integral factor in God's own self-determination, since God chooses to be completed through a created universe — or perhaps several universes. With regard to love as *eros,* it follows that God needs the world *because God freely chooses to be in need,* not because there is some intrinsic necessity of nature binding choice.[30] "God needs our love, because he is the loving God that he has freely decided to be."[31]

With regard to our discussion about the needs of love, this has the advantage that our *particular* world is necessary to God, through God's free choice. In God's eternal self-determination, God humbly chooses to need us as partners in the fellowship of love. This is in line with the biblical

27. Brümmer, *The Model of Love,* p. 229.

28. Vincent Brümmer, *Speaking of a Personal God* (Cambridge: Cambridge University Press, 1992), p. 102.

29. Karl Barth, *Church Dogmatics,* trans. G. Bromiley and T. F. Torrance (Edinburgh: T. & T. Clark, 1936-77), II/1, pp. 271-72.

30. I work this idea out fully in my book *The Creative Suffering of God,* pp. 63-71, under the heading "The Freedom of God to Be in Need." There is some affinity with the proposal of John Zizioulas that in God 'person' is the cause of 'nature': see *Being as Communion* (London: Darton, Longman and Todd, 1985).

31. This is a quotation from Vincent Brümmer, *The Model of Love,* p. 237, in a passage where he is commending and adopting the approach that I had developed in my book *The Creative Suffering of God,* pp. 66-68.

idea of election, which is an image for the particularity of God's questing love ("called according to his purpose" [Rom. 8:28-30]), though in the course of Christian history it has been sadly distorted into ideas of the predestination of people to alternative fates. The particularity of God's purpose does not of course mean that ours is the only world necessary to God; indeed, in the light of what we know about the universe this seems unlikely. But God's general will to direct love outwards to embrace created beings can at the very same time be conceived as specified to particular kinds of worlds. Moreover, this makes sense of creation itself as an act of kenosis, for in choosing to be a God with the needs of love, God willingly renounces self-sufficiency.

There are admittedly some logical strains in this solution, that God is entirely what God wills to be. Most evidently, it does not seem to square with the common-sense view that there must already be a nature in existence with powers of knowledge and intention in order to *make* choices. This critique has been effectively offered by Keith Ward, who therefore himself prefers the second approach mentioned above:

> God must have a given nature, which is not chosen, but which God possesses of necessity. It does not make sense to suppose that God chooses the divine nature completely, since *there must already be a choosing nature in existence to make such a choice.*[32]

Again he insists that "the creator cannot choose its own nature, since that nature must exist *prior to any actual choice being made.*"[33] But any talk about God stretches language, using it in an odd way; the question is what language is most adequate or least inadequate. To speak of God's "choosing to be in need" is certainly odd, but it is a linguistic attempt to divert us away from a view of God as some kind of substance that can be 'observed'[34] like other objects in the world, even as an object of perception in the mind. While this is doubtless also the aim of some who adopt the second approach sketched above, the advantage of beginning from the dynamic idea of God's 'willing' or 'choosing' is that it immediately speaks

32. Ward, *Religion and Creation*, p. 171.
33. Ward, *Religion and Creation*, p. 163; my italics.
34. Nicholas Lash uses the term 'spectatorial empiricism' in this context: see Lash, *The Beginning and the End of Religion* (Cambridge: Cambridge University Press, 1996), p. 79.

of God as an act or event. It therefore prompts us to think in a more 'participational' way, and to use language that reflects the reality of our engagement in God as an event of love.

That is, we find that we are summoned to be involved in a movement of divine being that is like the movement of a will, as we are summoned to share in movements of love and justice that are like relationships between persons. The model of God as Trinity is not an observational kind of language ("so, that is what God looks like") but a language of participation. When we pray to God as Father, for example, we find ourselves involved in a movement of responding and obeying like that of a son towards a father; this is interwoven with a movement of mission like that of a father sending out a son; and these movements are themselves interfused by a movement of discovery, opening up new depths of relationship, with a momentum like that of a fresh wind blowing, or water streaming or a searing fire burning (to use three biblical images for the Spirit). We are praying to the Father, through the Son and in the Spirit. The objection that there must be a nature to *make* choices is thus akin to the objection of advocates of a social doctrine of the Trinity, that there must be individual persons to "have relationships." If we think in a participatory way about God, we can only talk of being involved in movements of relational love, of choice and desire; the persons, as Augustine proposed, are nothing more or less than relationships.[35] This takes seriously the Johannine insight that "those who dwell in love dwell in God and God dwells in them" (1 John 4:16). Such indwelling, as we shall see, also has important implications for our understanding of the way that a God of love acts in the world.

There is, however, another possible strain in the account of God's 'choosing to be in need'. If God's will is not to be arbitrary then God's faithfulness must be unchanging. This may seem to require a nature possessing the quality of absolute fidelity, which exists as the *basis* for God's making of choices. However, it is possible to think of this 'covenant faithfulness' (*hesed*, in Old Testament faith) from the perspective of God's will;

35. Augustine, *De Trinitate*, 5.6. Augustine was, rather playfully, attempting to meet the alternative presented by the Arians, that 'persons' in God must be distinguished either by substance or accident; the former implied that there were three Gods, and the latter that the persons were not eternal. Augustine replied that the persons fell into neither category, but were relations, an idea later elaborated by Aquinas as 'subsistent relations': *Summa Theologiae,* 1a.29.4.

that is, God does not go back on the primal decision to be in need of a relationship with us and so to limit God's self in creation. God promises to be faithful to what God chooses to be, and we take a risk of faith on the consistent character of God's will which is manifested in the promise. Perhaps the idea of 'desire' that we have already explored may be of help here, not as an alternative to will, but as a dimension of it, expressing the 'settled quality' of God's will. It hints at something about God's choice that makes it infinitely different from our choosing between this and that, which might well be fickle and unstable. If God is choosing God's own being when God chooses us as covenant partners, then — as Karl Barth expresses it — "in the free decision of love God is God in the very fact that he *does* stand in this relationship with the other," so that "we cannot go back on this decision if we would know God and speak of him."[36] When we talk of God's eternal desire, I suggest, we are recognizing that God's decision to be in need of creation is the furthest frontier of our knowledge of God. We cannot "go behind it" and say "if God had not created, then *this* would have happened instead" or "God would be like *this* instead."

I incline, then, to the priority of God's will-as-desire over any 'essential nature' of God, though we might well speak of the result of God's willing and desiring as a 'nature' in the sense that we can identify *this* God as the one whom we worship. Giving this priority to the will of God has sometimes attracted the criticism that God is being projected as a larger version of Enlightenment Man, that is, as an absolute Subject dominating the world through an individual mind.[37] But I have placed the will of God in the context of threefold movements of relationship; we are engaged in complex movements of will that are also currents of self-giving love. 'God' means this triune communion.

4. The Risks of Love

We began this exploration of the analogy of love with a proposal, that God's creation 'out of love' involves the satisfying of divine needs. I then

36. Barth, *Church Dogmatics*, II/2, p. 6.
37. See the criticism of Jürgen Moltmann, in *Trinity and the Kingdom of God*, trans. M. Kohl (London: SCM, 1981), p. 139.

suggested that the problem this raises for the freedom of God can be resolved by affirming that God freely chooses to be in need, and this in turn can be best understood in the context of a triune God where 'persons' are movements of interweaving love. The very being of God is constituted by such relational activities as choosing, willing, desiring, and loving. In this sense, we may agree with the scholastic theologians that God is 'pure act', though not in the sense that God has no potentials to be realized. It remains then to be seen how this model helps us understand the action of God in the world, which is a continuous creativity.

If "God creates out of love," then the manner of God's action in the world is characteristic of love. That is, it cannot be coercive or manipulative but only persuasive, seeking to create response. Action through persuasion is necessarily hidden rather than obtrusive, and respects the considerable amount of self-creativity that created things possess. This is not the place to work out fully the implications of this for the nature of the cosmos, but I suggest that we can only make sense theologically of organic processes with their own inner capacity for evolution and self-development if we have a vision of the *whole* of nature, at every level, capable of response in its own manner to the desire of God. Beneath the surface of life, the cosmos at all levels is either responding to God's purpose for community, or drifting away so that things are out of joint. Attempts to describe this relationship are necessary myths to portray a reality, whether they be the biblical poetry of the trees of the field clapping their hands before the Lord, the floods roaring his praise and the universe groaning in the pains of childbirth,[38] or whether they be the process philosophy of a mental pole in subatomic particles, reaching towards satisfaction.

But how and where do created realities come up against this divine influence? The answer, I suggest, lies in the picture of the Trinity as interweaving movements of love in which we participate. In creation God limits God's self in 'making room' for creation to indwell the divine life, and in redemption God draws created beings ever more deeply into the communion of relationships in which God's being consists. The triune God might then be conceived as the environment, or 'field of force'[39] within

---

38. Psalms 96:12-13, 98:7-9; Romans 8:19-22.

39. This is how Wolfhart Pannenberg conceives the Spirit of God: see Pannenberg, *Systematic Theology*, vol. 1, trans. G. Bromiley (Grand Rapids: Eerdmans, 1991), pp. 382ff.

which the world develops; everything that exists is embraced within relational movements of self-giving and self-realizing love. We might say that God acts not by exerting force on things to move them mechanically (*A* 'pushing' or 'pulling' *B* with inevitable results) but by the influence of the divine movements and actions that surround all finite movements and actions, enticing them to conform to the purposes of love. This model combines ideas of both persuasion and attraction. The Neoplatonic vision of the 'One beyond Being' was of a God who moved all things through the *attractiveness* of the divine beauty, though without moving Itself; the dance of creation moved around a still center, which was "the love that moves the sun and the other stars" (Dante).[40] The picture I am sketching here combines the *attractiveness* of love with the *movement* of persuasion; the triune God moves all things precisely by being in movement, and attracting them into the movement of the divine dance. The patterns of action and behavior in human society and in the systems of the natural world are influenced by the patterns of God's own being,[41] and a significant pattern within the triune 'dance', as we have seen, is the healthy satisfying of needs; thus it is that created beings learn to 'want' as the creator wants.

Some such picture may help to place the action of God in the context of the network of causal relations in the world, where causality (as John Polkinghorne points out)[42] is 'holistic', and causal instances cannot be

40. Dante, *The Divine Comedy; Paradiso,* 33.145.
41. A. R. Peacocke has proposed that divine causality should be understood as an interaction of God with the pattern of the world-as-a-whole, resulting in a whole-part (or 'top-down') influence, and that this divine interaction should be understood as analogous to input of information: see Peacocke, "God's Interaction with the World," in R. J. Russell, N. Murphy, and A. R. Peacocke, eds., *Chaos and Complexity: Scientific Perspectives on Divine Action* (Berkeley: Vatican Observatory Publications, Vatican City State/Center for Theology and the Natural Sciences, 1995), pp. 263-64, 272-75, 285-87. Similarly, John Polkinghorne in *Belief in God in an Age of Science* (New Haven: Yale University Press, 1998), pp. 62-64, proposes that God acts upon pattern formation in the natural world *only* through a 'top-down' input of information, whereas creaturely acts mix energetic with informational causalities. In his essay in the present volume Polkinghorne now, however, modifies this view to allow for some energetic causation by God. My own argument here is that God's activity in pattern formation should be understood as activity through persuasion; if events are embraced in the movements of God's being, this opens up a kind of influence on patterns that is wider than the pure input of information.
42. Polkinghorne, *Belief in God in an Age of Science,* pp. 65-67.

186

disentangled from each other. God's interaction with the world also cannot be separated out, as it consists in a constant and hidden pattern-inducing influence. There is room in this model for what is sometimes called 'particular' as well as 'general' providence, since God can offer particular persuasive aims, specified to achieve a purpose in a definite historical context. Since all persuasion can be refused or modified by created entities, the offering of a particular aim or pattern does not infringe the integrity of creation; but if it is accepted there is the possibility of something new happening, even something unprecedented. This picture of the relation between the triune God and creation also enables us to speak of a deepening and ever-more costly kenosis of God, as God enters with empathy into the experience of the world, and feels with pain the brokenness of its patterns and the alienation at their heart. In Christ, we may say, this identification reaches the furthest point and so something new happens, for the relation of *this* son to God the Father is totally identical with the relationship of Son to Father within God's own being.

But if our affirmation of the 'needs of love' in God has brought us to an understanding of divine action as persuasion, the question arises urgently as to whether it is possible that God might fail to reach the satisfaction of love's needs and purposes. Can God, through persuasion alone, fulfill the divine project in creation, or is it feasible that evil might triumph? How much of a risk, then, does love take? We have seen that love in its two dimensions of *eros* and *agape,* both need-love and gift-love, does not calculate the gain to the lover but is open to rejection. Ought we then to conclude that God's love risks everything, that *total* loss must be one possible outcome, that love must face the possibility that "all has been given in vain"?[43]

First we must say that divine love takes a *real risk.* It is real in that suffering *can* 'befall' God, and it is real in that it *does.* I use the word 'befall' deliberately, as a way of signifying that God experiences suffering in relation to the world in a way that is not entirely under divine control. It 'happens' to God. Some writers on divine passibility do indeed take a qualified view of God's suffering, by proposing that God can always control the degree of hurt inflicted upon God's own self by others. Marcel Sarot, who takes this view, therefore prefers the term 'self-restraint' to

---

43. This is the view taken by W. H. Vanstone in his formative study, *Love's Endeavour, Love's Expense* (London: Darton, Longman and Todd, 1977), p. 77.

'self-limitation' with regard to divine kenosis, asserting that since God is the complete "master of his own passibility" and "remains in control" of it, he can "end his self-restraint whenever he wants to, and this means that he can interfere whenever he wants."[44] But in addition to the moral problems as to why God should apparently choose not to cut self-restraint short in face of an Auschwitz or a Rwanda, divine suffering would be very remote from our experience of suffering love if God were in complete control of the hurt others can inflict on God's self. We have no such securities. Sarot, and those who argue as he does, is rightly concerned that a suffering God should not become an object of pity to us as the eternal victim of the universe, and that God should have the joy of "knowing that he will reach his goal";[45] but these concerns, as I will suggest, can be safeguarded by other means than diminishing the vulnerability of God.

This divine capacity for suffering to 'happen' to God has its beginning in the very nature of creation. In making a free world that can lapse from divine purpose, God is exposed to the risk of something that God does not directly create, and that theologians have thus often called 'non-being'. That is, God is vulnerable to the emerging of something strange from the side of created beings — evil and gratuitous suffering. Here we may discern two kinds of pain, woven deeply into the development of organic life. First, there is a limited amount of suffering that will be an inherent part of any story of evolutionary emergence, and that might even be regarded as a kind of 'sacrifice' by some participants in the process for the sake of the future of others.[46] If we remember that God also shares this suffering, in empathy with created beings, then we can still affirm that evolution happens under the guiding influence of a good God. But second, there is a suffering in nature that is quite disproportionate to the process of the development of sentient beings. No excuse can be made for it in terms of education or nurture, and we may trace this pain and waste

44. Michel Sarot, *God, Passibility and Corporeality* (Kampen: Pharos, 1992), pp. 55, 41. Sarot's argument relies on what seems a tendentious understanding of a 'causal relation', as the causing of passion within a being by something outside it "overpowering its will" (p. 34); God then cannot be subject to causation from the world. But it does not follow that to be subject to *some* change outside one's control means being "*nothing more than a passive victim.*"

45. Sarot, *God, Passibility and Corporeality,* p. 64.

46. See A. R. Peacocke, *Creation and the World of Science* (Oxford: Clarendon Press, 1979), pp. 164-69, and the essays by Peacocke and Holmes Rolston in this volume.

to the drifting of creation away from the divine purpose, a resisting of the divine persuasion. If we have a vision of the whole of nature, at every biological level, as capable of response to God's influence, then we can also envisage it as tragically failing to respond. In fact, suffering as we know it is a blend of these two kinds of pain, appropriate and inappropriate, proportionate and disproportionate. In the world as it has become, we cannot separate them out, and it is this mixed pain with a dark center that befalls a loving God.

The vulnerability of love contradicts any idea that evil and the excessive suffering it causes are a logical entailment of creation, or a necessary educational program. To give priority to God's will-as-desire over an essential divine nature is thus to say that God chooses that suffering might *befall* God's own self; God chooses to be open to suffering with its final unpredictability. This means that the influence of the world upon God is certainly 'subject to his will', as Sarot insists,[47] but to an act of will made once for all and on which God will never go back.

This kenosis could also be understood in terms of the possibilities that are actualized in the cosmos. If we make a divine *nature* the ultimate reality, then we tend to think of an essential and eternal reservoir of all possibilities in God, even if God is continuously filling up the reservoir with newly imagined possibilities. Correspondingly, the freedom of the world is restricted to contributing to deciding *which* of the possibilities will be actualized. If we have a more dynamic view of the act of divine willing or desiring as ultimate, then there is scope for God to allow created beings to contribute to the very *making* of possibilities. New possibilities will emerge out of the interaction between God and the world in a genuine co-creativity. To adopt an image used by Charles Hartshorne, we may say that a particular shade of blue brushed on a canvas by an artist is not "haunting the universe from eternity" just waiting to be instantiated;[48] nor is it entirely created from the divine imagination. The possibility of this fraction of color emerges from cooperation between divine and human imaginations.

The risks of love are real, corresponding to the real gains of love. But the story of Jesus, and especially his death and resurrection, assures us that

47. Sarot, *God, Passibility and Corporeality,* p. 66.
48. Charles Hartshorne, *Creative Synthesis and Philosophic Method* (London: SCM, 1970), p. 59.

there is no greater power in the universe than empathetic love.[49] Identifying with the experience of another has the power to create response and to transform persons from their self-enclosed egocentricity to participants in communities of self-giving love. God has the power of universal identification, and so we can say consistently that God is both vulnerable *and* certain of final victory over evil and suffering. If we follow the view of divine omniscience proposed earlier, there is certainly something unknown lying ahead for God, but it is not unknown in the way that it is for us. God, unlike us, knows all the possibilities at any one time, however these have come into being; at the same time God knows the power of love to persuade and influence creation. In the triune life of God there is joy because of this secure hope that all things will be reconciled, and this joy does not cancel suffering but absorbs its sting.

God will fulfill God's own purposes, not *despite* the suffering of love, but *through* it. The reciprocity of love is not simply a romantic interplay of emotions; nothing else has the power to bring about the reconciliation of all things. Julian of Norwich sees this truth, when writing about the revelation she received about the desire of God. It is the "strength" of God's longing, embodied in the "spiritual thirst" of Christ, which is the cause of our longing for God; this thirst, she perceives, "lasts in him as long as we are in need, drawing us up to his bliss."[50]

The risk that God's love takes is thus real, but not total. Faith wagers that it is not possible, given the power of persuasive love, that God's venture in creation will fail. But there must still be something open and unknown about the fulfillment of God's purpose, because its *content* depends upon the response of the world. This is most evidently the case with God's project for the making of persons. There is no standard model of a personality that God is constructing like an artifact in a factory; our decisions and experiences shape what we are. So, not only the *route* to God's goal but the *content* of it is something that God has put into the hands of creatures. There is room then for tragedy as well as triumph in God's victory over suffering. God does take a risk, not only in being open to suffering along the way, but in the real possibility that there will be something 'missing' at the end of this world's day. While creatures will

49. For one attempt to describe the efficacy of empathy, see Edward Farley, *Divine Empathy* (Philadelphia: Fortress Press, 1996), pp. 303-15.
50. Julian of Norwich, *Revelations of Divine Love*, p. 84.

know bliss in the contemplation of their creator, God may know that they are not all that they could have been. There will be no deficiency in their beatific vision, for they will be perfectly related to God and God will have healed their past. But we can conceive of a blend of victory and tragedy in God's own experience of the end, a humble acceptance by God of the absence of some good that the world might have produced. This will not be the eternalizing of evil, but a recognition that not all potentials for good have been realized, due to failures of created beings to respond as fully as God desired.

So we return finally to the needs of love with which we began. Because true love does not *demand* the satisfaction of needs from the other, or manipulate the other in order to get it, there will always be the risk that some element of need will not be satisfied. By analogy, we may dare to say that in creating 'out of love' God is open to the risk of some unsatisfied desire. Although I have quoted with approval from two mystics of the positive way, Traherne and the Lady Julian, here I must part company with them a little. For Traherne, all the "wants" of God are eternally satisfied in a simultaneity of need and satisfaction; for Julian, God remains in unsatisfied "thirst and longing" only "as long as we are in need" of feeling the effect of it, which for her means the Day of Judgment.[51] But a Creator who chooses to be in need for the sake of love will also be ready for the eternal pain of noticing that some note is missing, some counterpoint lacking, some harmony not quite complete, in the song of praise arising from a reconciled creation. This is creation out of love and into love.

51. If, by contrast, we envisage eternity in a dynamic way, with opportunity for development of persons, then our need for the 'longing' of God will also continue.

Kenosis: Theological Meanings and Gender Connotations

SARAH COAKLEY

Christianity should have no hesitation in attributing to God that authenticity of love which it recognises in His Christ.

Love's Endeavour, Love's Expense, p. 59

The contributors to this book are all concerned with the technical theological question of kenosis (divine self-emptying) and its relation to the nature of divine love. But the term is used by our contributors in a number of different ways (even, it might be argued, in a bewilderingly different set of ways). It is thus the first, and major, task of this paper to provide a 'map' of these uses, and to chart what Wittgenstein would have called their 'family resemblances'; for we are dealing here with a sliding scale of uses that move us around the terrain of systematic theology in intriguing ways, from the doctrine of Christ, to the doctrine of the Trinity, to the doctrine of providence, to the doctrine of creation. And the matter does not stop there. For by unwinding the strings of implication, we see that this theme of kenosis has profound importance for how we perceive the *humanum* — how we think of the nature of human freedom and of the willed (and graced) response to God. This essay will thus attempt to show how decisions about our theological *starting point* vitally affect the way those strings of implication weave in with one another; and how our various contributors are differently affected by these starting points, and by their presumptions about authority and truth in matters of science and theology.

A second, and briefer (but no less exacting) task of this paper will be to draw out some of the gender implications, overt and covert, of the systematic choices made by our contributors. Kenosis has, of necessity, been a contentious theme in feminist theology in recent decades:[1] the call to 'self-effacement' or 'self-sacrifice' — whether in God or in the human — has the inevitable ring of 'feminine' abasement, which feminist theology from its outset has been concerned to expose and criticize. Can, then, this current project of valorizing the 'kenotic' be rescued from the feminist charge of 'false consciousness'? It is with that tricky matter that I shall be concerned in the latter sections of this paper.

I. *Kenosis:* Theological Meanings

But first we turn to the analytic task: that of charting the variety of meanings of kenosis in play in this book. Here we shall start with *christological* meanings (for in this area lie the origins of the technical term) and proceed via *trinitarian* meanings to more generalized senses relating to the doctrine of *creation*. As we shall show, it is a striking feature of this book that most of its contributors construe the significance of kenosis in this third, generalized, sense — addressing God's relation to the world — and tend to turn to christological or trinitarian meanings only as a subsequent — paradigmatic or illustrative — move. We shall be concerned to highlight what factors are determining this ordering of priorities, and to indicate the possible alternatives.

1. Christological Meanings of Kenosis

a. The New Testament: Philippians 2:5-11

As more than one of the essayists in this book remind us (see the essays by Moltmann, Ward, Polkinghorne),[2] the term *kenosis* ultimately derives

1. For a detailed examination of this issue as a feminist problem, see my earlier essay, "*Kenosis* and Subversion: On the Repression of 'Vulnerability' in Christian Feminist Writing," in Daphne Hampson, ed., *Swallowing a Fishbone? Feminist Theologians Debate Christianity* (London: S.P.C.K., 1996), pp. 82-111.

2. See Moltmann, Chapter 8 this volume; Ward, Chapter 9 this volume; Polkinghorne, Chapter 5 this volume.

from the use of the verb *kenoo* in Philippians 2:7: "he emptied himself." But the first, and most important, exegetical issue to note here is that the reference of the 'emptying' is not clear. What *is* being 'emptied' in this hymn? On one reading, which is the more obvious one if one assumes that the hymn is talking about Christ's personal pre-existence (see: "being in the form of God," v. 6), the 'emptying' refers to the moment of incarnation and the humility of the divine act in becoming human. But another reading (which is skeptical of there being a developed notion of 'incarnation' available at the time this hymn was composed) reads the emptying as *parallel* to the "he humbled himself" in v. 8, and so referring to the cross rather than to the incarnation.[3] On this latter view the hymn is based on the theme of Christ's recapitulation of Adam's role (on which Paul expands elsewhere in Rom. 5 and 1 Cor. 15); and the "being in the form of God" of v. 6 is an allusion to Genesis 1:26-27 and the creation of 'man' in the image of God.

While this New Testament interpretative debate cannot be settled here, it is worth noting the implications of this divergence of opinion for our systematic theological choices. If Philippians 2 is *not* talking about Christ's divine pre-existence, then the whole matter of kenosis is, from the start, not a matter of speculating about divine characteristics and the effect on them of the incarnation, but rather a *moral* matter of Jesus' 'self-sacrifice' *en route* to the cross. (When we come to look at what I have called 'generalized' readings of kenosis among our contributors we shall see that this view is attractive to many of them, even if they do not explicitly refer to Philippians 2.) If, on the other hand — as has been the more normal reading from early in the church's exegesis — pre-existence and incarnation are assumed to be at stake in the passage, then sooner or later the metaphysical question necessarily presses: What, exactly, has been 'emptied' at the incarnation? Is this merely a figure of speech, or does it connote an actual loss of divine power — temporary or otherwise? To this point we shall return shortly.

3. For this interpretation see especially J. D. G. Dunn, *Christology in the Making* (London: S.C.M. Press, 1980), ch. 4.

b. Pre-modern Exegesis of Philippians 2

To the early church, however, that last question had only one possible answer. For these patristic authors (whether under the influence of Platonic or Aristotelian metaphysics — on this particular point there was no divergence), God was by definition immutable, omnipotent, and omniscient.[4] Thus the most striking feature of the understanding of kenosis as developed under the influence of the great Alexandrian christologian, Cyril (d. 444), was that it involved a narrative of the pre-existent Word's coming amongst us, of his 'taking flesh', and so — most paradoxically — incurring for himself all the limitations of fleshly life, yet *without* any loss of divine characteristics. Indeed one could more truly say that kenosis involves gain rather than loss from this perspective: it is the taking on of flesh, rather than the abandonment of any aspects of divinity, that is the hallmark. But when Cyril writes in this mode, he is — as R. A. Norris has perceptively demonstrated[5] — not really interested in purveying a *theory* of Christ's personal make-up; what Norris calls the "two baskets" issue (how characteristics of humanity and divinity can be brought together) naturally concerns him at other times, but this is not at the heart of the story of kenosis for him, which has more the character of a narrative glorying in paradox than a metaphysical explanation. So indeed, in general, we search in vain in the patristic exegesis of Philippians 2 for an exacting account of *how*, precisely, the pre-existent Logos can also be a frail mortal human.

Moreover, the supposed 'solution' of the Chalcedonian 'Definition' of 451, which attempted a *rapprochement* between the warring christological parties of Alexandria and Antioch, did not itself, in its legitimation of the technical formula of "one *prosopon* and one *hypostasis* (person)" made known "in two *physeis* (natures)," actually explain how this could be accomplished, or how the divine and the human were to be conceived in their interaction.[6] This question of their mode of relation (the problem of

4. For a recent historical exploration and defense of these 'classical' divine attributes in the patristic period, see T. G. Weinandy, *Does God Suffer?* (Edinburgh: T. & T. Clark, 2000), esp. ch. 5.

5. See the important article, R. A. Norris, "Christological Models in Cyril of Alexandria," *Studia Patristica* XIII, Part 2, in *Texte und Untersuchungen* 116 (1971): 255-68; see p. 268 for the remarks about the 'two baskets' mode of christological thinking.

6. I discuss the problem of Chalcedon's explanatory limitations in my forthcoming ar-

the so-called 'communication of idioms') was speculated upon in a variety of ways both in the pre-Chalcedonian and post-Chalcedonian era; and, as may be obvious, a great deal hangs upon this from the point of view of the purported coherence of any *explanation* of the divine 'self-emptying'. Because divine immutability was not even considered negotiable in the pre-modern period, the possibilities on offer for interpreting the *communicatio idiomatum* were kept to three: first, a merely linguistic (rather than onto-logical) attribution of characteristics of the two natures to each other, in a mere 'manner of speaking'; secondly, a real communication of divine attributes to the human nature (but not *vice versa*); and thirdly, a communication of the attributes of the two natures to the 'person', but without mutual infection of the natures. While Zwingli was to come to favor the first, both classical Thomism and Calvinism opted for the last; but Luther, in entertaining the second for the purposes of his high eucharistic theology of 'real presence', opened the Pandora's box of direct mutual communication of the natures that was later to be pressed (by Thomasius) in the opposite direction: from the human to the divine.[7]

This is why the 'turn to the subject' in the modern period brings with it a new set of concerns where christology is concerned (and specifically, where the explication of the precise meaning of 'self-emptying' is in question).[8] As 'personhood' increasingly is conceived in terms of subjective consciousness, the Chalcedonian language of two 'natures' in one 'person' *(hypostasis)* comes to gather the connotations of psychological subjectivity and the expectations of clarified metaphysical explanation. It is in the light of this modernistic 'turn', I believe, that we should read the gathering debate in Reformation and post-Reformation Lutheran theology about kenosis (a matter discussed briefly in this volume by Moltmann and Ward[9]). For Luther it was enough to heighten the paradoxes charac-

---

ticle, "What Does Chalcedon Solve and What Does It Not? Some Reflections on the Status and Meaning of the Chalcedonian 'Definition'," in S. T. Davis, G. O'Collins, S.J., and D. Kendall, S.J., eds., *The Incarnation* (Oxford: Oxford University Press, forthcoming).

7. There is a brief but illuminating discussion of this history of the *communicatio idiomatum* in W. Pannenberg, *Jesus — God and Man* (London: S.C.M. Press, 1968), ch. 8.

8. This point is insightfully made by Graham Ward in his recent essay, "Kenosis: Death, Discourse and Resurrection," in Lucy Gardner, David Moss, Ben Quash, and Graham Ward, eds., *Balthasar at the End of Modernity* (Edinburgh: T. & T. Clark, 1999), pp. 15-68.

9. See Moltmann, Chapter 8 this volume; Ward, Chapter 9 this volume.

teristic of the Cyrilline kenotic tradition by replacing the focus of attention from the moment of incarnation to the theology of the cross: God's simultaneous 'absence' and revelatory presence at Calvary can be seen as a new version — albeit more tortured — of Cyril's kenotic narrative of the eternal Word who "suffered unsufferingly."[10]

c. The Modern Turn: Thomasius and Other 'True' Kenoticists

But another pressure from the Enlightenment period on was the emerging discipline of 'critical' New Testament study, which now refused piously to shelve questions about Jesus' supposed omniscience and self-consciousness (about his own status as divine, for instance, or about the timing of the Second Coming). Under these combined pressures, it was perhaps inevitable that the previously unthinkable should now be thought: that the divine attributes might *actually* and ontologically be modified and 'emptied' to some degree in the events of the incarnation.

The trouble with both Gottfried Thomasius's attempts in this direction (as Moltmann describes in this volume[11]), and with the work of the slightly later British kenoticists such as Gore, Weston, and Forsyth,[12] was that their attempts to explicate *what* features of divinity were actually relinquished or 'retracted' in the incarnation ran into as many logical oddities and paradoxes as the classical view of kenosis that they had forsworn. Indeed some of these authors (notably, Gore) found that in the end they did not really want to assert *true* 'abandonment' of divine characteristics in the incarnation, but rather a 'two levels of consciousness' model in Christ, with some features of divinity thus, as it were, pushed to the background.[13] It is a nice irony that contemporary analytic philosophers of religion who have taken up this distinctly *modern* task of explaining the relations of the two 'natures' of Christ in terms of conscious subjectivity

10. See Graham Ward, "Kenosis," pp. 25-28, for further analysis of Luther's position.

11. See Moltmann, Chapter 8 this volume.

12. In my article "*Kenosis* and Subversion" (see n. 1), esp. pp. 96-99, I discuss the position of the British kenoticists in greater detail.

13. See C. Gore, *Dissertations on Subjects Connected with the Incarnation* (New York: Scribner's, 1985), and my analysis in "*Kenosis* and Subversion," p. 97 and n. 33.

have often rejected a 'kenotic' account but relentlessly pursued Gore's analogy of a 'divided mind' in order to do it.[14] Other analytic philosophers who have *defended* the coherence of a form of kenosis tend to think of some features of Christ's divine powers as being temporarily unexercised (like a tennis player with one hand tied behind his back!) rather than completely relinquished.[15]

So far, then, we have shown that the christological uses of the language of kenosis in the history of Christian tradition shifted from its original hymnic celebration of Christ's exaltation through humility (a use at least capable of being read without necessary recourse to the notion of pre-existence), via its narrative application to the pre-existent Word who miraculously 'took flesh', and then on into the increasingly complex debates about the metaphysics of the relations of the 'natures', which became more problematic, not less, with the imposition of 'modern' notions of the subject on the classical category of *hypostasis*. It is a convoluted story, here told only in rough outline.

But it is, as we remarked a little earlier, a notable feature of the contributions to this volume that most of them (the exceptions are Moltmann and Ward) do not even regard the technical material on christological kenosis we have so far discussed as primary and central to their concerns *vis-à-vis* contemporary science and theology. Before we probe further into the reasons for this, we need to mention the *trinitarian* alternative on kenosis that both Moltmann (explicitly)[16] and Fiddes (more implicitly)[17] also reflect upon.

2. Trinitarian Meanings of Kenosis

As we have seen, christological readings of kenosis focus exclusively on the Son and particularly on the relation of his divinity to his humanity. But there is also a way of extending the reference of kenosis to the other

14. See the working out of this theme in T. V. Morris, *The Logic of God Incarnate* (Ithaca, N.Y.: Cornell University Press, 1986); D. Brown, *The Divine Trinity* (London: Duckworth, 1985); R. Swinburne, *The Christian God* (Oxford: Clarendon Press, 1994).

15. See S. T. Davis, *Logic and the Nature of God* (Grand Rapids: Eerdmans, 1983), p. 125.

16. See Moltmann, Chapter 8 this volume.

17. See Fiddes, Chapter 10 this volume.

two 'persons' as well, and to talk thus, as von Balthasar does, of the mutual disposition of self-giving within the Godhead:

> You, Father, give your entire being as God to the Son; you are Father only inasmuch as you give yourself; you, Son, receive everything from the Father and before Him you want nothing other than one receiving and giving back, the one representing, glorying the Father in loving obedience; you, Spirit, are the unity of these two mutually meeting, self-givings. . . .[18]

For Balthasar, in other words, the idea of kenotic self-surrender is too pervasive and important a characteristic of divine love to circumscribe its significance in christology alone; it is eternally true of the perichoretic and reciprocal interrelations of the persons of the Trinity, not something newly impressed on the divine by the events of the incarnation. And thus it colors all the divine acts *ad extra*: "the divine 'power' is so ordered that it can make room for a possible self-exteriorization even to the utmost point."[19] Although Balthasar is concerned to show that there are intimations of this trinitarian approach to kenosis in the Fathers, the shadow of Hegelian dialectics is cast more obviously across his path. Despite all his criticisms of Hegel, Balthasar centrally assimilates and accommodates what has been called Hegel's 'theology of hiatus': it is left to the Spirit to span the 'unimaginable gulf' between despair and hope in the Son's diremption from the Father in the cross.[20] That is why an understanding of kenosis focused on Christ's death must necessarily be conceived trinitarianly for Balthasar. And it is also why this 'trinitarian' perception of kenosis uncannily converges, as Moltmann brings out, with various modern, late-modern, and postmodern Jewish speculations about God's capacity to be in dialectical relation to God's self, or even to be found in 'absence'. As Lévinas puts it: "God manifests Himself *not by incarnation* but by absence . . . when He veils His face in order to ask everything, to ask the superhuman, of man."[21]

18. Quoted in *The Von Balthasar Reader* (Edinburgh: T. & T. Clark, 1982), pp. 428-29.

19. See Graham Ward's useful discussion of this theme, "Kenosis," pp. 44-46.

20. H. U. von Balthasar, *Mysterium Paschale* (Edinburgh: T. & T. Clark, 1990), chs. 1-2, spell out this characteristic theme of Balthasar; see esp. pp. 23-36 on *kenosis*.

21. Emmanuel Lévinas, "Loving the Torah More Than God," in Zvi Kolitz, *Yosl Rakover Talks to God* (New York: Pantheon, 1999), p. 85.

Despite the obvious (indeed profound) difference from Balthasar's Christian outlook, the shared theme is that of a dialectical break in the divine life. Thus if the christological notion of kenosis came to a head in modern accounts of subjective consciousness, so here the trinitarian account is focused instead on the postmodern obsession with 'difference', with acknowledging radical otherness even within God. To this point we shall return in our section on gender connotations of kenosis.

It is Moltmann's opinion, however, that Balthasar's trinitarian approach to kenosis leaves insufficient room for the place of creation "outside the triune God":[22] Balthasar's is indeed a participatory metaphysic, with strong influences from classic mystical theology. But why is it important to leave such 'room'? It is here that we pass to our third category of kenotic thinking, with which most of this book's contributors are concerned.

3. 'Generalized' Approaches to Kenosis: Doctrines of Creation and Providence

There are in our contributors' perspectives a range of overlapping and cumulative factors pressing them towards what they call a kenotic account of the creator's relation to the creation. Not all share the same metaphysical commitments (Barbour, notably, embraces an explicitly 'process' perspective, while others eschew it); and not all understand kenosis with precisely the same set of evocations. Here, without repeating the arguments of the essayists in detail, we shall concentrate on a brief analysis of the different uses of the term and of the principal factors propelling the authors in this direction. To anticipate: the factors uppermost in our authors' minds are the protection of human freedom, the alignment of 'scientific' and theological accounts of the cosmos, the desire for an adequate response to theodicy questions, and the demands of a theology of 'love'. To a much more minor extent feminist questions about the potential abuse of a theology of 'sacrifice' enter in (see Barbour), or the possibility of a 'maternal' understanding of the divine (Peacocke); but these reflections are not at the center of the discussion.

Thus Polkinghorne's contribution significantly sets the tone for many of the other essays. For him, kenosis primarily connotes the risk taken by

22. See Moltmann, Chapter 8 this volume.

the creator in submitting Godself to "the free process" of creation, which "qualif[ies]", in a kenotic way, the operation of God's power" (p. 96). Not only is this crucial in bringing the scientific story and the theological story into proper coordination, it also helps solve the pressing problems of theodicy. God is not an 'interventionist' God, but is subject to the vagaries of creaturely causality; indeed Polkinghorne is even willing to go so far as to aver that God "submits to being *a* cause among causes" (p. 104, my emphasis), a matter that for him finds paradigmatic expression in the incarnation. Ward's approach stops short of the "cause among causes" claim, but gives even more space than Polkinghorne to the significance for God of the gift to humanity of *libertarian* freedom: "not just the incarnation, but the creation of conscious and rational beings itself is a kenotic act on God's part" (p. 158). It involves "accepting many experiences of pain and suffering," "giving up of complete control," and of "complete knowledge"; but it also brings gain: "entering into relationship and communion" (pp. 158-59), something Ward presumes is somehow inhibited in God without the 'kenotic' act of risk.

Peacocke and Barbour repeat many of the same considerations, propelling them towards a 'kenotic' view of the divine; but Barbour makes explicit his 'process' metaphysic when he insists that kenosis [sc. "limitations of divine knowledge and power"] is a "metaphysical necessity rather than . . . voluntary self-limitation" (pp. 12-13). Thus "divine omnipotence is in principle impossible" (p. 13), not something surrendered as an earlier possession. Peacocke's 'panentheism' stops slightly short of this full-blown process view, but shares with it a definition of kenosis as "sharing in the suffering of God's creatures, in the very creative, evolutionary processes of the world" (p. 38). Like Polkinghorne, Peacocke sees the example of Jesus as thereby confirming this perspective on God's creativity as "self-limiting, vulnerable, self-emptying and self-giving" (p. 41).

Jeeves, Ellis, and Rolston all present subtly different emphases again. Jeeves does not actually speculate about kenosis in *God*, but instead reflects on "kenotic behavior" in a "kenotic community": the *penchant* towards "self-giving" and "self-limiting" which may have "genetic and neural substrates" (p. 88). Again, he brings in Christ only at the end of his argument as a unique "demonstration" of this capacity. Ellis also operates with a primarily ethical perspective on kenosis: letting go or giving up one's own desires for the greater good and on behalf of others (see p. 108), which nonetheless can also be secondarily applied to the "metaphysics of

201

cosmology" (p. 114). Unlike Barbour, Ellis insists that such 'letting go' must always be 'voluntary'; and unlike Peacocke and Barbour (who are aware of the feminist complexities of the appeal to 'self-sacrifice'), Ellis explicitly makes 'sacrifice' central to his notion of 'kenotic love'. By throwing such 'kenotic love' into explicit contradiction with any attempt to justify war, however (p. 123), Ellis reveals how complex the ethical appeal to 'sacrifice' can be: for has not death in battle traditionally been construed as the supreme 'sacrifice' for one's country? Again, christology is used here in an exemplarist mode for this notion of 'self-sacrifice', this time with the emphasis on Christ's forswearing of a triumphalist interpretation of Messiahship (pp. 110-12). Rolston takes a slightly different approach, and tackles the question of kenosis and 'nature' head-on. Initially defining kenosis as 'suffering love', he insists that "In nature, there is no altruism, much less kenosis" (p. 43); this is a "category mistake," just as talk of "selfish genes" is (p. 61). So Rolston prefers to keep the term *kenosis* for the *human* ethical capacity to "limit . . . human aggrandizement" for the sake of the planet — a supreme Christian task, he says, for the "next millennium" (p. 65).

Finally, we must look to the contributions of Fiddes, Welker, and Moltmann for more self-consciously *theological* starting points on the topic of kenosis. As systematic theologians (rather than scientists or philosophers), they all start from an analysis of the nature of divine love in Christian tradition and turn only then to questions of creation and cosmology. On this basis Fiddes (who only briefly uses the term 'kenosis', p. 190) argues for a 'panentheistic' notion of God's love that will fulfill its purposes "not *despite* the suffering of love, but *through* it" (p. 191), a method that involves significant 'risk'. Following Barth (rather than Balthasar: although one again suspects that Hegel hovers in the background), Fiddes thematizes this 'risky' form of love in explicitly trinitarian terms from the outset (see p. 186). Welker has a slightly different emphasis, defining kenosis as God's "willingness to meet creatures at their greatest distance from God," that is, in respect for the "otherness of the other" (p. 135). Finally, Moltmann, who provides the most nuanced account of different meanings of kenosis in Jewish and Christian tradition, opts himself for a multifaceted definition of kenosis as "self-giving," "self-limitation," and the "restriction of God's omnipotence, omnipresence, and omniscience" (p. 148). One may thus also appropriately speak of God's "self-humiliation" — that God chooses to "wait" for created beings

202

to "repent and turn back" to God (p. 149). Granted that "annihilation" is a real possibility, it is not entirely clear from this essay how the hope for final eschatological fulfillment can be a confident one.

Even this brief analysis of 'generalized' usages of kenosis in our volume has shown the 'family resemblance' sliding-scale of meanings from 'risk' to 'self-limitation' to 'sacrifice' to 'self-giving' to 'self-emptying' — and even to 'annihilation'. The metaphysical and moral baggage that these varying nodal definitions carry is not by any means the same in each case, as we have shown; and nor is the *basis* on which the case is made. Our systematic theologians are much more likely to acknowledge a prior commitment to the hermeneutical lens of christology or Trinity; whereas our scientists and philosophers are more inclined to argue from a particular understanding of human freedom (some form of 'incompatibilism' is favored by all, interestingly), or from the state of current scientific understanding of (say) chaos theory or genetics. The old debate, reaching back into medieval scholasticism, about the regrettable divide between discussion of *de deo uno* and *de deo trino* thus rears its head again here. Is a Christian doctrine of creation to be discussed *in advance* of reflection on trinitarian ramifications (as is the case in many of these essays)? Or does this leave the suspicion of a whiff of unreformed deism? Or again, as we have already mentioned in our foregoing analysis, is the original New Testament and patristic discussion of christological kenosis only to be seen as an optional resource, to be resummoned if it shows paradigmatic congruence with theological conclusions gleaned elsewhere? Or is this material in some sense normatively binding on our systematic reflections? The different answers reflected even in our different essayists in this volume show how complex and divergent can be our implicit attitudes to the authority of 'tradition'.

Other, vital, systematic divergences occur depending on the degree of 'mystery', on the one hand, or anthropomorphic symbolization on the other, that is felt to be tolerable in a doctrine of God. A number of our authors spend significant energy criticizing what is called a 'classical' account of divine attributes and divine providence (views associated especially with Augustine and later classical Thomism). This critique is indeed a notable *Leitmotif* of this distinguished collection of essays, since all are agreed that the classic divine attributes of omnipotence, omniscience, and immutability must be challenged. While this huge concatenation of theological questions cannot be reopened at this point, it is worth reminding ourselves that Aquinas himself would have strongly refused the anthropomorphism inherent in the suggestion that God is 'absolute ruler' of the universe (see Barbour, p. 1), or that the understanding of human freedom he espoused would suggest inhibiting 'control'.[23] We are dealing with subtle matters here about where we are willing to concede mystery and wonder in our system, and where the system appears to break down under the impact of cumulative criticisms. Suffice it to say that Thomism is not without intelligent answers to the 'kenotic'-related questions pressed in this volume about theodicy, cosmology, human freedom, and the accommodation of Jesus' human weakness and suffering in the christological realm by means of the *communicatio idiomatum;* but it has not been the task of this volume to explore those alternative 'classical' perspectives in any depth.[24] That would have produced a very different — and much longer — book. I have already suggested above that the striking commitment in this book to a *libertarian* view of freedom may be the linchpin holding several other systematic choices (about kenosis, theodicy, cosmology, and divine characteristics) together. And that, as it happens, provides an immediate bridge into our last section on the gender connotations of kenosis in this volume and elsewhere.

II. Kenosis: Gender Connotations

As we have already hinted at points in this discussion, gender themes are entangled with the theological matter of kenosis in a number of interesting — and not always obvious — ways. In this closing section we shall enumerate three such ways that gender issues intersect with our theological choices in this area, and attempt some adjudication.

1. Kenosis and Libertarian Freedom

To most of the writers in this volume it is taken as an axiomatic good that humans should enjoy a type of freedom that places limitations on God's

23. On this theme in Aquinas, see Herbert McCabe, *God Matters* (London: Mowbray, 1987), ch. 2 ("Freedom"); and Brian Davies, *The Thought of Thomas Aquinas* (Oxford: Clarendon Press, 1992), ch. 9 ("Providence and Freedom").

24. Compare for instance Herbert McCabe's defense of a 'classical' alternative on these themes, in *God Matters,* ch. 4 ("The Involvement of God").

power and foreknowledge. For many this supposition is driven by the theodicy question: If God is powerful enough to eradicate evil and suffering, then why does God not do so? It must be, the argument runs, that God has placed limitations on God's own power in this area. The 'space' granted to humans by God to exercise freedom — for good or ill — is, as we have indicated, an important component in the 'generalized' notion of divine kenosis that is dominant in this book. But it is worth underscoring here that the authors who propose this view assume that the 'freedom' thus exercised by humans must be of the 'incompatibilist' sort, that is, the type supposedly free from conditioning control by another. The visual picture here, in other words, is of a (very big) divine figure backing out of the scene, or restraining his influence, in order that other (little) figures may exercise completely independent thinking and acting.

But why and how is this picture of freedom 'gendered'? The answer lies in the significance granted, in this particular 'picturing' of freedom, to an act of total independence from restriction, conditioning, or the admission of dependence; and this is a vision deeply reminiscent, to those schooled in pyschoanalytic theory, of the male child's repudiation of the power of the mother. Thus, to the French feminists, especially, this kind of picture of 'adult' independence is actually an intrinsically 'male' fantasy — a rejection and repression of the maternal; it is the antithesis of the willing acknowledgment both of our mutual human dependencies and of our continuing need for divine sustenance.[25] The underlying symbolism — this argument goes on — is of a normative 'masculine' self who gains independence by setting himself apart from that which gave him life and indeed continues to sustain him.

But what, then, would be the alternative? 'Incompatibilist' views of freedom are not the only ones on offer philosophically (indeed, interestingly, these are increasingly decried by secular philosophers); various forms of 'compatibilism' are also possible — views of freedom that do not attempt to abstract from the conditioning and even 'determining' factors that continue to be in effect even as a 'free' act is undertaken. For secular philosophers the debate here focuses on the extent of physiological and social determinism that can co-exist with an authentically 'free' act; but

---

25. I have explored this critique of incompatibilist freedom in relation to French feminist thought in my chapter, "Feminism," in C. Taliaferro and P. Quinn, eds., *A Companion to Philosophy of Religion* (Oxford: Blackwell, 1997), pp. 601-6.

for *theistic* compatibilists a picture is conjured in which I am most *truly* 'free' when I am aligned with God's providential and determining will for me (the God "whose service is perfect freedom," as the Cranmerian collect runs). But this approach, as we have noted above, is part of the so-called 'classical' vision of divine interaction with the world that most of the contributors to this book are concerned to decry; and this is especially so if they continue to 'picture' such determinism as the inappropriate and restrictive control of individual humans by some sort of divine dictator.

But it is an interesting irony that also present in this volume is a competing 'picture' of divine-human exchange that undoes this assumption about the supposedly strangling effect of a continuous dependence on the divine. Thus Ian Barbour, as already mentioned, can write positively about the 'maternal' symbolism of a God conceived not as "overpowering but as empowering" (p. 15), as constantly loving us into being rather than repressing human freedom and initiative. In Barbour's 'process' analysis this is a view aligned with an already-assumed repudiation of 'classical theism'; but it is worth underscoring that Julian of Norwich's treatment of a parallel theme (alluded to by Paul Fiddes, pp. 175, 191) accepts a 'classical' vision of God but writes into it a notion of divine desire that finds its *completion* in human responsiveness rather than setting itself in competition with it.

In short, the decisions we make theologically about divine (or human) kenosis are shot through with gender associations and overtones, whether acknowledged or not. If we think of divine kenosis as required for a God who must *get out of the way* in order that 'freedom' be enacted, then one sort of gendered picture is probably in play; whereas if we think of God as nurturing and sustaining us *into* freedom (of a different, 'compatibilist', sort), then it may be that another set of gender associations are present in the background. For the latter view, we should note, it is not *God* who is in need of restriction or 'emptying', but rather a false form of hubristic *human* power — a form that many feminists would dub 'masculinist'. While Rolston and Jeeves do not explore these gender associations, what they do underscore is that kenosis as a human undertaking must acknowledge the profound dependencies we have on God, on the earth, and on each other.

206

2. Feminism and Kenotic 'Self-sacrifice'

At this point, however, it might be objected that this gender analysis assumes precisely the sexual stereotypes that it should be attempting to upend. Is all nurturing 'maternal', and all false jostling for power 'masculinist'? Surely not; no physiological 'essentialism' is either implied or condoned by these remarks. Yet such gender *associations* are undeniably still abroad in our culture, and thus worthy of bringing to consciousness when they may be impinging on theological choices. The same issue presses when we turn to the related question of kenosis and 'self-sacrifice'. For here there has been a long-standing critique by feminist theologians of 'kenotic' christology on the grounds that it may make normative for women forms of 'self-sacrifice' and 'self-abasement' that keep them in subordinate roles, and can even lead to the condoning of abuse. Whereas men may need to learn forms of moral kenosis that compensate for their tendency to abuse power (this argument runs), women can be endangered by an emphasis on 'self-emptying' that is already damaging to their sense of identity. As Daphne Hampson has written:

> That [kenosis] should have featured prominently in Christian thought is perhaps an indication of the fact that men have understood what the male problem, in thinking in terms of hierarchy and domination, has been. It may well be a model which men need to appropriate and which may helpfully be built into the male understanding of God. But . . . for women, the theme of self-emptying and self-abnegation is far from helpful as a paradigm.[26]

This argument is initially well taken, especially when aimed at the British christological kenoticists of the late nineteenth and early twentieth century (Gore, Weston, Forsyth), whose images and illustrative narratives for kenosis are indeed replete with sexist and classist assumptions, as I have demonstrated elsewhere.[27] But we should again beware of reinforcing the gender stereotypes that this illuminating form of critique seeks to

26. Daphne Hampson, *Theology and Feminism* (Oxford: Blackwell, 1990), p. 155; discussed at length in connection with other feminist perspectives in my "*Kenosis* and Subversion" (see n. 1), *passim*.

27. See the detailed analysis in my "*Kenosis* and Subversion," pp. 96-99.

question. As with our discussion of kenosis and freedom, so here: the undeniable danger of using the appeal to 'kenotic' self-sacrifice as a means of subordinating, or even abusing, Christian women should not be confused with the attempt to reconsider the status of kenosis as a legitimate spiritual goal for both men and women (a task undertaken by several contributors in this volume). The danger lies in refusing even to face what the 'hermeneutics of suspicion' lays before us for consideration; it does not therefore follow that *all* attempts to rethink the value of moral kenosis, or of 'sacrificial' love, founder on the shoals of gender essentialism — as Hampson's critique would appear to suggest. Indeed, as I have argued elsewhere, the *repression* of questions of kenotic 'vulnerability' in much feminist theology to date is a worrying trend if what it disallows is an admission of creaturely dependence in women as well as men.[28] Nonetheless, this admission should not cause a new lurch towards the 'safety' of a theological approach that *denies* gendered difference, as our last consideration will show.

3. Gender and 'Otherness'

A final way in which questions of gender impinge on the theological discussion of kenosis returns us to the issues of fracture or 'hiatus' *within* the divine; we saw how in this generation this theme has exercised the Jewish philosopher Lévinas as much as the Christian theologian von Balthasar, although with different metaphysical resolutions. It is, arguably, in the dialectical break between 'God' and 'God', between divine absence and divine presence, that 'kenotic' space is made for the recognition of the 'other' *as* other.[29] But who is this 'other', precisely? As the French feminists Luce Irigaray and Julia Kristeva have in different ways illuminated, the question of the 'other' cannot be divorced from questions of gender: the gendered identity of the child is initially formed precisely in its negotiation of the crisis of recognizing its own difference from the mother, and its introduction into the world of language. For Kristeva, such a passage is 'kenotic' in a particular sense: it involves an

28. See "*Kenosis* and Subversion," *passim*, but esp. pp. 106-11.
29. Graham Ward explores this theme at length, in an interesting comparison of Balthasar and Julia Kristeva, in "Kenosis," pp. 40-68.

'abjection' from the mother which is the precondition of entry into the social world of communication, termed by Kristeva (following Lacan) the 'symbolic' law of the father. The negotiation of this crisis itself involves deep loss, and thus implicitly summons the hope of a future reparation, even of a 'resurrection'.[30]

Even if we are not inclined to accept the full package of Lacanian assumptions here encoded, it may be seen that kenosis from this perspective involves a discussion of the deep difficulties of recognizing 'otherness' without swallowing the other into a preconceived category or an item of personal need. The moral integrity of the 'other' is only maintained by a *deliberate* act of space-making, or perhaps — as Irigaray will have it — of mutual 'ecstasy', which waits on the other's difference without demand for egotistical control. As such, this respectful space-making mirrors the dialectical gap in the divine that von Balthasar sees only as bridgeable by the Holy Spirit; and so too for Irigaray, in parallel argument, sexual love at its best is represented as ineluctably triadic in structure, the two lovers both distinguished and joined by the 'third', which represents their mutual "standing out of themselves" (ecstasy).[31]

But if we ask, finally, what such concern with gendered 'otherness' has to do with the themes of kenosis in this book, we shall be led back first to Welker's concerns with divine respect for 'otherness' and Moltmann's brief discussion of Balthasar's 'kenotic' trinitarianism: the 'genealogy' of these concerns, with their roots in Hegelianism, is now clearly seen to be closely connected with the contemporary French feminist debates about gendered 'otherness'. And if the French feminists have convinced us at all of the significance of early child-development for this capacity to respect 'otherness', then the concerns of Rolston, Jeeves, and Ellis about moral kenosis are surely worthy of supplementation and reconsideration along these gendered lines.

30. See Graham Ward, "Kenosis," p. 62, for a discussion of this theme in Kristeva, transposed into psychoanalytic categories.

31. See Luce Irigaray's exploration of the 'trinitarian' nature of sexual love at its best in her "Questions to Emmanuel Lévinas," in Margaret Whitford, ed., *The Irigaray Reader* (Oxford: Blackwell, 1991), p. 180.

Conclusions

In this necessarily brief analysis of the usages of the term *kenosis* in this volume, we have attempted to distinguish and categorize a range of meanings and associations of the term, and to chart the 'family resemblances' between them. Along the way we have indicated some of the systematic choices made by the essayists, their presumed sources of authority in theological matters, and their respective starting points and chief concerns. While making no extended defense of 'classical theism', so-called, we have drawn attention to the dangers of caricaturing its perception of divine power and control, but have also recapitulated some of the cumulative and important reasons why most of the contributors to this book eschew such 'classical' views of divine omnipotence in favor of what I have termed a 'generalized' notion of divine kenosis. Finally, by educing a number of gender associations, both explicit and implicit, in the understandings of kenosis in play in this book, we have sought to draw attention to the seemingly inexorable way in which gender associations attach themselves to the matter, and to urge a deeper consideration of the theological significance of these gender themes for a contemporary theology of science and creation.